Here's what your colleagues are saying
about the fifth edition of
Learning and Behavior:

"*Dr. Chance's book is the best there is-- clearly written, comprehensive, accessible, and up-to-date. I've used this book in all of its editions without a single negative comment turning up on student evaluations. I can't think of another textbook that has so consistently pleased my students while serving my instructional needs.*"

> Robert Epstein, Ph. D.
> Editor-in-Chief, Psychology Today, and
> University Research Professor,
> California School of Professional
> Psychology at
> Alliant International University

"*The fifth edition of* Learning and Behavior *is a thoughtful and well-written textbook... Its primary strength is its breadth and interrelatedness to human experience and application. The examples are clever and intriguing. The variety of the research quoted in the text really shows the author's scholarship.*"

> Mark Reilly, Ph. D.
> Arizona State University

"*Wonderful! Four thumbs up! (Including my hand thumbs and foot thumbs.) My students come into the class not knowing much about experimentation, but by the end of the semester they know a lot!*"

> Margaret Thomas-Jenkins, Ph.D.
> University of Central Florida,
> Orlando

Instructor's Manual with Test Bank

for

Learning and Behavior

Fifth Edition

INSTRUCTOR'S MANUAL WITH TEST BANK

FOR

LEARNING AND BEHAVIOR

FIFTH EDITION

Paul Chance
Cambridge Center for Behavioral Sciences

With Diane Chance

Includes an Introduction to *Sniffy, the Virtual Rat*
Prepared by
Michael Snyder
University of Alberta

THOMSON
WADSWORTH

Australia • Canada • Mexico • Singapore • Spain • United Kingdom • United States

Printed in the United States of America
1 2 3 4 5 6 7 06 05 04 03 02

Printer: Globus Printing Company, Inc.

ISBN: 0-534-59869-2

For more information about our products, contact us at:
Thomson Learning Academic Resource Center
1-800-423-0563

For permission to use material from this text,
contact us by:
Phone: 1-800-730-2214
Fax: 1-800-731-2215
Web: http://www.thomsonrights.com

Asia
Thomson Learning
5 Shenton Way #01-01
UIC Building
Singapore 068808

Australia
Nelson Thomson Learning
102 Dodds Street
South Street
South Melbourne, Victoria 3205
Australia

Canada
Nelson Thomson Learning
1120 Birchmount Road
Toronto, Ontario M1K 5G4
Canada

Europe/Middle East/South Africa
Thomson Learning
High Holborn House
50/51 Bedford Row
London WC1R 4LR
United Kingdom

Latin America
Thomson Learning
Seneca, 53
Colonia Polanco
11560 Mexico D.F.
Mexico

Spain
Paraninfo Thomson Learning
Calle/Magallanes, 25
28015 Madrid, Spain

CONTENTS

Appendix

* Figures are intended for use as transparencies. Numbers in parentheses indicate
  most relevant chapters in *L&B*.

PREFACE

This instructor's manual is meant to accompany the fifth edition of *Learning and Behavior* (Wadsworth, 2003). *L&B* is intended primarily for the introductory course in learning principles, although it is sometimes used in other courses, such as experimental psychology.

Each chapter in this manual provides an outline of the corresponding text chapter, a summary of the main points covered in the chapter, class notes, answers to chapter review questions, a key to the chapter practice quiz found in the text, and a ready-to-use chapter quiz and its key. This edition also includes an appendix with several items some instructors may find useful.

Class notes. The class notes include ideas that may be of some interest to the instructor in planning lessons. It also includes ideas for exercises set off in boxes. Most of these exercises are intended for use in the classroom and are designed to demonstrate topics covered in the chapter. Some of the exercises can be conducted by the students outside the class. Although I hope the suggestions offered here will be of interest to all users of *L&B*, they are addressed in particular to the instructor who is relatively new to the learning course.

Some of the exercises are based on *Sniffy the Virtual Rat* (Alloway et al., 2000). This is a software program published by Wadsworth that simulates a laboratory rat in an experimental chamber. The rat is remarkably realistic as it wanders about the chamber, grooms itself, drinks water, and eats food from a food tray. (I have never noticed Sniffy eliminating wastes, however. This precludes the necessity of cleaning up after him, and is apparently an important advantage that silicon rats offer. Sniffy is also completely odorless, another virtue of silicon life forms.)

The software now comes in two versions, Lite and Pro. The former focuses on the basic learning procedures, whereas the latter includes exercises on habituation, stimulus generalization, and other topics. The choice of programs, it seems to me, depends on the time available and the extent to which the instructor sees the class as a laboratory course. My only objection to the Sniffy software is the fact that the program creates graphs that purport to show mental states, such as the degree to which Sniffy associates a CS with a US. In other words, inferences from Sniffy's behavior are reported as though they were observatios. Despite this flaw, I urge instructors to try the program because I think it is an excellent teaching tool, especially when an animal lab is not available.

Review questions. Each chapter includes 20 review questions. Some of these are straightforward factual questions, but many require critical or creative thinking. The questions are intended primarily to enable students to review the chapter and assess their mastery of it, and to provide material that will lead to interesting and useful classroom discussions. Feedback from instructors and students alike suggests that the questions serve both purposes well. Although a few instructors have said that certain items are too difficult for undergraduates, I have been impressed by the sophistication of the thinking prompted by the questions. Some instructors have created listservs through which the members of a learning class exchange ideas related to review questions. I urge techno-savvy instructors to explore this idea.

Practice quiz key. This manual includes keys to the practice quizzes in *L&B*. The quizzes are intended primarily to help students assess their mastery of the chapters, but some instructors may want to require students to complete the quizzes and submit them for inspection, while others may want to use them as pop quizzes.

Chapter quiz. This manual includes an additional quiz for each chapter of the text. The quizzes are double-spaced so that they may be photocopied or used to create transparencies for use on an overhead projector. A key is also provided and includes page references to make it easier to locate the relevant passages.

<u>Test bank</u>. In addition to the chapter quizzes, there is a test bank organized by chapter at the end of this manual. There are 659 questions in this bank: 422 multiple choice, 113 true-false, 64 completion, and 60 short answer. There is some repetition across question types, of course; i.e., a given point might be asked about in both a multiple choice question and in a true-false question.

The fifth edition of *L&B* has extensive footnotes. In general, this is information that is supplemental to the text. Some instructors will want students to be familiar with the content of all footnotes; other instructors may tell students to ignore certain footnotes. The attention students give to footnotes will, of course, depend on the guidance of the instructor and the extent to which instructors test on that material. The test bank includes questions on many of the footnotes.

<u>Appendix</u>. The appendix to this manual includes several items that may be useful in teaching the learning course. Perhaps the most important of these is Michael Snyder's *Introduction to Sniffy the Virtual Rat* . Snyder has used the Sniffy software for many years and offers guidance that should be very helpful to those less familiar with the program. Other appendix items include key search terms for each chapter; a set of figures that might be used to make transparencies for use in class lectures or exercises; and a few short handouts.

Each edition of *L&B* changes in response to feedback from students and instructors who have used it. The same can be said of this manual. If you have suggestions for its improvement, I hope you will contact me. You can reach me by emailing me at PBchance@aol.com.

I look forward to hearing from you

Paul Chance
Senior Fellow, Cambridge Center for Behavioral Studies
Author, *First Course in Applied Behavior Analysis* (Wadsworth, 1998)

1

Introduction: Learning to Change

Chapter Outline

Main Points

Change is the only constant. Organisms cope with change through evolution and learning. Evolution depends on variation and natural selection. Natural selection has produced reflexes, fixed action patterns, and general behavior traits that help organisms adapt to their environments. Natural selection is slow, since it necessarily takes place over generations, and is of no value to the individual in coping with change. (E.g., if the climate turns suddenly colder, natural selection will not come to the individual's rescue.) Learning, defined here as a change in behavior due to experience, resembles natural selection in that it is a mechanism for adapting to change. Learning is more rapid than natural selection and helps the individual to survive. The nature-nurture debate wrongly implies a choice whereas in fact the two are inextricably intertwined, like the fibers of a rope; it is never entirely clear where one leaves off and the other begins.

Class Notes

<u>Background</u>: Most of us think of changes in our environments as exceptional events, so when learning is described as a means of coping with change it may seem rather unimportant to some students. "We need to know how to learn in case something in our environment changes," they may say. It is for this reason that the chapter begins by proposing that our environments are *constantly* changing. You may want to draw attention to the fact that the very first word in the chapter is *change*.

<u>Natural selection:</u> The first query appears in this section, and it may be worthwhile to spend a moment on it to encourage students to make use of the queries as they read. (This might also be encouraged by using some query items in quizzes and exams.)

    Robert T. Fancher (1992), in a letter to *The Sciences*, writes that "evolution is grossly inefficient: as long as organisms survive and propagate, evolution does not make much difference in what else happens" (p.4). This is a good point. Natural selection selects one characteristic over another only if one leads to an increased tendency to reproduce.

    The point that evolution does not imply an intelligent agent will be difficult for some students to grasp. Richard Dawkins, in *The Blind Watchmaker*, deals with this problem nicely, and sections of his book might be read in class or assigned. His analogy of the segregation of stones on the beach shows how complex ends can be achieved through simple natural forces. Of course, the student may answer (as Newton did long ago) that God established the forces in the first place. The point is that we can account for natural phenomena (including evolution and learning) in a scientific way.

Although it is a sensitive issue, it may be worth bringing attention to footnote 3 and the point that belief in evolution is not necessarily incompatible with belief in God. Many students assume that to accept scientific concepts such as evolution, you have to be an atheist. But while most scientists probably are not religious in the traditional sense, many do believe in God. In 1995, Richard Malott of Western Michigan University did an informal survey of people attending a professional meeting on the teaching of behavior science and found that 31% said they believed in God. (I believe that that is about the same proportion found among physicists and other natural scientists.)

It is hard for some students to believe that mutations can play a role in evolution. You might want to emphasize that the vast majority of mutations are harmful or of no consequence. It is also helpful to remind students that evolution is a play in which a single act may last millions of years.

Because fixed action patterns are sometimes very complex, students may have a hard time believing that the behavior is not learned. Dawkins' beach stones may be useful again here.

In discussing evolution, I say nothing about "punctuated equilibrium," the idea that evolutionary change may occur in fits and starts: i.e., sometimes rapidly and sometimes slowly. It might be worth mentioning this in classes since learning often follows a similar pattern, with behavior sometimes changing rapidly, sometimes slowly.

Exercise: Nature's Sieve

Instructors who enjoy photography might want to produce slides of beach stones as they are segregated by size by the action of the waves. (Photos might be taken at, say, 24 hour intervals.) These might then be shown to the class to illustrate order arising out of an unintelligent process.

It probably bears repeating that what I have called general behavior traits are behavioral tendencies, not specific acts. They include the dispositions that people have in mind when they speak of temperament, and it is clear that to some extent these dispositions -- aggressiveness, fearfulness, activity level, and so on -- are products of heredity.

Lee Cronk's article, *Old Dogs, Old Tricks*, is a wonderfully readable discussion of how evolved behavior can fail to meet the needs of current environments. Students should be encouraged to read it, and instructors may want to read parts of it aloud in class.

The Trut article on the fox farm study is available online at www.edu/~blackmark/jsk/canid.htm. This is an important study, and I am grateful to Carl Cheney of Utah State University for bringing it to my attention.

Learning: Evolved modifiability. It might be well to underline the point that learning is itself a biological mechanism that is the result of natural selection. Along with reflexes, fixed action patterns, and general behavior traits, animals have evolved a special mechanism for coping with change: learning. Strum's work is cited here mainly because it runs counter to the popular notion that in nature, might makes right, and might is largely the result of heredity. Strum argues that the most successful strategies were kinder and gentler, and probably had to be learned.

It is one thing to speak of learning as animal training or the acquisition of academic skills in the classroom. It is quite another to suggest, as the text does, that what we are as a species and who we are as individuals is largely the product of learning. This is a disturbing idea for some students. The idea that experience shapes behavior also wreaks havoc with traditional notions of responsibility, guilt, and innocence. These issues must be treated with sensitivity. Students should be shown that this new approach to behavior actually increases autonomy and holds the promise of improving our effectiveness.

Nature and nurture. Simplifying complex matters is evidently intrinsically reinforcing, since people often do it even when the simplification are distortions. Biological determinism is one form of oversimplification; environmentalism is another. Interactionism can also be a form of oversimplification.

Education provides ample evidence of the interaction of nature and nurture. Some research in education (that of the late Benjamin Bloom, for instance) has shown that when fast and slow learners begin a lesson with similar competence on prerequisite skills, their learning rates become similar. This suggests that different learning rates may depend less on innate ability than on previous learning.

Exercise: Photographing Change

One way of getting students to appreciate the pervasiveness of change is to show the students an old photograph of someone they know and ask them if they recognize the person. (A childhood photograph of yourself should work nicely, but you could use a figure from politics or entertainment.) You might show a series of photos, each one taken several years after the last. Once the students have guessed the answer, ask them to identify in what ways their own appearance has changed in the past 24 hours. The discussion should help the students begin to appreciate the fact that changes are taking place constantly, and we are constantly adapting to them.

Exercise: Exit Quiz

I don't know who is to credit for this idea, but I have used it with very satisfactory results: Five minutes before the end of class, I take a position by the door, and explain that I will ask each student a question on the day's lesson. To leave the room, they must answer the question correctly. I ask basic questions that can be answered in a few words (e.g., What is learning? What does FAP stand for? What are the two essential elements of evolution?). If a student answers incorrectly, I send him to the end of the line (or the back of the pack), and then ask the next student the same question. I usually ask no more than half a dozen different questions. Most students seem to enjoy the activity, and since I start five minutes before class ends, they are not delayed.

Key to Review Questions

<u>Note:</u> Review questions are intended partly to help students digest the material in the chapter, and partly to prompt them to think critically about what they have read. Some instructors require students to provide written answers to all review questions, some assign a few questions, but probably most use selected questions as a way of initiating class discussions. Some of these are very difficult; some, in fact, do not have satisfactory answers. Some instructors believe it is a mistake to ask students questions they cannot answer, but we cannot expect students to believe that a field is challenging if we ask them only easy questions.

1. Define the following terms. Give an example or illustration of each that is not taken from the text.

<u>Fixed action pattern</u>: Any largely inherited series of interrelated acts, usually elicited by a particular stimulus (the releaser); formerly called instinct.

<u>General behavior trait</u>: Any general behavioral tendency that is strongly influenced by genes. Examples include introversion and general anxiety. GBTs are more variable than FAPs and are not dependent on a releasing stimulus.

<u>Habituation:</u> A decrease in the intensity or probability of a reflex response resulting from repeated exposure to a stimulus that elicits that response.

<u>Learning</u>: A change in behavior due to experience. Some instructors like to say that learning is a "relatively enduring change" in behavior. I do not favor this modification because there is no consensus about what enduring means. Other instructors like to say that learning is due to "certain kinds of experience." While this is true, it doesn't seem to add much unless you specify the kinds of experience, in which case the definition becomes unwieldy.

<u>Mutation</u>: Any change in a gene. When the mutation occurs in a reproductive cell, the mutation may be passed on to offspring. The term *mutation* may have a negative connotation for students (film monsters are sometimes mutants), but from the standpoint of science *mutation* is a neutral term.

<u>Natural selection</u>: The tendency for characteristics that contribute to the survival of a species to persist, and for those that do not to disappear.

<u>Reflex:</u> A relationship between a specific event and a simple response to that event. It may be worth emphasizing that the term *reflex* refers to the relationship, not to the response, per se. The patellar reflex is not the knee jerk itself, but the relation between the blow to the patellar tendon and the movement of the foot.

<u>Releaser:</u> Any event that reliably elicits a fixed action pattern. The light from which the cockroach runs is a releaser.

<u>Sensitization:</u> An increase in the intensity or probability of a reflex response resulting from earlier exposure to a stimulus that elicits that response.

2. What is the mechanism by which species change as their environments change?

Species change by means of natural selection. (Individuals change by means of learning.)

3. Are humans still evolving? Explain.

Some students think of evolution as a process that took place in the past, and we and other creatures are its finished products. They need to understand that so long as environments change, evolution will continue.

4. Why has the field mouse not evolved into an animal as large and ferocious as the grizzly bear?

The first thing that might be said is that perhaps it has! A mouse the size of a grizzly bear might once have evolved and then died out, replaced by today's diminutive creature. The point is that evolution does not require getting bigger and stronger; it requires surviving long enough to produce offspring that will survive. Whatever contributes to the survival of the species, whether it be bigness and ferocity or smallness and timidity, will persist. If the field mouse has not evolved into a large, ferocious animal, it is because being a small, timid animal works.

5. In what sense is natural selection the product of experience?

Experience refers to changes in environment, and it is the environment that selects characteristics.

6. In what sense is learning the product of natural selection?

Learning ability is the product of natural selection. Therefore it can be said that learning is indirectly the product of natural selection.

7. How are reflexes and fixed action patterns like the ROM (read only memory) of a computer?

ROM is hard-wired. Reflexes and fixed action patterns are also "hard wired" -- they are part of the genetic programming of the individual. Also, like material in ROM, reflexes and FAPs cannot be easily "reprogrammed."

8. Invent a new reflex, one that would be helpful to humans.

The point of this question is to help students appreciate that evolution is a very effective mechanism: It is very difficult to think of useful reflexes that humans do not already have. An example might be gagging induced by eating food contaminated by botulism. People happily eat contaminated food, and the body does not react in a timely fashion. A gagging response to botulin-contaminated food could save lives. Another lifesaving reflex might be awakening from exposure to smoke. Many people die during their sleep as the result of smoke inhalation during house fires. If smoke caused people to awaken, fewer would die.

In discussing proposed reflexes, it might be useful to ask why they have not evolved. Part of the answer lies with the fact that evolution is not an intelligent process in which the environment decides what a species needs and then builds that characteristic. Another part of the answer may have to do with the proposed reflex involving low incidence events. It would certainly be useful to have a gagging reflex in response to botulin-contaminated food, but since botulism is relatively rare and since most people affected survive, the proposed reflex would have limited survival value for the species. In other words, if we designed a couple with the gagging reflex, their offspring might not be significantly more likely to reproduce and rear young than other children.

9. One learning specialist (Rachlin, 1976) refers to fixed action patterns as complex reflexes. Do you favor this idea? Explain.

There is no right answer to this question. The point is to get the student to think about the similarities and differences of reflexes and fixed action patterns. The latter can certainly be viewed as reflex chains in which one reflex is the elicited stimulus, or creates the eliciting stimulus, for the next reflex.

10. Who said change is the only constant, and what did he mean?

Lucretius; see the quotation at the beginning of the chapter. Lucretius' point was that everything in the universe is in a state of flux.

11. Why is natural selection "behind the times?"

The evolution of a useful feature typically requires many generations, but the environment can change dramatically within a single generation.

12. During wars, some soldiers sacrifice themselves to save their comrades. Some behavior scientists believe such altruistic behavior is the product of natural selection. How can this be, when the altruistic act ends the person's opportunities for reproduction?

Any act that improves the chance of survival of one's racial, ethnic, or political group also contributes to the survival of genes shared with that group. In addition, the success of an army indirectly ensures the survival of the individual soldier's blood relatives. (Winning armies do not usually return home and slaughter their own people.) Thus, soldiers who sacrifice their lives to save their comrades may increase the chances that their blood relatives at home will survive and reproduce.

13. How are reflexes, fixed action patterns, and general behavior traits alike? How do they differ?

All are, in general, less variable and more dependent on genes than other forms of behavior. They differ chiefly in the degree to which they vary and in the degree to which they can be modified by experience. Reflexes are less variable and generally less malleable than general behavior traits, with fixed action patterns falling between the two.

14. How would the length of a species' life span affect its chances of adapting to change through natural selection? Hint: Consider fruit flies in the dark.

Generally speaking, the shorter the lifespan, the faster we might expect a species to adapt to changes. Evolution takes place across generations, so the more generations produced in a given period of time, the more likely adaptable characteristics are to be selected. The reference to fruit flies is to the study described on page 5 of the text; it was possible to study several generations because of the short lifespan of the flies.

15. A person is asked to blink his eyes and does so. Is this a reflex act? Explain.

This question anticipates the distinction between Pavlovian and operant procedures, and is here partly for that reason. (Some instructors may want to use this question as a way of introducing respondent and operant behavior.) But the main reason for the question is to get students thinking about behavior and the difficulty of classifying behavior into categories such as reflexive and voluntary.
  Probably the best answer, from the standpoint of behavior science, is that blinking in response to a request is not a reflex response. For one thing, babies blink, but not in response to requests. That implies that requests to blink are not eliciting stimuli for the blinking reflex. Also, there probably are measurable differences between an eye blink elicited by a puff of air (for example), and an eye blink elicited by a request. (Verbally-elicited blinks may be slower and have longer latencies, for example.) Students might be encouraged to observe their own voluntary and involuntary blinking to see if they can detect such differences.

16. Why are most mutations unhelpful?

Mutations are more or less random events. Since species alive today are the products of millions of years of evolution, it is unlikely that any one random change in genes would be an improvement on eons of evolution.

17. In an unchanging world, would an organism with appropriate innate behavior need to learn?

Presumably the answer is no. Learning is a mechanism for coping with a changing environment. If there are no changes in the environment, there would be no need for (indeed, no opportunity for) learning.

18. Under what circumstances might learning be *mal*adaptive?

Learning is an adaptive mechanism, but it is not perfect. There are many instances in which learning is not only nonadaptive, but maladaptive. Among people, most superstitions, phobias, and prejudices have limited adaptive value, and some interfere with efficient functioning.

19. Captive animals behave very differently from animals in the wild. In which circumstance is their true nature revealed? Where should one look to see true human nature?

This is another of those questions that keep philosophers awake at night. There is probably no right answer, and the point of asking the question is to encourage students to wrestle with the nature-nurture problem, for that is what the question is really about.

Many ethologists assume that one sees true animal behavior only in the wild, in the organism's "natural" habitat. Some anthropologists argue that we see true human behavior only in pre-industrialized societies, our species' "natural" habitat. But while the behavior of lions in zoos is in many respects different from the behavior of lions in African savannas, both are lions. Similarly, the behavior of humans in cities is often different from that of humans in tribal villages, but we are talking about people in both situations. We cannot arbitrarily say, "We will accept the behavior of this organism in situation X as representative of the species, but we reject the behavior of this organism in situation Y." What situations X and Y reveal is not natural behavior and unnatural behavior, but the powerful effects of environment on behavior.

20. People sometimes suggest that one thing that separates humans from other animals is the tendency of people to believe in God. Is this distinction valid? If so, is the belief in God innate?

The fact that most people the world over believe in a deity of some sort is consistent with the idea that there is an inherited tendency toward the belief. On the other hand, there are a lot of atheists. This and the fact that religious beliefs are obviously related to instruction (children in Catholic families rarely grow up to be Moslems, for example) suggests that belief in God is dependent on learning.

This question has become the subject of empirical research. Some students may want to read Why God Won't Go Away: Science and the Biology of Belief *(Newberg, et al., 2001). See the review by Michael Shermer in the December, 2001 edition of* Psychology Today.

Key to Practice Quiz

1. Learning is a <u>change</u> in <u>behavior</u> due to <u>experience</u>.

2. The human fondness for sugar and <u>salt/sex</u> illustrates that behavior that has survival value at one time may be harmful at another time.

3. The sight of a chick with an open mouth reliably results in an adult bird providing food. The chick's open mouth is an example of a <u>releaser</u>.

4. Evolution is the product of <u>variation</u> and <u>natural selection</u>.

5. A reflex is a <u>relation</u> between a specific <u>event/stimulus</u> and a simple response.

6. In *The Blind Watchmaker*, Richard Dawkins suggests that the arrangement of <u>stones</u> on a <u>beach</u> demonstrates how order can come out of disorder without intelligent intervention.

7. <u>Habituation</u> is a reduction in the intensity or probability of a response due to repeated exposure to stimulus that elicits that response.

8. Peter and Rosemary Grant demonstrated natural selection in finches on the Galapagos Islands. They found that during <u>drought</u>, finches with larger beaks survived and reproduced, while those with smaller beaks died off.

9. The chief limitation of natural selection as a mechanism for coping with change is that it is <u>slow</u>.

10. An aversive event is one that is <u>escaped/avoided/painful/ unpleasant</u>.

Chapter 1 Quiz: Learning to Change

1. Learning is a _____ in _____ due to

    _____.

2. Fixed action patterns are elicited or induced by events called _____.

3. Evolution is the product of _____ and

    _____.

4. _____ said, "Change is the only constant."

5. Repeated exposure to a stimulus that evokes a reflex response results in

    _____.

6. _____ may be thought of as evolved modifiability.

7. Freud did not believe that human's have an instinctive opposition to _____.

8. Harry and Margaret _____ demonstrated that the early experiences of

    monkeys affect adult adaptation.

9. Instincts are now often called _____.

10. The author of your text believes that learning is an evolved mechanism for coping with

    _____.

Key to Chapter 1 Quiz

<u>Note</u>: Some quiz items in chapter quizzes may be from the practice quiz or from the test bank. Other questions may be based on footnotes. Both practice quizzes and chapter quizzes are meant to include items that vary widely in difficulty. Numbers in parentheses indicate the pages on which the answers may be found.

1. Learning is a <u>change</u> in <u>behavior</u> due to <u>experience</u>. (24)

2. Fixed action patterns are elicited or induced by events called <u>releasers</u>. (12)

3. Evolution is the product of <u>variation</u> and <u>natural selection</u>. (4)

4. <u>Lucretius</u> said, "Change is the only constant." (2)

5. Repeated exposure to a stimulus that evokes a reflex response results in <u>habituation</u>. (10)

6. <u>Learning</u> may be thought of as evolved modifiability. (24)

7. Freud did not believe that human's have an instinctive opposition to <u>incest.</u> (17)

8. Harry and Margaret <u>Harlow</u> demonstrated that the early experiences of monkeys affect adult adaptation. (28)

9. Instincts are now often called <u>fixed action patterns</u>. (12)

10. The author of your text believes that learning is an evolved mechanism for coping with <u>change/a changing environment</u>. (24)

2

The Study of Learning and Behavior

Chapter Outline

Main Points

The text takes the natural science approach to learning and behavior. With regard to the study of learning, this means looking for relations between environmental and behavioral events. Learning is a change in behavior due to experience (stimulus events). Changes in the rate of behavior can be monitored on a cumulative recorder. Various kinds of evidence contribute to our understanding of learning: anecdotes; case studies; descriptive studies; between-subjects and within-subject experiments. Each has its strengths and weaknesses. The use of animals in learning research is controversial, but there are good reasons for it. The remainder of the text deals with five questions having to do with the kinds of learning experiences; the tendency of learned behavior to spread (generalization and discrimination); reinforcement schedules; forgetting; and the limits of learning.

Class Notes

Background: The fundamental lesson to be learned from this chapter is that behavior can be studied with the same basic approach used in the natural sciences. It is well to emphasize to students that this does *not* mean denying that people think and feel. One way to begin discussing this chapter is to consider the Huxley quotation on the first page.

Learning defined. Some psychologists prefer to modify the word *change* with the phrase, *relatively permanent*. This is meant to exclude transitory changes in behavior such as those associated with habituation (see Chapter 1). Others (e.g., Thompson, 2000) consider habituation a primitive form of learning, and would not want it excluded. There is also the problem of defining *relatively permanent*; personally, I don't see how we could reach consensus on what the term means.

I discuss the meaning of learning in some detail because most students come to the course with certain ideas about learning that are at odds with the way psychologists use the term. For example, students typically think of learning as the acquisition of knowledge or skill. The notion of operational definitions of behavior is also apt to be foreign to students.

Measuring learning. Students have a hard time thinking of learning as the *decrease* in any measure of behavior; this issue might deserve special attention.

Sniffy Exercise: Observing Behavior

Careful observation is fundamental to science, so it may be useful to introduce the students to *Sniffy the Virtual Rat* by asking them to observe Sniffy's behavior for two minutes. Students might list all the things Sniffy does during this period: scratch, walk around, groom, raise up on his hind legs, etc. After discussing the observed behaviors with the class, ask the students to observe Sniffy again, this time counting the number of times one particular behavior (such as scratching) occurs in a five minute period. If the students work in pairs or small groups, they should compare their results with their partners, and report them to the class as a whole. Counts will tend to differ, even though the students are watching the same "rat." The possible reasons for these discrepancies should be discussed. Each group's count may then be averaged and the data from the class as a whole tabulated and plotted on the blackboard as a frequency graph.

Sniffy Exercise: The Slope of Learning

Each time that Sniffy presses the lever, that behavior is reflected on a cumulative record. This record then serves as a handy way of demonstrating how a cumulative record is produced, and how it is interpreted. In addition to allowing students to observe the formation of a cumulative record by a lever-trained Sniffy, the instructor might provide printouts of cumulative records (from Sniffy or a real animal). The class might be asked to identify when the behavior rate slows, when it increases, and when it is steady.

Research designs. Statistics are sometimes useful in interpreting data, but it is important for students to realize that they do not compensate for methodological weakness. If the data obtained in a series of interviews or a survey or in direct observations are inaccurate, no statistical test will improve them. If people do not answer interview questions honestly, for example, then statistical analysis becomes a mathematics of lies.

Animal research and human learning. Students are increasingly concerned about animal rights. The issue is difficult, and it may be well to bring the issues out into the open now, especially since some experiments the students will read about involve the use of strong aversives with animals.

Some instructors may want to point out that students who use cosmetics or soap, take medications, or undergo surgery, radiation or other medical treatments are benefiting from animal research. Eye shadow, for instance, is routinely tested on rabbits to make sure it is safe, often to the great discomfort of the animals. Students who wear wool clothing or eat meat also support treatment of animals that is typically far worse than the treatment animals receive in research labs.

Some students find it demeaning to them to suggest that their behavior follows the same basic rules followed by rats and pigeons. It may be worth pointing out to them that chimpanzees and humans share 98% of their genes, yet there are major differences between them. Wolves and dogs are also nearly identical genetically, yet the small difference in genes makes a big difference in behavior. The fact that humans and many other animals learn in similar ways does nothing to detract from the fact that people learn a great deal more from their experiences.

One topic that always seems to come up in discussions about animal research is the use of computer simulations. Since computer simulations are used to predict the course of weather systems, for example, why not write computer simulations to predict how a rat would behave? If simulations could anticipate new findings, medical researchers would have given up doing animal research years ago.

It should be noted that the text includes many basic and applied studies with human subjects. This is worth emphasizing since students seem inclined to think the learning course deals only with animal learning. If instructors want their students to believe that the principles covered in their course apply to humans as well as animals, then they will do well to call attention to experiments that use human subjects.

Questions about learning The questions in this section are intended to provide an overview of the remainder of the text. The first question makes the point that the next few chapters deal with the kinds of experiences that produce learning.

Key to review questions

1. Define the following terms in your own words. Give an example or illustration of each that is not provided in the text.

ABA reversal design: A type of within-subject experiment in which behavior is observed before (A) and after (B) an experimental manipulation. The original (A) condition is restored, sometimes followed again by the experimental (B) condition. Instructors may want to ask students when it might be appropriate to restore the experimental condition. It may not occur to them that in therapeutic situations it is often very important to do so.

Anecdotal evidence: First- or secondhand reports of personal experience.

Baseline period: In a within-subject experiment, a period of observation (often designated "A") during which no attempt is made to modify the behavior under study. The notion that the baseline period provides a basis for comparison should be stressed.

Behavior: Anything a person or animal does that can be measured. This definition does not exclude thinking and feeling, but in practice the term usually refers to publicly observable behavior.

Between-subjects experiment: An experimental design in which the independent variable is made to vary across two or more groups of subjects. Also called between-treatment or group design.

Case study: Detailed study and description of a single case. Usually used in clinical settings.

Control group: In a between-subjects experiment, those subjects not exposed to the independent variable.

Cumulative record: A graphic record of behavior, each point of which reflects the total number of times the behavior has been performed as of that time.

Cumulative recorder: An apparatus (or software) that records every occurrence of a behavior, thereby producing a cumulative record.

Dependent variable: The variable by which the outcome of an experiment is measured. It is expected to vary with (to depend on) the independent variable.

Descriptive study: A study in which the researcher attempts to describe a group by obtaining data from its members.

Experiment: A research design in which the researcher measures the effects of one or more independent variables on one or more dependent variables.

Experimental group: In a between-subjects experiment, those subjects exposed to the independent variable.

Independent variable: In an experiment, the variable that the researcher controls. The independent variable is usually expected to affect the dependent variable.

Matched sampling: A procedure for reducing extraneous differences among subjects in between-subjects experiments, by matching those in the experimental and control groups on specified characteristics, such as age, sex, and weight.

Operational definition: A definition that specifies the operation (procedure) by which a term will be measured.

Stimulus: Any event that affects, or is capable of affecting, behavior. Normally refers to environmental events, but can also refer to physiological events.

Within-subject experiment: A research design in which the independent variable is made to vary at different times for the same subject. Students are often unfamiliar with this kind of experiment. It may be a good idea to emphasize that each subject acts as both experimental and control subject. Some people prefer the terms single-subject or single case experiment.

2. A muscle on your hand twitches involuntarily. Is the muscle twitch behavior, or is it physiology?

This is one of those questions that may not have an answer. On the one hand, it is something an organism does that is measurable, which is the definition of behavior. On the other hand, such twitches are the very substance of physiology; if it isn't physiology, what is?

3. What are the principal similarities between within-subject and between-subjects designs?

I emphasize similarities here because the differences are fairly obvious. Students might mention that both are experimental designs and both involve comparisons between experimental and control conditions.

4. When would it not be possible to use an ABA design in the study of behavior?

Within-subject experiments compare subjects before and after an intervention. The intervention cannot be "undone," and this sometimes makes reversal inappropriate. We can, for example, remove a person's appendix to determine the effects of the procedure on certain symptoms, but we cannot restore the appendix to see if the symptoms return. Similarly, we cannot teach a person to read and then "restore" illiteracy by terminating instruction.

5. We humans see only a small part of the spectrum of light waves. Do light waves that fall outside of our detectable range qualify as stimuli?

The point here is that only stimuli that affect or are capable of affecting behavior qualify as stimuli. Therefore, what is a stimulus for one individual may not be for another individual. This implies that the "same" environment may be quite different for different individuals or for the same individual at different times.

6. Give an example of human learning measured as a *decrease* in the intensity of a behavior.

Answers will vary, of course. A masseur may learn to exert less pressure when massaging a person's back; a parent may learn to strike a child less forcefully; a person may learn to exert less pressure when brushing his teeth; and so on.

7. How could you quantify the changes in topography associated with learning to speak a foreign language?

One way would be to record the student's speech over a period of weeks or months and then present the tapes in random order to experts in the language. The degree to which the average ratings go up would reflect learning. Another approach might be to compare the sound wave patterns of the student with those from a native speaker. If the discrepancy diminishes over a period of time, the student's proficiency has improved.

8. A psychologist studies maze learning in rats by running 50 rats through a maze, one at a time. He does this 10 times. Then he computes the average time for all rats on each run and plots this on a graph. What sort of study is this?

Some students may say it is a within-subject design, since the rats were run one at a time. This is not, however, a defining feature of this design. There is no mention of any independent variable: rats simply run a maze 10 times. What the researcher seems to be doing is compiling norms for maze running in rats. If so, this makes it a descriptive study, rather than an experiment. If it is an experiment, it is a between-subjects design.

9. Some people dismiss research evidence by saying, "Oh, you can prove anything with research." How would you reply to this comment?

Perhaps the most obvious reply is, "What is better proof?" Often the people who reject scientific evidence readily accept anecdotal evidence, which is demonstrably less reliable. Other points that might be made are that scientific method has a very long track record of producing useful findings, that science is self-correcting, and that, in fact, you cannot "prove anything" with research.

10. Explain how the rate of behavior is reflected on a cumulative record.

The idea here is for students to describe in their own words how to interpret a cumulative record. Answers should mention the fact that the ink pen moves across the page each time a response occurs, so that the steeper the resulting line, the higher the response rate.

11. What is the chief virtue of matched sampling?

Matching reduces the amount of uncontrolled variability between groups.

12. Give an example of an event that would be a stimulus for one person but not for another.

The only difficulty here is to come up with an example not included in the text. Some people have poorer night vision than others, so an object one can see clearly may go undetected by another. There are also differences in sensitivity to pitch. Sexual stimulation may provide another example: Photographs of nude males may be sexually arousing to homosexual males and heterosexual females, but not to heterosexual males and homosexual females.

13. Does the term *toothache* refer to a stimulus or a behavior?

It seems to me the answer is open to debate. "I have a toothache" may mean, "I am responding to a stimulus in the proximity of my tooth." Thus, the toothache may be considered a response. However, toothache also refers to an abscess or other aberration, and this aberration excites pain receptors; things that excite pain receptors are usually considered stimuli.

14. What is wrong with defining learning as the acquisition of new behavior?

This question is asked because students tend to think of learning as the acquisition of new behavior, and it's important for them to realize that learning has a broader meaning. Answers should mention the fact that certain instances of learning (e.g., changes in behavior rate or latency) do not involve acquiring new behavior.

15. A researcher has 20 rats in a large cage, and he wants to assign them to two groups. He puts the first rat he catches in the experimental group, the second into the control group, and so on. Why is this bad science?

Without the hint, many students would think this procedure a good example of random assignment. The reason it is not has to do with the fact that the experimental group will systematically differ from those in the control group: The former are, on average, those caught more readily. These animals might be less healthy, less timid, or less active than those caught later. If students have a hard time seeing this, you might ask them if there would be any bias in putting the first 10 rats into the experimental group and the next 10 in the control group. Alternating is a milder form of the same biased procedure.

16. You are studying cocaine addiction in rats. An animal rights activist accuses you of animal cruelty. How can you defend your work?

Answers might mention that animals provide less variability in genetic and learning backgrounds than humans, are less expensive, and provide insights that may ultimately help animals as well as humans.

17. You are attempting to discover learning principles by studying the effects of experience on the eye blink. A friend says that eye blinking is a trivial kind of behavior, not worth studying. Defend your work.

Again, the object is to get students to play Devil's advocate since many students think that eye blinking and the like are trivial subjects for study. The hope is that students will learn that simple responses such as eye blinks and lever presses are merely convenient ways of rigorously studying fundamental principles.

18. A teacher says that learning researchers rely too much on animal studies and adds, "You can't tell anything about people from research on rats." How could you defend "rat psychology" against this criticism?

In answering this question, students might mention biomedical research in which animal analogues are used very effectively to better understand human disease processes and treatments. They might also mention that research done with animals is often replicated with humans, and this confirms the validity of animal research.

19. Some researchers argue that learning is a change in the brain produced by experience. Discuss the virtues and weakness of this definition.

Students might discuss the fact that learning may be said to occur without any apparent change in behavior. They might also talk about the problems with the notion of potential (which is implicit in such definitions), particularly the fact that a potential for behavior is never identified until the behavior occurs.

20. Why is random assignment of participants unnecessary in experiments with a within-subject design?

Subjects are not being compared with one another, and they are not assigned to different treatment groups.

Key to Practice Quiz

1. This book takes the <u>natural</u> science approach to behavior, the approach that focuses on identifying physical events that affect behavior.

2. One reason that many learning studies use animals is that with animals it is possible to control <u>variability/heredity/learning experiences</u>.

3. In an <u>operational</u> definition, a behavior is defined by the procedure used to measure it.

4. Changes in behavior due directly to the effects of an injury do not qualify as learning. A change in behavior caused by <u>maturation/disease/aging</u> also does not qualify as learning.

5. The kind of experiment that can be likened to turning a light switch on and off is an <u>ABA reversal</u> design.

6. <u>Between-subjects/group design</u> experiments assume that there are no important differences among participants.

7. A change in <u>topography</u> involves a change in the form a behavior takes.

8. Fluency combines errors and <u>speed</u>.

9. If there is a reduction in the time that passes before a behavior occurs, we say that learning is measured in terms of <u>latency</u>.

10. The cumulative recorder is used to measure learning as a change in <u>rate</u> of behavior.

Chapter 2 Quiz: Study of Learning and Behavior

1. _____ is the number of correct performances per minute.

2. When a concept is defined in terms of the procedure by which it is measured, the definition is said to be _____.

3. A change in _____ involves a change in the form a behavior takes.

4. In a _____ record, learning is indicated by a change in the rate at which a behavior occurs.

5. The essential element of a between-subjects design is that the independent variable varies across _____.

6. In a within-subject experiment, each subject's performance during a treatment period is compared to that subject's performance during a _____ period.

7. A _____ is an environmental event that is capable of affecting behavior.

8. Behavior can be defined as anything an organism does that can be _____.

9. A person who argues that something is true because "Everyone knows that..." is relying on _____ evidence.

10. Response _____ refers to the time that passes before a behavior occurs.

Key to Chapter 2 Quiz

1. <u>Fluency</u> is the number of correct performances per minute. (46)

2. When a concept is defined in terms of the procedure by which it is measured, the definition is said to be <u>operational</u>. (38)

3. A change in <u>topography</u> involves a change in the form a behavior takes. (42)

4. In a <u>cumulative</u> record, learning is indicated by a change in the rate at which a behavior occurs. (45)

5. The essential element of a between-subjects design is that the independent variable varies across <u>participants</u>. (50)

6. In a within-subject experiment, each subject's performance during a treatment period is compared to that subject's performance during a <u>baseline</u> period. (52)

7. A <u>stimulus</u> is an environmental event that is capable of affecting behavior. (40)

8. Behavior can be defined as anything an organism does that can be <u>measured</u>. (37)

9. A person who argues that something is true because "Everyone knows that..." is relying on <u>anecdotal</u> evidence. (47)

10. Response <u>latency</u> refers to the time that passes before a behavior occurs. (44)

3

Pavlovian Conditioning

Chapter Outline

Main Points

Pavlov's discovery of S-S learning came out of his effort to understand digestion. Pavlovian conditioning involves the pairing of two stimuli, CS and US. The US is contingent on the CS; neither stimulus is contingent on behavior. Conditioning is often measured as response latency or response strength. In higher-order conditioning, the CS is not paired with a US but with a well-established CS. The most important variable affecting Pavlovian conditioning is the way in which the CS and US are paired; the most effective procedures are trace and delayed. Other variables affecting learning rate are the degree of CS-US contingency; CS-US contiguity; various stimulus features (one stimulus may overshadow another); prior experience with CS and US (which can produce latent inhibition and blocking); number of CS-US pairings. Putting a CR on extinction means presenting the CS without the US. Pavlov's stimulus substitution theory has given way to preparatory response theory.

Class Notes

<u>Background</u>. Discussions of Pavlov's work too often neglect the fact that he was a physiologist trying to understand the workings of glands. His work illustrates the value of following interesting leads.

Pavlov's remark about the glands having "a kind of intelligence" strikes me as important; not only did the glands behave differently to different stimuli, but their behavior changed as the result of experience. This meant that "psychic reflexes" were to be explained in terms of learning.

Basic procedures. Instructors may want to emphasize that Pavlovian conditioning is sometimes called S-S learning because the experiences that produce learning involve the pairing of stimuli. It might be a good idea to indicate that Pavlov's unconditional reflexes are the innate reflexes discussed in the first chapter.

Exercise: Food for Thought

Bring a lemon to class and, in the course of the lesson, casually cut it into slices and take a bite. Then ask the students what reaction they had. Would a person who had never seen a lemon react in the same way? What accounts for the difference?

Some students find the flow charts on identifying elements of and types of conditioning (the boxed material adapted from Hummel, et al.) very helpful. It may be useful to go through these boxes in class.

The text describes Pavlov's early work in some detail in order to give students an idea of the rigor of his methods. Toward this end, it may be useful to read certain passages of *Conditioned Reflexes* aloud or to assign one chapter of Pavlov's text.

Exercise: Reinventing Pavlov

Ask students to invent a new terminology of Pavlovian conditioning. That is, replace all the terms in the section on basic procedures with new terms. (E.g., the conditional stimulus might be called an acquired signal.)

Higher-order conditioning. The significance of higher-order conditioning is apt to escape many students. If they dismiss it as trivial, they may learn an important lesson about the value of basic research when they get to the work of Staats and Staats on prejudice in Chapter 4.

Variables affecting Pavlovian conditioning. Many authors discuss the various ways of pairing CS and US (trace, delayed, etc.) in the discussion of basic procedures. I treat them here to emphasize that how the CS and US are paired affects the rate of learning.

Exercise: Delaying Pavlov

Ask the students to speculate on how long a CS-US interval might be and still produce a CR. Eating and becoming ill might be used as an example: If you ate a hot dog and immediately became sick, you might feel queasy the next time you tasted a hot dog. What if you ate the hot dog and became sick 20 minutes later? An hour later? Two hours later? Two days? A month? What are the limits, and how would you go about defining them?

The sections on contingency and contiguity provide the opportunity to discuss these fundamental concepts. They form part of a precise description of experience. It is one thing to say that learning is due to experience; it is quite another thing to describe experience in an objective way. Again, the boxed material adapted from Hummel et al. may be a useful instructional tool.

Papini and Bitterman (1990) raise doubts about the role of contingency in Pavlovian conditioning. This topic seems to me to be beyond the scope of an undergraduate course in learning principles, but some instructors may want to pursue it.

Exercise: Personality and Conditioning

There is a very nice figure on page 74 of Eysenck (1965) showing eye blink conditioning in introverts and extroverts. Instructors might ask students to theorize about whether introverts or extroverts are more "conditionable" and, if so, why. The students might be given the raw data and be asked to plot it, draw curves that typify the performance of the two groups, and interpret the results.

In considering the effects of the number of CS-US pairings, it is worth noting that each successive pairing has less impact on behavior. What this means is that experience modifies not only behavior, but the effect that later experiences will have on behavior.

Extinction of conditioned responses. The concept of extinction is introduced in this chapter. Instructors may want to discuss the distinction between the extinction and forgetting.

Concerning the box on Edwin Twitmyer, it might be interesting to ask students if his decision to give up work on patellar conditioning might itself have been partially a result of Pavlovian conditioning. After all, talking about his conditioning experiments was paired with a humiliating experience at the APA meeting chaired by William James. Perhaps talking (and thinking) about conditioning became CSs for feeling humiliated and/or depressed. Speculation, of course, but interesting speculation.

Theories of conditioning. The discussion of preparatory response theory provides a good opportunity for considering the evolutionary value of Pavlovian conditioning.

My hope is that the box on awareness will provoke stimulating class discussion on the nature of conditioning. There is little doubt that humans undergoing conditioning sometimes "catch on" to the relation between CS and US, but there are problems with assuming that this understanding is essential to the appearance of the CR. The awareness issue also raises questions about what constitutes an explanation of conditioning.

The idea of "psychic reflexes" may seem antiquated and naive to some students, rather like the ancient belief that sight was the result of light emanating from the eye. It might therefore be useful to point out that the popular view of Pavlovian conditioning (i.e., the bell makes the dog think of food, and thinking of food makes it salivate), is merely a variation of the psychic reflex concept.

Key to Review Questions

1. Define the following terms:

Backward conditioning: A Pavlovian conditioning procedure in which the US precedes the CS.

Blocking: Failure of a stimulus to become a CS when it is part of a compound stimulus that includes an effective CS. The effective CS blocks the formation of another CS.

Classical conditioning: A synonym for Pavlovian conditioning; the procedure of pairing a neutral stimulus with a US.

Compound stimulus: Two or more stimuli presented simultaneously, often as a CS.

Conditional reflex: A reflex acquired through Pavlovian conditioning and consisting of a CS and a CR.

Conditional response: The response part of a conditional reflex; the response elicited by a CS.

Conditional stimulus: The stimulus part of a conditional reflex; the stimulus that elicits a CR.

Contiguity: Nearness of events in time (temporal contiguity) or space (spatial contiguity).

Contingency: A dependency between events. An event may be stimulus-contingent (dependent on the appearance of a stimulus) or behavior-contingent (dependent on the appearance of a behavior).

Delayed conditioning: A Pavlovian conditioning procedure in which the CS starts before, and then overlaps with, the US.

Extinction: In Pavlovian conditioning, the procedure of repeatedly presenting the CS without the US.

Higher-order conditioning: A variation of Pavlovian conditioning in which a neutral stimulus is paired, not with a US, but with a well-established CS.

Intertrial interval: The interval separating the trials of a discrete trial procedure.

Latent inhibition: In Pavlovian conditioning, the failure of a CR to appear as a result of prior presentation of the CS in the absence of the US.

Overshadowing: Failure of a stimulus that is part of a compound stimulus to become a CS. The stimulus is said to be overshadowed by the stimulus that does become a CS.

Preparatory response theory: Theory of Pavlovian conditioning that proposes that the CR prepares the organism for the occurrence of the US.

Pseudo conditioning: The tendency of a neutral stimulus to elicit a CR when presented after a US has elicited a reflex response.

Sensory preconditioning: A procedure in which two neutral stimuli are paired, after which one is repeatedly paired with a US. If the other stimulus is then presented alone, it may elicit a CR even though it was never paired with the US.

Simultaneous conditioning: A Pavlovian conditioning procedure in which the CS and US occur together in time.

Spontaneous recovery: The sudden reappearance of a behavior following its extinction.

Stimulus substitution theory: The theory that the CS substitutes for the US. Assumes that the CR is essentially the same as the UR.

Test trial: The procedure of presenting the CS on some occasions without the US to determine whether learning has occurred.

Trace conditioning: A Pavlovian conditioning procedure in which the CS begins and ends before the US is presented.

Unconditional reflex: A synonym for reflex. An unconditional reflex consists of a US and a UR.

Unconditional response: The response elicited by a US. Often called an unconditioned response.

Unconditional stimulus: The stimulus that elicits a UR. Often called an unconditioned stimulus.

2. What did Pavlov mean when he said that glands seemed to possess intelligence?

Pavlov was impressed by the fact that the glands responded differently, depending on the stimulus: sand produced a lot of saliva, marbles produced very little. The "intelligence" of the glands is really the "intelligence" of evolution.

3. One of Pavlov's most important discoveries was that salivation could be attributed to events occurring in the dog's environment. Why is this important?

Pavlov's discovery showed that salivation (and by implication other kinds of behavior) could be understood in terms of functional relations between behavior and physical (as opposed to mental) events. This helped lay the groundwork for a natural science of behavior.

4. Why do you suppose Pavlovian conditioning is also called classical conditioning?

Classical means the original or standard form, and Pavlovian conditioning was the first form of learning studied in a rigorous scientific manner.

5. Explain the use of test trials in the measurement of Pavlovian learning.

Answers should describe how test trials are conducted and note that they are a way of determining whether learning has occurred.

6. Why is pseudoconditioning a problem for researchers?

Pseudo conditioning is a problem because it is false (pseudo). It involves changes in behavior that may be mistaken for conditioning. It is analogous to false positives on medical tests.

7. Give an example of higher-order conditioning from your own experience.

The object here is to induce the students to examine their own behavior in terms of a new concept. This is very different from memorizing the examples given in a text. Answers should be scrutinized to ensure that they do not represent instances of direct (lower order) conditioning.

8. Give an example of overshadowing.

Any example that meets the definition will do. If thunder were always preceded by the sound of a buzzer as well as lightning, it is likely that we would jump at the sound of a buzzer and not notice the lightning flash. The buzzer would overshadow the lightning.

9. How is overshadowing different from blocking?

Answers should mention that blocking involves a stimulus that is already a CS, while overshadowing involves two or more neutral stimuli one of which becomes a CS.

10. Why is it a mistake to speak of *simple* Pavlovian conditioning?

The text makes the point that Pavlovian conditioning is affected by a number of variables and so is far less simple than people imagine.

11. Explain the differences among trace, delayed, simultaneous and backward conditioning procedures. Illustrate each procedure with an example not given in the text.

This is straightforward, but students should describe the different procedures in their own words.

12. If you wanted to establish a conditional eye blink in response to a light, what procedure (from among trace, delayed, etc.) is least likely to be successful.

There might be room for debate, but the best answer is probably backward conditioning.

13. What is the principal flaw in Pavlov's stimulus substitution theory?

One candidate is that evidence indicates the CR and UR are not identical. This pretty much shoots down Pavlov's idea that the CS is merely a different way of eliciting the UR. An argument can also be made for citing circularity as the chief flaw, since there is no independent evidence for the proposed physiological events.

14. In what sense is a CR a preparatory response?

The fact that the CR is different from (sometimes the opposite of) the UR raises the possibility that it prepares the organism for the US. This is supported by a number of studies.

15. How would you determine the optimum intensity of a CS for eyelid conditioning?

There may be many ways to do this, but a fairly simple procedure would be to conduct a group design experiment in which each group received conditioning trials but with different intensities of CS.

16. Peggy Noonan, a political speech writer, reports that soon after she had a baby she returned to the campaign trail. One day she saw something in a crowd and began lactating. What did she see?

Some students are bound to complain, "There is nothing in the book about lactating speech writers!" Of course, they are right. The point is to be able to apply principles that are in the chapter to situations never encountered before. In this case, the student needs to think about the stimuli normally present during breast feeding. The answer, of course, is a baby, and that is what Ms. Noonan saw in that crowd. (The example comes from Noonan's 1990 book about her experiences with the Reagan administration, What I Saw at the Revolution.*)*

17. Some dentists ask their patients to listen to music through headphones while having their teeth worked on. The idea is to help the patient relax, thereby reducing the painfulness of the procedure. Should people who do this listen to music they like, or music they dislike?

Many students have probably experienced this procedure first hand, and very likely have never questioned the wisdom of listening to preferred music. But if music is paired with painful stimuli, might not the music lose its appeal? Anyone who has to have a lot of painful dental work done might be unwise to listen to their favorite music.

18. Some victims of insomnia sleep better at strange hotels than they do in their own bedroom. Explain why.

Again, there is nothing in the chapter about insomnia, so the student is required to apply principles to a new problem. The phenomenon might better be accounted for in terms of operant stimulus control, but it's worth considering the potential role of classical conditioning. The student's reasoning should probably run something like this: Any stimuli associated with sleepless nights are apt to become conditional stimuli for sleeplessness. The bedroom therefore becomes a CS for wakefulness. To the extent that a hotel bedroom provides different stimuli from our familiar bedroom, it will be less effective as a CS for wakefulness.

19. In 1957, an amateur psychologist named James Vicary flashed imperceptible messages on a screen during showings of the film, *Picnic*. The messages were "Hungry? Eat popcorn" and "Drink Coca-Cola." Although Vicary claimed these "subliminal ads" increased sales of popcorn and Coke ®, research proved him wrong. However, the ads did have the effect of arousing hostility toward Pavlovian conditioning. Was Vicary's amateur experiment really a study of Pavlovian conditioning?

Many students have heard of Vicary's experiment, or at least they've heard of subliminal ads, and this question is here partly in the hope that some misunderstandings might be corrected. I encourage instructors to make three points in discussing the question: First, the original experiment was not done by a trained researcher and probably lacked proper controls. Second, subsequent research showed that subliminal ads do not work. Third, Vicary's experiment did not involve Pavlovian conditioning. He presented a stimulus ("Eat popcorn"), but did not pair that stimulus with a US. The procedure is actually based on the assumption that previous operant learning would incline people to respond to discriminative stimuli for eating. Since weak discriminative stimuli are less effective than stronger ones, it is likely that Vicary would have gotten much better results by displaying "Eat popcorn" on the screen for several seconds before or after the film.

20. How has the study of Pavlovian conditioning altered your view of human nature?

This is another question that is meant to challenge basic ideas and assumptions. Many students are inclined to think that Pavlovian conditioning has nothing to say about human nature. Once encouraged to think about the issue, however, they may recognize that Pavlov's work means that certain kinds of behavior can be attributed to specific kinds of experiences. Further, this realization gives us some power since it means that we can produce certain kinds of behavior by providing certain experiences. Before Pavlov, fear, anger and many other responses originated in the mind; after Pavlov, they originated in experience.

Key to Practice Quiz

1. The conditional response is so named because it depends on many <u>conditions</u>.

2. In higher-order conditioning, the CS is paired with a well-established <u>conditional</u> stimulus.

3. <u>H. G. Wells</u> thought Pavlov was one of the greatest geniuses who ever lived.

4. Pavlovian conditioning usually involves <u>reflexive</u> behavior.

5. In Pavlovian conditioning, the appearance of the US is normally <u>contingent/dependent</u> on the appearance of the CS.

6. Generally speaking, the shorter the CS-US interval, the <u>faster</u> the rate of learning; the shorter the inter-trial interval, the <u>slower</u> the rate of learning.

7. Braun and Geiselhart found that older subjects acquired conditional responses <u>less</u> rapidly than younger subjects.

8. Siegel's research on drug effects supports the <u>preparatory response</u> theory of conditioning.

9. The least effective form of Pavlovian conditioning is probably the <u>backward</u> procedure.

10. Latent <u>inhibition</u> is the result of the CS having appeared alone before conditioning trials.

Chapter 3 Quiz: Pavlovian Procedures

1. In Pavlovian conditioning, the appearance of the US is normally _____ on the appearance of the CS.

2. _____ inhibition is the result of the CS having appeared alone repeatedly before conditioning.

3. Pavlov called reflexes present at birth _____ reflexes.

4. Research suggests that poor conditioning results in _____ people may be associated with dementia.

5. The time between conditioning trials is called the _____.

6. The researcher who nearly became the American Pavlov was Edwin

   _____.

7. Pavlov won the Nobel Prize for his research on _____ _____.

8. Conditional reflexes are so named because they depend on many _____.

9. In delayed conditioning the CS and US _____.

10. Each pairing of a CS and US is one _____.

Key to Chapter 3 Quiz

1. In Pavlovian conditioning, the appearance of the US is normally <u>contingent/dependent</u> on the appearance of the CS. (81)

2. <u>Latent</u> inhibition is the result of the CS having appeared alone repeatedly before conditioning. (86)

3. Pavlov called reflexes present at birth <u>unconditional</u> reflexes. (70)

4. Research suggests that poor conditioning results in _____ people may be associated with dementia. (89, n11)

5. The time between conditioning trials is called the <u>intertrial interval</u>. (89)

6. The researcher who nearly became the American Pavlov was Edwin <u>Twitmyer</u>. (94)

7. Pavlov won the Nobel Prize for his research on <u>physiology</u>. (69)

8. Conditional reflexes are so named because they depend on many <u>conditions</u>. (70)

9. In delayed conditioning the CS and US <u>overlap</u>. (79)

10. Each pairing of a CS and US is one <u>trial</u>. (72)

4

Pavlovian Applications

Chapter Outline

Main Points

Pavlovian conditioning is important to survival and has many practical applications in modern society. It helps account for phobias, prejudice, advertising effects, some paraphilias, taste aversions, and the functioning of the immune system. Through counterconditioning, Pavlovian conditioning can often undo the damage of natural learning experiences.

Class Notes

<u>Background</u>. The text tries to convey the notion that Pavlovian conditioning is not only a vibrant research area, but a topic of considerable practical importance. The popular view that all Pavlov did was train dogs to salivate at the sound of a bell is unfortunately perpetuated in the press and even in some psychology texts. Some instructors are reluctant to give attention to applications in what they consider a course on basic research, but I believe that helping students see how Pavlovian conditioning affects their lives will give them an appreciation for the laboratory research from which those benefits stem.

Exercise: Pavlov in the Papers

Ask students to scan a newspaper for items that in one way or another reflect the importance of Pavlovian conditioning, and share those items with the class. Selected items might include articles about racists, "crimes of passion," display and classified ads that use Pavlovian principles to sell products and services, certain medical treatments, and the arrangement of article topics (e.g., the fact that crimes are not covered in the cooking section).

Fear: The Little Albert study offends many students today. It may be worth discussing the fact that standards of treatment of children were very different in Watson's day. It should also be noted that Watson planned to eliminate Albert's fear, but the child and his mother, who worked at the hospital, left before this could be done.

Exercise: Watson on Trial

It might be fun to have a mock trial of John Watson on charges of child abuse for the experiment with Little Albert. Some students would serve as prosecuting attorneys, others as defense attorneys, one or two as judges, and the remaining students would serve as the jury. If you are willing to get into the act, you might make yourself available as an expert witness. One class period might be devoted to the trial, or you might set aside 15 minutes at the end of each of three or four class periods. Today's students really enjoy this kind of activity. In the course of the trial, all students will become acquainted with the original research and the ethical dilemmas that are almost intrinsic to behavioral research.

Prejudice: Student often acknowledge that people acquire prejudices when they suggest that people are prejudiced "because that's how they were brought up." They seldom consider precisely what "how they were brought up" means. What sort of experiences do families provide that convey prejudice? Can these experiences be described in terms of Pavlovian procedures?

The text gives considerable space to the work of Staats and Staats. Some texts never even mention this work, but in my opinion it is every bit as important as that of Garcia on taste aversion, which is routinely covered. I hope instructors will discuss the Staats's work and its significance.

Exercise: Word Judging

Announce that you will read several words aloud, and ask the students to rate each word on a 1 to 4 scale from positive to negative. The words should include some that are likely to have emotional significance, such as baby or failure. It will be important to provide sheets with the scales, to insist that students circle only one number, and to emphasize that they should answer quickly. Two students might then tabulate the scores to determine each word's "affective value." It might also be interesting to look for differences in the ratings of men and women. (They might rate the words *man* and *woman* differently, for example.)

Advertising: Some instructors may want to take up the topic of "placement advertising," the practice of providing exposure to brand name products in media, particularly films. For example, a popular actor portraying a protagonist in a film might drink a brand name soft drink during a scene; there may or may not be any mention of the product, which is typically unimportant to the story line. Do such ads utilize Pavlovian principles? Are they likely to be more or less effective than traditional ads? Do they raise any special ethical questions?

32

Dave Barry (1992), the humorist, pokes fun at the ads for Timex watches in which people who have survived terrible accidents endorse the watches. He writes that the message he gets from these ads is that if you wear a Timex watch, something bad will happen to you. He adds that he finds himself edging away from Timex display cases for fear that a great white shark may come around the corner. Barry's spoof makes a good point: Ads can backfire if the product is paired with stimuli that have unintended negative effects, such as eliciting fear. Along these lines, it might be noted that O. J. Simpson, who had been a frequent figure in television commercials, apparently lost much of his appeal to advertisers after his arrest for murder.

The paraphilias: The role of learning in sexual behavior tends to be neglected in learning courses, possibly because sex is a controversial topic, and possibly because the role of learning is so subtle. It might be interesting to ask students when they first became aware that they were male or female. Other questions to ask: What sort of experiences do parents provide that convey gender identity? How might sexual orientation be influenced by learning experiences? What is a sexual aberration? How can "normal" sexual behavior be distinguished from "abnormal" sexual behavior? Who decides when someone needs treatment? Does society have the right to prescribe treatment for pedophilia? for rape? What about cross-dressing, exhibitionism, masturbation, and homosexuality?

Taste aversion. Research on the role of Pavlovian conditioning in taste preferences has focused on taste aversions. Yet it is clear that people come to like certain foods just as they come to dislike others. It might be interesting to ask students to identify the CS and US that might be involved in a person's preference for, say, chocolate. Preference for sweets is certainly influenced by evolution (see Chapter 1), but there are cultural differences as well, which means learning is involved. Many traditional treats in Japan are not what Americans would call sweet.

Immune function. Note that to say that an illness is partly the product of experience does not mean that it is not real. Too many physicians (and future physicians taking learning courses) look with contempt on people whose illnesses are primarily the products of learning. This may have to do with the word psychosomatic, which laymen take to mean "in the mind." The implication is that psychosomatic illnesses are somehow less real than those caused by disease or injury. This is not always the case.

Key to Review Questions

1. Define the following terms and provide an example of each:

   Aversion therapy: A form of counterconditioning in which a CS is paired with an aversive US, often a nausea-inducing drug.
   Conditioned emotional response: An emotional response to a stimulus that is acquired through Pavlovian conditioning.
   Conditioned suppression: A reduction in the rate of responding due to the non-contingent presentation of an aversive CS.
   Conditioned taste aversion: An aversion, acquired through Pavlovian conditioning, to foods with a particular flavor.
   Counterconditioning: The use of Pavlovian conditioning to reverse the unwanted effects of prior conditioning.

2. Suppose your doctor advises you to eat liver, which you despise. How might you overcome your aversion to liver?

   Students should be able to recognize that this problem involves a stimulus (liver) producing an undesired response (aversion). If so, they should be able to devise a way of altering the response by pairing consumption of liver with some desirable stimulus, such as some enjoyable food. The student might, for instance, take a bite of mashed potatoes and gravy (a favored food) immediately after eating a bite of liver. Increasing the level of food deprivation might also be helpful.

3. You are the dietitian in charge of cancer patients at a hospital. How might you apply your knowledge of taste aversions to improve the health of your patients?

   Some students may suggest an approach similar to that suggested for the previous item. However, in this instance the problem may be better viewed as a matter of helping patients avoid taste aversions. One way to do that might be to ask oncologists to require patients to eat a certain food (e.g., strawberry ice cream) before each chemotherapy or radiotherapy treatment. The patients should develop a strong aversion to that particular food item, but might not develop other taste aversions.

4. Pavlovian learning usually requires CS-US intervals of no more than a few seconds. Taste aversion conditioning is an exception. Why does this exception exist?

   This question is meant to remind the student that learning is a biological mechanism that evolved because it contributed to survival. Food-induced illness typically follows eating after several minutes or hours. Presumably long CS-US intervals work in taste aversion learning because individuals capable of learning under such circumstances were more likely to survive and reproduce.

5. A man of about 80 named Albert walks into a psychologist's office asking for help in overcoming an irrational fear of white, furry creatures. What can the psychologist do to help him?

   The student's reply should probably focus on counterconditioning, perhaps along the general lines of the procedure used with Peter.

34

6. How can you increase the likelihood that your child will share your devotion to jazz music?

Many people seem to think of tastes in music as innate. While there may be innate predispositions to like certain kinds of music, learning is almost certainly involved. Answers should suggest pairing jazz music with pleasant experiences at an early age. Students might suggest, for example, playing a jazz tape while nursing the infant.

7. You are in charge of rehabilitating criminals convicted of various hate crimes. Can Pavlovian learning help?

The key word here is hate. Emotional reactions to certain groups (Whites, African-Americans, homosexuals, etc.) are learned. Emotional learning is probably largely a matter of Pavlovian conditioning. A rehabilitation program for those guilty of hate crimes might include Pavlovian procedures meant to help inmates unlearn their hatred. Some students may want to read Hate Crime: The Story of a Dragging in Jasper, Texas *by journalist Joyce King. It not only examines the crime itself, but reveals how prisons contribute to race hatred.*

8. What do salivating dogs have to do with masochism?

Answers should describe the role of Pavlovian conditioning in the behavior of people who obtain sexual pleasure from pain or humiliation.

9. It has been said that people who have amorous encounters under clandestine conditions are sometimes later unable to enjoy amorous experiences under more ordinary conditions. Explain why.

The clandestine conditions presumably become a CS for erotic arousal through their pairing with amorous experiences. Safe conditions have not had the opportunity to become CSs for sexual arousal. One person who has written about this curious phenomenon is Bertrand Russell; unfortunately, I cannot provide the source for his comments.

10. What does the work of Staats and Staats lead you to predict about the backgrounds of Ku Klux Klan members?

The work of Staats and Staats suggests that Ku Klux Klan members have a history of exposure to racial and ethnic slurs. For example, their parents may routinely have complained about how a given group "is ruining the country," have "stolen" the good jobs, etc.

11. In what sense are psychosomatic illnesses caused by events outside the patient's body?

If an illness is psychosomatic, then it is at least partly the product of experience. Most such experiences involve stimuli outside the patient's body.

12. Invent a better term for the disorders known as psychosomatic illnesses.

Psychosomatic suggests that the disorders are "in the mind," or the result of mental processes. The evidence indicates that they are due largely to experience. Proposed terms should reflect this fact. Perhaps ecogenic *or* envirogenic *would be appropriate.*

13. Why is it a mistake to speak of simple Pavlovian conditioning?

The same question was asked in Chapter 3. Again the answer should get at the complexity of Pavlovian learning. Students might cite some of the variables that affect Pavlovian learning or point to the variety of things that can be learned through Pavlovian procedures.

14. What sort of procedure (trace, backward, etc.) did Garcia use in his experiments on taste aversion?

The text reports that the rats were irradiated while they drank sweet-tasting water. Since the CS (sweet water) and US (radiation) overlap, a delayed procedure is involved.

15. Why are people more likely to develop aversions to foods they have not often eaten?

Students might be encouraged to apply the concept of latent inhibition. In any case, their answers should make note of the fact that familiar foods are eaten many times without being paired with illness and this history makes the food resistant to conditioning.

16. How is Pavlovian conditioning used to sell beer?

All students have seen the magazine and TV ads in which a particular kind of beer is paired repeatedly with positive stimuli, particularly young, attractive people having a great time in recreational settings.

17. What is the essential difference between the way Peter and Albert acquired their fears?

Probably the essential difference is that Albert's fear of the rat was established deliberately and systematically, while Peter's fear of the rabbit was "natural" -- i.e., the product of unplanned experiences. Both almost certainly involved the same sort of Pavlovian procedures.

18. What is a euphemism? Why are euphemisms used?

The word euphemism does not appear in the chapter, but the concept is discussed. (See, for example, the box, Bite Your Tongue.) *The point of this exercise is to get students to take a fresh look at an everyday experience, in this case the use of euphemisms. As words acquire aversive qualities, other more neutral words are used in order to avoid undesirable effects. No one likes to speak of killing unwanted pets, for example, so we talk of "putting them to sleep."*

19. Many people hate groups of people with whom they have had no direct experience. How can Pavlovian conditioning account for these emotions?

Here again the work of Staats and Staats is important. We can learn to hate people we've never met if the words that name those people are regularly paired with unpleasant words or images.

20. How has reading this chapter altered your view of Pavlovian conditioning?

I hope that students will feel more positive about Pavlovian conditioning and will see it as a richer, more complex phenomenon than they had previously.

Key to Practice Quiz

1. The phenomenon of latent <u>inhibition</u> suggests that we are more likely to develop aversions to novel foods than to familiar ones.

2. People used to believe that children were instinctively afraid of fire, animals, and many other things. John Watson and Rosalie <u>Rayner</u> found that many such fears were acquired through conditioning.

3. The first person to use counterconditioning to treat a phobia was probably <u>Mary Cover Jones</u>.

4. The work of Staats and Staats suggests that prejudice may be partly the result of <u>higher</u>-order conditioning.

5. Dana Bovbjerg and her colleagues found that women receiving chemotherapy in a hospital later showed decreased functioning of their <u>immune</u> systems when they returned to the hospital.

6. Gorn influenced product choice by pairing pens of a certain color with certain kinds of <u>music</u>.

7. In <u>aversion</u> therapy, a stimulus that elicits an inappropriate response is paired with an aversive stimulus such as shock or an emetic drug.

8. The pairing of a particular food with nausea-inducing stimuli often results in a conditioned <u>taste aversion</u>.

9. Carl Gustavson did research aimed at reducing predation of <u>sheep</u> by coyotes.

10. Masochism may be the result of pairing stimuli that cause <u>pain/humiliation</u> with those that cause <u>pleasure/sexual</u> <u>arousal</u>.

Chapter 4 Quiz: Pavlovian Applications

1. The first person to use counterconditioning to treat a phobia was probably

   _____.

2. Conditioned suppression is used as a measure of _____.

3. Sexual offenders are sometimes treated with a form of counterconditioning called

   _____ therapy.

4. The CS and US in the Little Albert experiment were a _____ and

   _____, respectively.

5. Elnora Stuart paired _____ with pleasant scenes.

6. Carl Gustavson studied conditioned _____ _____ in coyotes.

7. *Conditioned Reflexes and Psychiatry* was written by _____.

8. Prejudice is an example of a conditioned _____ _____.

9. A recent variation of counterconditioning uses _____ reality.

10. The work of _____ and _____ suggests that prejudice may be

    partly the result of higher-order conditioning.

Key to Chapter 4 Quiz

1. The first person to use counterconditioning to treat a phobia was probably <u>Mary Cover Jones</u>. (109)

2. Conditioned suppression is used as a measure of <u>fear</u>. (112)

3. Sexual offenders are sometimes treated with a form of counterconditioning called <u>aversion</u> therapy. (120)

4. The CS and US in the Little Albert experiment were a <u>rat</u> and <u>loud sound</u>, respectively. (107)

5. Elnora Stuart paired <u>toothpaste</u> with pleasant scenes. (116)

6. Carl Gustavson studied conditioned <u>taste aversions</u> in coyotes. (125)

7. *Conditioned Reflexes and Psychiatry* was written by <u>Pavlov</u>. (130)

8. Prejudice is an example of a conditioned <u>emotional response</u>. (111)

9. A recent variation of counterconditioning uses <u>virtual</u> reality. (110)

10. The work of <u>Staats</u> and <u>Staats</u> suggests that prejudice may be partly the result of higher-order conditioning. (111)

5

Operant Reinforcement

Chapter Outline

Introduction
Box: E. L. Thorndike: What the Occasion Demanded
Basic Procedures
Box: B. F. Skinner: The Darwin of Behavior Science
Discrete Trial and Free Operant Procedures
Operant and Pavlovian Learning Compared
Primary and Secondary Reinforcers
Shaping and Chaining
Box: Tips for Shapers
Variables Affecting Reinforcement
Contingency/Contiguity/Reinforcer Characteristics/Task Characteristics/Deprivation
Level/Other Variables
Box: Octopi Individuality
Extinction of Reinforced Behavior
Theories of Reinforcement
Hull's Drive-Reduction Theory/Relative Value Theory and the Premack
Principle/Response Deprivation Theory
Theories of Avoidance
Two-process Theory/One-process Theory
Recommended Reading
Review Questions
Practice Quiz
Query Answers

Main Points

Thorndike's early work led him to formulate the law of effect, one of the fundamental principles of behavior. Skinner built on this foundation: He invented most of the terms of operant learning used today, and described the basic procedures, including shaping and chaining. Operant and Pavlovian procedures differ in several ways, most notably in the fact that operant procedures involve response-contingent events, whereas Pavlovian conditioning involves stimulus-contingent events. The rate of operant learning is affected by the degree of contingency and contiguity, reinforcer characteristics, and other factors. The extinction of an operant response involves the withholding of reinforcing consequences. There are three main theories of positive reinforcement: drive-reduction; relative value (which produced the Premack Principle); and response deprivation. There are two theories of avoidance: two-process and one-process.

Class Notes

Background. Thorndike's work is often given little more than a paragraph before going on to Skinner, yet it was Thorndike who formulated the law of effect and laid the foundation for the work of Skinner and others who followed. Thorndike's work is primitive by today's standards, but it is seminal and deserves careful consideration.

40

Texts usually take up operant learning after Pavlovian conditioning, which gives the impression that Pavlov had historical primacy. However, Thorndike and Pavlov were doing their classic work at about the same time. Thorndike published his dissertation in 1898, about the same time Pavlov was studying salivary conditioning. Pavlov's work was not published in English until 1927, so Thorndike probably did not know about it until then. Likewise Pavlov (1927) notes that he was unaware of Thorndike's work when he was doing his early studies.

Sniffy Exercise: Reinforcement

It may be useful to start the Sniffy program on a computer at the front of the classroom and allow the students to observe Sniffy for a moment so that they can see that he has no particular inclination to press the lever. Then set the computer to reinforce lever presses, cover the computer screen so that the students are not distracted, and go on with the lecture or other lesson activities. (You may want to mute the feeder mechanism if it becomes distracting, but the increased frequency of reinforcement indicated by the sound may prove useful: Students can *hear* learning taking place. Toward the end of the class period, uncover the computer so that the students can again observe Sniffy's behavior and cumulative record. By the end of the period, the rate of lever pressing is likely to be considerably higher than it had been, despite the fact that no one had attempted to train Sniffy. This should make a nice lesson in the power of reinforcement by the "natural" environment. Time permitting, you might want to ask, "Who trained Sniffy to press the lever?"

Basic procedures. The opening quote ("Nothing succeeds like success") might be discussed in detail. What does success mean? How does it "succeed?" Is the tendency to be influenced by success part of human nature? Why would such a tendency have evolved? Is the French proverb a form of the law of effect?

Reinforcement is most often equated with increased behavior rate. In recent years, however, other measures of strength (fluency, intensity, resistance to extinction) have been getting more attention.

Some students, particularly those majoring in education, will have been told that reinforcement undermines intrinsic motivation. They are referring to the work of Ed Deci, Mark Lepper and others showing that under certain circumstances rewards reduce participation in the rewarded activity. Many of the studies are problematic. (For instance, many fail to grasp the difference between rewards and reinforcement, and use rewards that are not reinforcers. Many studies reward behavior that is already occurring at a high rate. Etc.) The "dangers" of reinforcement (and even of rewards) have been hugely exaggerated in education with the result that many teachers are even reluctant to praise student success. Students, especially those preparing for careers in education, should be encouraged to read articles that question the uniform condemnation of rewards (see, for example., Chance, 1992, for a nontechnical analysis).

I have tried to keep L&B tightly focused on behavior and environment relationships. However, neuroscientists are beginning to understand the biological aspects of some learning principles and some students may want to pursue this topic. A good place to start is with *Highjacking the Brain Circuits with a Nickel Slot Machine* by Sandra Blakeslee. The article ran in NYTimes.com on February 19, 2002 and is available online at www.nytimes.com.

Discrete trial and free operant procedures. The distinction between discrete trial and free operant procedures is somewhat arbitrary. For instance, lever press training is usually considered a free operant procedure, but if the rat is removed from the chamber after each lever press, it becomes a discrete trial procedure. Similarly, Thorndike's puzzle boxes experiments are usually characterized as discrete trial, yet the animals were free to engage in any behavior within the box. Nevertheless, some instructors consider the distinction important and applied work, especially with children with severe behavior disorders, is increasingly divided between those who favor traditional discrete trial training and those who favor more incidental "free operant" training.

Operant and Pavlovian procedures compared. An interesting lesson to be learned from reading the early learning literature is that people did not at first see a clear distinction between Pavlovian and operant procedures. To many people, Thorndike was merely pairing two stimuli, a treadle (for instance) and food.

Some instructors may want to note that there are some researchers who argue that Pavlovian and operant procedures are really different aspects of the same phenomenon. Taste aversion provides an example. This subject is usually considered the product of Pavlovian conditioning. It is possible, however, to consider it a form of operant learning: Eating a particular flavor is punished by nausea. Thus, whether learning is Pavlovian or operant may depend on how one looks at the events.

Primary and secondary reinforcers. I have limited the discussion of conditioned reinforcers to the conventional view. Some instructors may want to have students do some reading on alternative views.

Shaping and chaining. Instructors may want to draw a parallel between shaping and evolution. When behavior is shaped by a trainer, there is a clear goal, which distinguishes it from evolution. However, behavior is often shaped by the environment without any predetermined target; in these instances behavior is selected in much the same way as is involved in evolution. It is sometimes useful and entertaining to invite students to describe unintentional shaping of undesirable behavior (such as tantrums) that they have witnessed.

Exercise: The Training Game

Karen Pryor (1984) conducts an exercise called the Training Game. A volunteer is taught to perform some simple act, such as marching in place, picking up an object, or leaning against a wall. Students can reinforce approximations by shouting "Yes" or some other word to reinforce successive approximations of the desired behavior. (Of course the volunteer does not know in advance what the target behavior is.) Students are inclined to use punishment (shouting *wrong* for example) and must be cautioned beforehand against this. I have conducted this exercise many times; it is always great fun and makes a compelling case for the value of shaping and reinforcement. I serve as the subject the first time; it seems to reduce anxiety about volunteering.

As a follow-up exercise, students might be asked to shape lever-pressing or some other behavior in Sniffy.

In discussing chaining, I always suggest that it is really a kind of shaping. The value of primary reinforcement of the last response in the chain might be discussed. It may be fun to ask students to give examples of behavior chains from their own experience.

Exercise: The Chain Ladder

This can be done as a "thought experiment" in class. The initial question is: How do you train a dog to climb a three-step ladder? What is the first thing you do? Students often think you start by reinforcing approximations, but what about a task analysis? What about modifying the situation to make it easier? (E.g., start with standing on a "step" that is merely a tread lying on the floor, then raise it one inch.) What reinforcers should you use? What problems might you have with food reinforcers? And so on. Once a detailed plan has been worked out for training, one or two students may want to attempt the training at home. If so, they should arrange to have the training sessions videotaped, if possible. (In my experience, students nearly always can arrange to have training sessions videotaped.) The video can then be played in class, and students can assess the methods used. Did the trainer make good use of reinforcers? Of shaping? Did she break the task into suitable links?

Variables affecting operant learning. Students tend to find the discussion of controlling variables rather uninteresting. Exercises and class discussions help make it more appealing.

Exercise: Intermittent Shaping

Repeat the Training Game, but this time reinforce approximations intermittently. In my experience, the best way to do this is to designate one student as the trainer, and instruct the trainer to reinforce every second approximation of the desired behavior. (Of course, the student being trained would not be informed of this rule.) This usually results in markedly slower learning, and helps students understand why their own efforts to reinforce behavior are often unsuccessful.

Students might be asked to perform a similar exercise with Sniffy outside of class and share the resulting cumulative record at the next class meeting.

Exercise: Delayed Reinforcement

Repeat the Training Game but delay reinforcement by two seconds. (The student being trained should not be told reinforcement is being delayed.) The delay in reinforcement slows or prevents learning and typically produces obvious frustration in both the student and trainer. It might be fun to have two students trained at the same time, with one receiving immediate reinforcement and the other receiving reinforcement delayed two seconds.

This is another exercise that might be replicated outside of class with Sniffy, and once again the students might be asked to share the cumulative records produced.

Extinction of reinforced behavior. The problem here is to help students avoid confusion between extinction following Pavlovian conditioning and extinction following operant reinforcement. One possible solution is to note that extinction means withholding something. In Pavlovian extinction it means withholding the stimulus (US) that was contingent on a stimulus (the CS); in operant extinction it means withholding the stimulus (the reinforcer) that was contingent on a behavior.

Operant extinction produces effects not ordinarily associated with Pavlovian extinction. One of these, resurgence, has important implications for the use of extinction in applied settings.

Sniffy Exercise: Extinction

Start Sniffy at the beginning of class, and let the students observe a lever-trained Sniffy for a moment. (Sniffy's lever-pressing should have been maintained on CRF prior to class.) Cover the computer and discontinue all reinforcement while you go on with the lesson-- which will ideally include a discussion of extinction. (Again, you may want to set the software on mute.) Toward the end of class, uncover the computer and let the students again observe Sniffy and the cumulative record. Have the students look at the record for signs of an extinction burst and spontaneous recovery.

Theories of reinforcement. Some instructors may believe that drive-reduction theory need not be covered, but most students implicitly accept the idea that behavior is driven by internal states or needs, so there is a case to be made for reviewing the theory, including its weaknesses.

Handouts

The columns of Anne Landers and Abigail Van Buren are rich sources of material to stimulate class discussions while demonstrating to students the practical significance of learning principles. One column, for example, was about a four-year-old boy who, while in a grocery store, nagged his mother for a candy bar (Van Buren, 1995). She steadily refused, whereupon the youngster hit her in the stomach with his fist-- after which she bought him the candy he wanted. Reading a column such as this is almost guaranteed to get a good discussion going without much probing, but certain questions are worth raising: What's your best guess about why the boy behaved this way? Why do you suppose the mother gave in? The woman was pregnant-- does that shed any light on her behavior? On the boy's behavior? If this woman were your friend and asked for help in dealing with her son, what would you suggest?

Theories of Avoidance. Perhaps the key to introducing the theories of avoidance is to be sure students understand the problem to be solved: Escape can be understood in terms of reinforcement, but why does the organism avoid the aversive stimulus? What is the reinforcer? Murray Sidman's question, How can something that did not happen be a reinforcer?, is well worth exploring.

Key to Review Questions

1. Define the following terms in your own words:

Backward chaining: A chaining procedure in which training begins with the last link in the chain and adds preceding links in reverse order.

Behavior chain: A series of related behaviors, the last of which produces reinforcement.

Chaining: The procedure of establishing a behavior chain.

Conditioned reinforcer: See secondary reinforcer.

Discrete trial procedure: An operant training procedure in which performance of a behavior defines the end of a trial.

Drive: In Hull's theory of reinforcement, a motivational state (such as hunger) caused by a period of deprivation (as of food).

Drive-reduction theory: The theory of reinforcement that attributes a reinforcer's effectiveness to the reduction of a drive.

Escape-avoidance learning: A form of negative reinforcement in which the subject first learns to escape, and then to avoid, an aversive.

Escape training: See negative reinforcement.

Extinction: In operant training, the procedure of withholding the reinforcers that maintain a behavior.

Extinction burst: A sudden increase in the rate of behavior during the early stages of extinction.

Forward chaining: A chaining procedure in which training begins with the first link in the chain and adds subsequent links in order.

Free operant procedure: An operant training procedure in which a behavior may be repeated any number of times.

Instrumental learning: See operant learning.

Law of effect: The statement that behavior is a function of its consequences.

Negative reinforcement: A reinforcement procedure in which a behavior is followed by the removal of, or a decrease in the intensity of, a stimulus.

Negative reinforcer: Any stimulus which, when removed following a behavior, increases or maintains the strength of that behavior.

One-process theory: The view that avoidance and punishment involve only one process, operant learning.

Operant learning: Any procedure in which a behavior becomes stronger or weaker (e.g., more or less likely to occur), depending on its consequences. (Any suggestion that the term applies only to animal learning should be corrected.)

Positive reinforcement: A reinforcement procedure in which a behavior is followed by the presentation of, or an increase in the intensity of, a stimulus.

Positive reinforcer: Any stimulus which, when presented following a behavior, increases or maintains the frequency of that behavior.

Premack principle: The observation that high-probability behavior reinforces low-probability behavior.

Primary reinforcer: Any reinforcer that is not dependent on another reinforcer for its reinforcing properties.

Reinforcement: The procedure of providing consequences for a behavior that increase or maintain the strength of that behavior.

Relative value theory: Theory of reinforcement that considers reinforcers to be behaviors rather than stimuli and that attributes a reinforcer's effectiveness to its probability relative to other behaviors.

Response deprivation theory: The theory of reinforcement that maintains that a behavior is reinforcing to the extent that the organism has been deprived (relative to its baseline frequency) of performing that behavior.

Resurgence: The reappearance during extinction of a previously effective behavior.

Reward training: See positive reinforcement.

Secondary reinforcer: Any reinforcer that has acquired its reinforcing properties through its association with other reinforcers.

Shaping: The reinforcement of successive approximations of a desired behavior.

Sidman avoidance procedure: An escape-avoidance training procedure in which no stimulus regularly precedes the aversive stimulus.

Task analysis: The procedure of identifying the component elements of a behavior chain.

Two-process theory: The view that avoidance and punishment involve both Pavlovian and operant procedures.

2. Apply Thorndike's reasoning about animal anecdotes to anecdotes about other remarkable phenomena, such as telepathy, astrology, and dreams that "predict" the future.

Thorndike's point is that anecdotal reports tend to be biased. For instance, people are more likely to report dreams that come true than those that do not.

3. Thorndike objected to the term *"trial-and-error" learning.* Why do you suppose he did so?

Thorndike believed that we learn through "trial and success." It was success that "stamped in" behavior. (We would today say that reinforcers strengthen behavior.) Error merely "stamps out" ineffective behavior; it teaches us what not to do. Students often think of operant learning as involving random behavior, so that learning is a matter of luck. (Thorndike contributed to this notion by using the phrase, "trial and accidental success.") But behavior is the product of learning history and biology and is not random.

4. One of Skinner's chief contributions to psychology is said to be the use of behavior rate as a dependent variable. How does this approach differ from Thorndike's studies of chicks running mazes?

Students will find this problem difficult, but it should help them to see the fundamental difference between the discrete trial approach of Thorndike and the free operant approach of Skinner.

5. How was the "Skinner box" an improvement over Thorndike's puzzle boxes?

Personally I think Thorndike's puzzle boxes are underrated. However, success does remove the animal from the learning situation so puzzle box research is limited to the discrete trial approach; it is possible to do discrete trial and free operant work in the Skinner box. Thorndike's procedure also confounds escape learning and reward training, since the cat both escapes confinement and obtains food. The Skinner box can involve behavior rate as the dependent variable; puzzle boxes are not suited for behavior rate measures. The Skinner box also reduces distractions by events outside the box and makes automatic recording of responses possible.

6. Explain the difference between negative and positive reinforcement.

The answer is straightforward enough. The reason for asking the question is that students have a hard time remembering that both strengthen behavior and that the key difference is in whether a stimulus is removed or added. A less important point has to do with the nature of the stimulus: Negative reinforcement involves stimuli the organism avoids or escapes, given the opportunity, while positive reinforcement involves stimuli the organism ordinarily seeks out.

7. In the "experiment" in which Skinner turned on a light when his baby daughter moved her arm, did Skinner shape Deborah's arm movements or did Deborah shape Skinner's light switching?

This question gets at the question of control. Students tend to think of operant training as manipulative and controlling, but when one person reinforces another the relationship is necessarily reciprocal. In this instance, Skinner's efforts to reinforce arm movements produced arm movements and that reinforced his behavior. Both were influencing the behavior of the other. Students have a hard time seeing this, so the topic deserves special attention.

8. What is the single most important difference between Pavlovian and operant learning?

Probably the most important difference is that in Pavlovian conditioning a stimulus (the US) is contingent on the appearance of another stimulus (the CS), whereas in operant learning a stimulus (the reinforcer or punisher) is contingent on a behavior.

9. A worker used to slip away from the plant every afternoon to hunt rabbits. When his employer found out, he gave the man a raise "as an incentive to work harder." What do you think of the employer's action?

Strictly speaking, nothing can be said to have been reinforced until some behavior has been shown to be stronger. However, it is likely that slipping away from work has been reinforced since money is usually a powerful reinforcer, and money was made contingent on leaving work. Some students may say that working harder was reinforced since that is what the employer meant to reinforce. In this case the instructor might ask the student to identify the employee behavior that led to the raise, and note that reinforcement refers to a relationship between behavior and consequences, not behavior and intentions. Incidentally, the incident described in this question actually occurred.

10. Does the children's game, "Hot and Cold," make use of shaping?

The answer depends, of course, on how the game is played. The object of the game is for the seeker to find an object with "hints" (reinforcers and punishers) from others. If the reinforcers are provided for any slight behavior in the right direction and then only for more precisely appropriate behavior, shaping is involved. However, it is possible for people to find objects without benefit of shaping. The "cold" part of Hot and Cold involves punishment, and shaping normally involves only positive reinforcement.

11. How could a Spanish instructor use shaping to teach a student to roll r's?

The answer should get at the notion that rolling r's can be performed first in a very crude way and then gradually refined through reinforcement. The teacher might begin, for example, with ordinary short r sounds, such as that in fertile, and gradually move to words with longer r sounds. Or the teacher might ask the student to stretch a short r, as in ferrrrtile.

12. Describe the procedure you would use to train a dog to retrieve the morning newspaper from your front lawn.

The student should be able to break the task into links and identify how the links would be reinforced.

13. How is chaining a form of shaping?

Chaining might be said to be a form of shaping in that it builds up behavior.

14. Some teachers object to the use of shaping and chaining in classroom instruction because the procedures have been used to train animals. How would you defend their use?

If students have difficulty with this item, you might refer them to the discussion of animal research in Chapter 2. Perhaps the main point is that what matters is whether a procedure works with humans, not whether it was originally demonstrated with humans.

15. What is one characteristic that influences the reinforcing power of touch?

This question probably seems harder than it is. Intensity is one factor: too little pressure may be annoying, as can too much pressure. Another factor is friction, or the roughness of the surface touching the skin.

16. Why is the Premack Principle sometimes called Grandmother's Rule?

Grandmother's Rule is never mentioned in the chapter, so the student is asked to do some problem solving. In Grandmother's day, when families actually ate meals together, Grandmother insisted that kids eat their vegetables or they wouldn't get dessert. A high probability behavior was made contingent on a low probability behavior.

17. Design an experiment to determine the optimum amount of food to use in training rats to perform a new behavior. Plot a hypothetical graph of the data you would expect to obtain.

The experiment may be either single-case or group design, and should involve varying amounts of food as the dependent variable. It may be useful to have students describe their hypothetical experiment and draw their data graphs on the black board.

18. What are the problems with the drive-reduction theory of reinforcement?

The text mentions the fact that some reinforcers seem not to depend on conditioning, yet do not reduce any physiological drive. Another problem is circularity. Achievements, for example, are said to be reinforcing because they reduce the need for achievement, but the need for achievement is said to exist because achievements are reinforcing!

19: What is the chief difference between Premack's relative value theory and Timberlake and Allison's response deprivation theory?

Perhaps the chief difference is the fact that response deprivation theory takes baseline responding into account, while Premack's theory does not.

20. How has your study of operant learning changed your views of human nature?

The hope is that answering this question will help students to see the relevance of operant learning to their own lives. Thorndike and Skinner showed that behavior is not capricious, but lawful. This means not only that a science of behavior is possible, but that such a science can help us solve individual and societal problems.

Key to Practice Quiz

1. Reinforcement is the process of providing consequences for a behavior that <u>strengthen</u> the behavior.

2. Thorndike's early research used a <u>discrete</u> trial procedure, whereas Skinner used a <u>free</u> operant procedure.

3. Secondary reinforcers are also called <u>conditioned</u> reinforcers.

4. Shaping is the reinforcement of <u>successive approximations</u> of a desired behavior.

5. The first step in building a behavior chain is to do a <u>task</u> analysis.

6. Kennon Lattal found that he could not shape disk pecking in pigeons if the reinforcer was <u>delayed</u>.

7. The reappearance of previously effective behavior during extinction is called <u>resurgence</u>.

8. According to David Premack, reinforcement involves a relation between two <u>behaviors/responses</u>.

9. According to <u>response-deprivation</u> theory, an activity becomes reinforcing when the organism is prevented from engaging in it at the baseline rate.

10. The two processes of the two-process theory of avoidance are <u>Pavlovian conditioning</u> and <u>operant reinforcement</u>.

Chapter 5 Quiz: Reinforcement

1. Reinforcement is the procedure of providing consequences for behavior that increase or maintain the _____ of that behavior.

2. Thorndike's studies of learning started out as an attempt to understand animal

    _____.

3. The law of _____ says that behavior is a function of its consequences.

4. Operant learning is also referred to as _____ learning. (135)

5. According to the _____-process theory of avoidance, the avoidance response is reinforced by a reduction in the number of aversive events.

6. Thorndike's experiments with puzzle boxes used a _____-trial procedure.

7. Charles Catania identified _____ characteristics that define reinforcement.

8. The contingency square shows that there are _____ operant procedures.

9. The opposite of a primary reinforcer is a _____ reinforcer.

10. Schlinger and Blakely found that preceding a reinforcer with a stimulus reduced the negative effects of _____.

Key to Chapter 5 Quiz

1. Reinforcement is the procedure of providing consequences for behavior that increase or maintain the <u>strength</u> of that behavior. (141)

2. Thorndike's studies of learning started out as an attempt to understand animal <u>intelligence</u>. (134)

3. The law of <u>effect</u> says that behavior is a function of its consequences. (137)

4. Operant learning is also referred to as <u>instrumental</u> learning. (139)

5. According to the <u>one</u>-process theory of avoidance, the avoidance behavior is reinforced by a reduction in the number of aversive events. (182)

6. Thorndike's experiments with puzzle boxes used a <u>discrete</u>-trial procedure. (144)

7. Charles Catania identified <u>three</u> characteristics that define reinforcement. (141)

8. The contingency square shows that there are <u>four</u> operant procedures. (141)

9. The opposite of a primary reinforcer is a <u>secondary/ conditioned</u> reinforcer. (149)

10. Schlinger and Blakely found that preceding a reinforcer with a stimulus reduced the negative effects of <u>delay/delayed reinforcement</u>. (162)

6

Operant Punishment

Chapter Outline

Main Points

Use of punishment is widespread; although it is used less and less by psychologists as a treatment tool, it is frequently used by parents, teachers, employers, supervisors, legislators, international bodies, and others. It is important to understand a procedure that plays so prominent a role in our lives. A distinction can be made between positive and negative punishment; although the terms are troublesome, they are analogous to positive and negative reinforcement. Punishment and negative reinforcement both involve aversives, but punishment reduces the frequency of behavior whereas negative reinforcement strengthens it. The variables affecting punishment include contingency and contiguity, the intensity of the punisher, the initial level of punishment used, and alternative means of obtaining reinforcement. Attempts to explain punishment include two-process and one-process theories. Punishment can produce unwanted side-effects: escape, aggression, apathy, abuse, and imitation of the punisher. Alternatives to punishment include response prevention, extinction, and various forms of differential reinforcement.

Class Notes

<u>Background</u>. One problem with including a chapter on punishment is that it may actually increase the tendency of students to use it. I have therefore attempted to stress the negative aspects of punishment.

<u>Basic procedures</u>. It should be noted that punishment always works, by definition. A punisher is defined by its effects on behavior, not by its apparent aversiveness. Studies of punishment may often underestimate its effects. This is because punishment is usually studied in combination with reinforcement. For instance, a researcher may punish lever pressing that is reinforced with food. This is done because if the behavior resulted <u>only</u> in aversive consequences, it would not persist.

Exercise: The Punishment Game

Ask the students to shape the behavior of a volunteer (as in the exercises in Chapter 5), but instead of reinforcing successive approximations, punish "inappropriate" behavior. Every time the volunteer does anything that is not an approximation of the desired behavior, students should shout, "No!" Learning usually proceeds slowly, if at all. The exercise illustrates that punishment teaches what not to do, not what to do. (Eventually the student may escape the aversives by performing the desired behavior, so response acquisition is due to negative reinforcement rather than to punishment.) If the volunteer fails to perform the target behavior, ask the class to switch from punishment to positive reinforcement. Typically the behavior shapes up quickly. The contrast in the effectiveness of the two procedures as ways of shaping behavior is impressive.

Punishment and negative reinforcement compared. Students (and even some psychologists) routinely confuse these two procedures, so it may be worth spending some time to make sure students grasp the difference.

Variables affecting punishment. The Training Game (see the previous chapter) can be used to demonstrate the effects of varying levels of punishment, punishment delays, and other variables.

Theories of punishment. The theories of punishment are essentially the same one-process and two-process theories connected with avoidance.

Problems with punishment. I devote considerable space to the problems associated with punishment. It may be worthwhile to have a class discussion about the distinction between abuse and punishment (see review question 11). Elsewhere (Chance, 1998) I argue that if a procedure causes prolonged discomfort or risks permanent injury, it is abuse, not punishment. To some extent the complaints about the clinical use of punishment may be due to a failure to distinguish clearly between punishment and abuse.

Exercise: Finding Alternatives

Provide examples of everyday situations (child rearing, teaching, employee absenteeism, etc.) involving behavior that people try to change using aversives. (For instance, a roommate repeatedly fails to lock the door when leaving. Typically we lecture, nag, and perhaps threaten bodily harm.) Then ask students to work in pairs or groups of three to come up with nonaversive alternatives. (The roommate problem might be solved through response prevention by installing a lock that automatically locks the door whenever it is closed.) Share the various solutions to the problems.

<u>Alternatives to punishment</u>. I begin this section with response prevention because it is often the most desirable and simplest solution to the problem of unwanted behavior. The use of noncontingent reinforcement as an alternative to punishment is exciting, but it seems to me there is considerable risk of misuse by students since "noncontingent" rewards can be unintentionally contingent on undesirable behavior.

Punishment is probably most often abused when the unwanted behavior is reinforced in some way. (If there were no reinforcement contingency, it is unlikely the behavior would occur often enough to be a problem.) It is therefore important that students understand the value of identifying the reinforcers that maintain an undesirable behavior before attempting to modify the behavior.

Key to Review Questions

1. Define the following terms:

    DRA: A form of differential reinforcement in which a behavior that is different from an undesired behavior is systematically reinforced. (The procedure provides an alternative means of obtaining reinforcement.)

    DRI: A form of differential reinforcement in which a behavior that is incompatible with an unwanted behavior is systematically reinforced.

    Positive punishment: A punishment procedure in which a behavior is followed by the presentation of, or an increase in the intensity of, a stimulus.

    Punisher: Any consequence of a behavior that decreases the strength of that behavior.

    Response prevention: The procedure of altering the environment so as to prevent unwanted behavior from occurring.

2. Why do people rely so much on punishment?

    Lots of answers are possible, but the hope is that students will look to the consequences of using punishment, rather than attribute causes to "character" (e.g., "People are mean"). Punishment is used because it usually has immediate, reinforcing consequences for the punisher.

3. Benjamin Franklin said that we hate those whom we fear. Do you think he was right? Explain.

    The issue is empirical, but the question is designed to get students to think about the adverse effects of aversives. Certainly we fear those who use or threaten to use aversives, and one side effect of aversives is aggression. Aggression and hate are closely related behaviors.

4. What is the key difference between positive and negative punishment?

    Students have a hard time giving up the circular idea that positive reinforcement involves "positive" events and negative reinforcement involves "negative" events. The actual distinction has to to with whether something is added to the situation or removed from it.

5. Many people believe that raising the price of cigarettes will reduce smoking. If so, does this constitute punishment?

    This question may lead to an interesting discussion. Any procedure in which a consequence of behavior reduces the frequency of the behavior is, by definition, a form of punishment. However, the example is unlike most examples of punishment. For one thing, the contingency is between paying for and receiving cigarettes, not between smoking and paying.

6. Why is it important to use extinction in conjunction with differential reinforcement?

    So long as a behavior produces reinforcing consequences the punishment. Moreover, after punishment is discontinued, the behavior will immediately increase in frequency.

7. If you were the only person in the world, could you still be punished?

In ordinary parlance, punishment implies a punisher, but among researchers punishment implies only a contingency between a response and a suppressive consequence. If a person drives fast and is injured, that consequence may make him less likely to drive fast in the future; no one else need be involved.

8. What is the key difference between negative reinforcement and punishment?

One answer is that negative reinforcement increases a response whereas punishment suppresses it. Some students may say that negative reinforcement means the removal of an aversive stimulus, while punishment means the addition of an aversive. One problem with this answer is that there are two kinds of punishment, and this distinction applies only to type 1 punishment.

9. People often say they seek "open, honest relationships." Why are such relationships so rare?

The phrase implies saying hurtful things. (E.g., "I hate to say this, but that dress makes you look fat.") Although not meant to injure, such comments are nevertheless apt to be punitive. Punishment has negative side effects, including the tendency to retaliate. (E.g., "Thank you for telling me. By the way, did you cut your own hair, or were you in an accident?") There may also be a tendency toward escalation, which is not conducive to friendship.

10. What is the key difference between the two-process and one-process theories of punishment?

This is straight from the text: One-process theory relies on operant learning; two-process theory relies on Pavlovian conditioning as well as operant learning.

11. How would you distinguish between punishment and abuse?

This is another question that is likely to lead to an interesting discussion. Abuse may be defined as procedures that cause prolonged discomfort or permanent injury. Abuse might also be thought of as use of aversives that is out of proportion to its benefits. (A strong contingent electric shock might suppress thumb sucking, but most people probably would not consider it appropriate. On the other hand, contingent shock to suppress tooth pulling might be acceptable.) It might also be noted that punishment must reduce the frequency of the unwanted behavior, whereas abuse often does not.

12. Why do you suppose it took researchers so long to appreciate the power of punishment?

It is difficult to say, since everyday experience would seem to convince us that punishment is powerful. Perhaps the fact that early work by prominent researchers (particularly Thorndike and Skinner) showed only temporary effects made it difficult for others to take contrary views.

13. Some psychologists have suggested that people could reduce unwanted behavior in themselves, such as nail biting, by wearing a rubber band around their wrist and snapping it against their skin whenever they perform the unwanted behavior. What do you think of this technique?

Students might note that since people can avoid the aversive stimulus by not snapping the band, the technique might not be implemented for long. I believe this has been the problem with this technique. The technique is self-punishing!

14. Five-year-old Mary has misbehaved. Her father spanks her and sends her to her room. Has Mary been punished?

The definition of punishment requires that the behavior involved occur less often; the question does not provide that information so it is impossible to say if Mary was punished. It can also be argued that behaviors are punished, not people, so that Mary has not been punished regardless of the change in her behavior.

15. How might David Premack define a punisher?

For Premack, a reinforcing stimulus is any relatively high-probability behavior. An aversive stimulus would then be any relatively low-probability behavior.

16. Give examples of the side effects you might expect if you used punishment to control the behavior of a spouse or friend.

Examples might include verbal or physical attacks, avoidance, the "silent treatment," stuttering, apathy, abandonment (escape), and so on.

17. If you were a practicing physician, how would you alter the behavior of an elderly person who frequently comes in with vague, inconsequential symptoms?

Many physicians have to deal with this problem. It is a difficult problem because, on the one hand, such patients take time away from those who need attention; on the other hand, "vague, inconsequential symptoms" sometimes reflect the early stages of disease. Thus, merely setting up a punishment contingency may lead to the suppression of reports of important symptoms. A better approach might be to ask what reinforcers maintain doctor visits in the absence of real medical need. Often the answer is attention from others. The doctor might then have a nurse or physician's assistant interview the patient and do a preliminary examination (thus providing attention without using up the doctor's time), and review their notes and follow up on them with a brief interview.

18. Suppose you are a pediatric dentist, and many of your patients constantly suck their thumbs, a practice that may cause dental problems. What would you do?

The problem is to reduce the frequency that a child's thumb spends in the child's mouth. There is only so much the dentist can do first hand, but he or she might instruct the parents in an effective procedure. One possibility is to coat the child's thumb with a foul-tasting material. Sucking the thumb is then punished by a bad taste. One problem with this technique is that the child may suck some other digit. Another approach is to give the child a treat or attention periodically, but only if he is not sucking on a thumb. This procedure should be effective without the negative side effects of punishment.

19. How could a principal use differential reinforcement to reduce the use of punishment by her teachers?

One possibility is to provide reinforcement (praise, time off, and written commendations are likely possibilities) contingent on the use of procedures other than punishment.

20. You are preparing guidelines for the use of corporal punishment in a reform school. What one point will you emphasize most?

This question is apt to produce a wide variety of answers. Some might emphasize the conditions under which corporal punishment may be used (e.g., to stop behavior that is injurious to the child or others); some might stress the problems associated with punishment; others might set limits on the severity of punishers, etc.

Key to Practice Quiz

1. The first formal studies of punishment were probably done by <u>Thorndike</u> around the turn of the century.

2. Positive punishment and <u>negative reinforcement</u> are often mistakenly thought to refer to the same procedure.

3. Murray Sidman, an expert on punishment, wrote a critique of the subject called <u>Coercion and Its Fallout</u>.

4. According to the two-process theory, punishment involves two procedures: <u>Pavlovian</u> and <u>operant learning</u>.

5. Punishment is more likely to suppress a behavior if the organism has <u>alternative/other</u> means of obtaining reinforcement.

6. Benjamin Franklin observed that people who are feared are <u>hated</u>.

7. David Camp and his colleagues found that a delay of 30 seconds greatly reduced the effects of contingent shock. They found that even a delay of <u>two</u> seconds made shocks less effective.

8. In using punishment, it is best to begin with a punisher that is <u>slightly stronger</u> than the minimum required to suppress the behavior.

9. The fact that an annoying behavior occurs implies that it has <u>reinforcing</u> consequences.

10. Five problems are associated with punishment. Three of these problems are <u>escape/aggression/apathy/abuse/imitation (any three of the forgoing)</u>.

Chapter 6 Quiz: Punishment

1. Five problems are associated with punishment. Three of these problems are

    _____

    _____.

2. David Camp and his colleagues found that even a _____-second delay in punishment reduced its effectiveness.

3. Negative punishment is also called _____ training.

4. One alternative to punishment is response _____.

5. Positive punishment necessarily involves _____.

6. _____ is often an appropriate alternative to punishment, but it is sometimes slow.

7. Punishers are defined by their effects on _____.

8. Punishment is often confused with _____ reinforcement.

9. Differential reinforcement of _____ is the procedure of reinforcing behavior that cannot be performed at the same time as the unwanted behavior.

10. Differential reinforcement is used in combination with _____ .

Key to Chapter 6 Quiz

1. Five problems are associated with punishment. Three of these problems are escape/aggression/apathy/abuse/imitation (any three of the forgoing). (203-205)

2. David Camp and his colleagues found that even a two-second delay in punishment reduced its effectiveness. (195)

3. Negative punishment is also called penalty training. (191)

4. One alternative to punishment is response prevention. (209)

5. Positive punishment necessarily involves aversives. (191, n5)

6. Extinction is often an appropriate alternative to punishment, but it is sometimes slow. (211)

7. Punishers are defined by their effects on behavior. (190)

8. Punishment is often confused with negative reinforcement. (192-193)

9. Differential reinforcement of incompatible behavior is the procedure of reinforcing behavior that cannot be performed at the same time as the unwanted behavior. (212)

10. Differential reinforcement is used in combination with extinction. (211)

7

Operant Applications

Chapter Outline

Main Points

Behavior evolves in much the same way that species evolve; it is selected by its consequences. Operant learning helps explain not only the behavior of laboratory animals in experimental chambers, but "real-world" behavior problems, including animal care and training, self-awareness, verbal behavior, insightful problem solving, creativity, superstition, and some forms of "abnormal" behavior.

Class Notes

<u>Background</u>. I love the opening quote from Huxley, "The great end of life is not knowledge, but action." It might be worth discussing what Huxley meant. The traditional approach sees problems as emanating from within the individual, and assumes that something inside the individual must be changed in order to change the behavior. This has proved to be a largely ineffective approach to behavior problems large and small. The natural science approach suggests that we may often change behavior by changing the person's environment; it leads to *action*.

It is difficult to get students to appreciate that "simple" operant procedures can account for important human activities, or that they can provide solutions to complex human problems. The principal goal of this chapter is to help the instructor do just that.

<u>Animal care and training</u>. Some instructors may want to assign readings from Hal Markowitz's book, *Behavioral Enrichment in the Zoo*. Before Markowitz began doing research on the problem of improving the quality of life for captive animals, most efforts focused on trying to increase the similarity of the animal's environment to its natural habitat (e.g., making synthetic rocks look realistic), or providing some form of "stimulation" (e.g., a ball to play with or a television set to

watch). Markowitz showed that it is important to make reinforcing events (such as eating food) contingent on the animal's behavior (such as foraging). If you see less perseverative pacing of animals in zoos today than in decades past, it is likely that much of the credit goes to Markowitz.

Students tend to underestimate the difficulty of shaping new behaviors. After discussing the example of shaping the behavior of an elephant, you might ask, "How would you train an elephant to ride a tricycle?" One answer is provided in *The American Animal Trainer Magazine* and is available on their website at www.animaltrainermagazine.com/article2.htm.

Another article on animal training that is well worth assigning is Susan Friedman's *The Help at Hand*, which appeared in the May, 2000 issue of *PsittaScene*, a magazine for parrot owners. Friedman reviews some common training procedures and interesting resources for students.

I have wanted to write a section on the applications of operant procedures to child rearing and/or education, but have not managed to do it. Numerous resources are available in the area. Carl Cheney has an unpublished article called *Mechanically Augmented Human Toilet Training, or The Electric Potty Chair*. In it Cheney describes an apparatus he built and used to toilet train his children. When a child uses the potty, a circuit is closed and a clown face on a box lights up.

Self-awareness. This section attempts to get students to think about self-awareness in a new way. It proposes that "we are what we do." Therefore, to be aware of oneself is to be aware of one's behavior.

The research on self-awareness should provide ample stimulus for class discussions. However, the significance of the work of Gallup and of Epstein and his colleagues on self recognition in animals will not be immediately obvious to all students.

Exercise: Lost Awareness

Ask the students to think of a time when they were completely unaware of themselves, when they were so unselfconscious that, when they once again became aware of themselves, they realized they had been in a different sort of state. Ask the students to share these experiences. It is likely that they will have in common intense focus on some activity. In these instances we say that we "lose ourselves" in the activity. (Psychologist Mihaly Csikszentmihalyi calls such experiences "flow.")

Self-awareness is closely related to self-concept. The idea that we are dependent on others for both raises a question that might form the basis for an interesting class debate: What sort of self awareness and self concept would a person have who, though provided with adequate care, had no social intercourse with other humans? If, as sociologist Charles Horton Cooley (1902) said, we see ourselves in the looking glass that others hold before us, what would happen if there were no one to hold up a looking glass?

So far as I know, no one has replicated or extended Mary Boyle's work with comatose patients mentioned in the box on shaping awareness. Instructors whose students have access to *Science Citation Index* might want to encourage a student to search it for more recent research. Some students may be aware of hospitals that play recorded music for patients who are in coma. However, students should be made aware of the difference between playing music noncontingently and making music contingent on behavior.

<u>Self-Control</u>. The chief point of this section is that self-control is not due to some inner condition, such as "willpower," but is learned. The emphasis is on practical self-control techniques, rather than experimental research. Students who want to read the research literature may be advised to search data bases for work by Walter Mischel, Sidney Bijou, and Donald Meichenbaum.

Some students may have read Daniel Goleman's book, *Emotional Intelligence*. Some of the work Goleman discusses is about learning self-control, and may provide the basis for interesting discussion.

<u>Verbal behavior</u>. Some students may object to the operant analysis of verbal behavior. They may cite some statement such as, "The sky is blue," and ask what change in behavior such a statement produces. What reinforcer is provided? But the instructor might ask in turn under what circumstances such a statement might be made. One does not walk up to a stranger and say, "The sky is blue." An exploration of the circumstances under which statements are made should provide hints as to the reinforcing effects such statements produce. In addition, it should be noted that people bring to every situation the effects of long histories of reinforcement for verbal behavior.

Some students may argue that conversing cannot be accounted for in terms of reinforcement contingencies because when people speak they do not simply repeat sentences that were reinforced in the past. As "proof" of this argument, they may invent an absurd statement such as "In the moonlight, chocolate smells like Italy." At this point some instructors may want to discuss the concept of response class. Along these lines, they may want to note that when Verplanck reinforced opinion statements, he got more opinion statements, not the *same* opinion repeated over and over again. Along these lines, the Lanza (Lanza et al., 1982) experiment on lying in the pigeon is fun.

Exercise: A Reinforcing Chat

Verplanck's experiments on the reinforcement of conversational speech beg to be replicated as a student exercise. Students might attempt to reinforce comments on a particular topic or the use of particular words or phrases. A student whose roommate tends to talk too much about himself, for instance, might reinforce the use of pronouns other than I. To get the most from the exercise, students should get a baseline rate and record data in a subtle manner.

<u>Insightful problem solving</u>. People often speak about solving problems "through insight" as if there were an "insight procedure" or algorithm. But insight is not a way of solving problems; it is a reaction to *having solved them*. This is a foreign point of view to most students and will not be readily embraced by them. If students insist that some problems are "solved by insight," the burden is on them to describe what that means. When they attempt to do so, they are likely to describe the experience of *having reached* a solution, not the means by which the solution was reached.

The importance of the Epstein, et al. banana experiment will escape some students. "But the birds still had to have insight to put the two ideas (moving the box and climbing the box) together," they may say. This complaint really gets at the nature of scientific explanation. In science, explanation means identifying the variables that control the phenomenon to be explained. One way of determining whether we have identified the right variables is to attempt to produce the phenomenon. That is what Epstein and his colleagues did, and that is why their work is important.

Exercise: Mental Sets

One way to convey the importance of learning history to insightful problem solving is to show how learning history interferes with problem solving. One way to do this is to induce a response bias (aka, "mental set") that interferes with performance. This can be done with a series of 10 anagrams, the first 9 of which require the same sort of response. (The solutions may have something to do with nature, or they may all start with a hard consonant sound.) The last item requires a different sort of solution, and is therefore much more difficult than it would otherwise have been. Students might work on the exercise in pairs, with one student solving anagrams and the other timing solutions.

Creativity. Novel behavior can be treated as a response class and strengthened through reinforcement. The work of Karen Pryor et al. (1969) is, I think, as important to creativity as it is entertaining. It is perhaps worth mentioning that training in creative pursuits, such as painting or creative writing, can either reduce or increase the originality of a student's work. The outcome depends on the extent to which the instructor reinforces "mainstream" versus novel performances. In the latter case, the instructor often says that her approach is "to help the student find *his own way*." In other words, instead of reinforcing imitation of what others have done, they reinforce novel production.

Exercise: Uses for a Telephone

Reinforcement for novel behavior is not the only factor in creativity. Ask students with different backgrounds to come up with creative uses for a familiar object, such as the telephone. The exercise may help students appreciate the value of diverse learning experiences in creative problem solving.

Superstition. The debate over whether Skinner's superstition experiment really produces complex, organized behavior, such as clockwise turns, is an interesting example of how science works. Students tend to view debates and contradictory findings in science as signs of weakness. We need to help students understand that this is the way discovery works; only religion offers simple, absolute truths, and the truths of religion do not enable us to build refrigerators, put people on the moon, prevent polio, or treat behavior disorders effectively.

Exercise: Everyday Superstitions

Ask students to list things that they do with some regularity even though they do not appear to produce reinforcing consequences. To protect their anonymity, you might ask students to write about them on slips of paper. Share some of these revelations with the class --without identifying the students.

Exercise: Superstition Experiment

Fred Keller describes an experiment on superstition that you may want to perform in class. Keller asked a boy to say words one after another, but to avoid sentences or phrases. Keller explained that as the boy was doing this, he (Keller) would now and then drop a penny into a cup, and that later the boy would get to keep the pennies. "All you have to do," Keller said, "is say words." Once the boy started, Keller picked the word *flower* at random for reinforcement. Thereafter, each time the boy said *flower*, Keller dropped a penny into the cup-- but he did this 10 seconds after the word appeared. One result was the appearance of superstitious behavior: The boy would say "ship, sea, beautiful, red, flowers." Since reinforcement was contingent only on saying flower, the sequence of words that preceded it was superstitious.

I have never tried this experiment in class, but I'm fairly confident it would prove interesting. You need only ask one student to serve as the volunteer, and have that student wait outside while you explain the experiment (but not necessarily the expected findings) to the class. Then either do the training yourself or have a student do it. This is also an exercise that some students may want to try outside of class as a project. As always, it's best to have the students videotape the training if possible.

Learned helplessness and depression. In accounting for learned helplessness, Seligman (1991) does not restrict himself to the experiences that reliably produce it. Instead, he writes that learned helplessness is due to "the belief that whatever you do doesn't matter" (p.15). He adds that, "The very thought 'Nothing I do matters' prevents us from acting" (p.7). But Seligman's dogs became helpless when given experiences in which, in fact, they *were* helpless. In my view, "the belief that whatever you do doesn't matter" is *part* of learned helplessness, not its cause.

Outside Project: Vulnerability

As an outside project, ask students to research old newspaper articles on suicides following the stock market crash of 1929. Were there any commonalities among them? Were they, for example, middle class or wealthy? Had they always been wealthy or did they acquire their wealth recently? Research on learned helplessness and learned industriousness both suggest that a little failure now and then may be a good thing. It may well be that those who committed suicide after the crash were those who had always been wealthy and successful. Another example of this may be the case of Vincent Foster, the Clinton advisor who committed suicide. Foster's friends and associates commented that Foster was someone who was *always* successful, who never had even small setbacks. Yet another possible example is Edwin Twitmyer, who gave up research on Pavlovian conditioning after the failure of his speech on the subject (see Chapter 4). Could too much success make people vulnerable to depression and helplessness when a serious failure occurs? T. H. Huxley once observed, "There is the greatest practical benefit in making a few failures early in life."

Delusions and hallucinations. It should be noted that hallucinations and delusions may be products of organic brain disease. The purpose of this section is not to argue that such behavior is always learned, but to show that learning may be involved-- even when there is an underlying organic impairment.

Self-injurious behavior. I have included self-injurious behavior here partly as a way of providing an example of the useful application of punishment, and as a way of demonstrating that problems formerly solved with punishment are now typically dealt with in other ways.

Key to Review Questions

1. Define the following terms in your own words:

   Learned helplessness: The failure to escape an aversive following exposure to an inescapable aversive.
   Superstitious behavior: Any increase in the strength of behavior that is due to coincidental reinforcement.

2. In what sense is the relationship between an organism and its environment reciprocal?

   It is important that students break free of the notion that operant learning involves control in only one direction, from the environment to the organism. A good example might be a teacher and pupil. Students might be asked to change perspectives, to move from the pupil's shoes to those of the teacher. They might then see that the teacher's behavior is often under the reinforcing control of the student.

3. How is self-awareness like the awareness we have of others? How is it different?

   Both involve observation of behavior, but self-observations are often not independently verifiable.

4. Janet hypothesizes that people who are good at observing others are good at observing themselves. Design a study to test her hypothesis.

   One way to go about this would be to compare self observations of two groups, those identified as good at observing others and those who are not. The problem is to figure out a way of measuring observational abilities. That might be done by, for example, having subjects participate in a roundtable discussion and then giving a test on various aspects of the participants' behavior. (E.g., "Which person in the group tended to interrupt others most often?" "Which person was most ambivalent about his position on X?") Self-observation would have to be similarly defined and measured.

5. Does the use of a mirror by Gallup's chimps imply a concept of self?

   This is a controversial issue, and there is probably no simple answer. The point is that self concept is not a separate entity reflected by behavior; it is behavior.

6. How is an operant analysis of verbal behavior different from the traditional approach to language?

   The student should note that traditionally language is thought of as information transfer, while the operant analysis looks at verbal behavior as a special class of behavior that is shaped and maintained by its consequences, especially its effects on other people.

7. Given the role of reinforcement in verbal behavior, what reasons can you give to explain why some people talk to themselves when alone?

   The consequences of talking aloud are different from those of talking silently. There is some evidence, for instance, that thinking aloud while working on a problem is helpful in reaching a solution.

8. In supporting the operant view of verbal behavior, which research described in this chapter is more important, that of Quay or that of Verplanck?

This is obviously a matter of opinion, but the point is to get the students to think about the contributions of these two figures.

9. Occasionally the solution to a problem comes to a person in a dream. Can you account for this in terms of operant learning?

I believe the weight of evidence favors the view that dreams are essentially meaningless. The real object of this question is to get students to speculate a bit about a mysterious phenomenon. They might, for instance, propose that dreams are behavior and that good ideas produce similar effects whether the person is asleep or awake when the ideas occur.

10. Why is insight not an adequate *explanation* of problem solving?

To achieve insight means to reach a solution. Using insight as an explanation amounts to saying that we solve problems because we solve problems.

11. Studies show that students who have difficulty learning higher level skills, such as algebra, often perform poorly at lower level skills. Explain why.

Lower level skills, such as addition and subtraction, are often components of higher level skills, such as algebra. Inability to perform one component efficiently interferes with the ability to perform other components. (For more on this, see Johnson and Layng, 1992.) The point is that learning depends partly on previous learning. Students may see this readily as a general principle, yet fail to see it when it comes to insightful problem solving.

12. You head the product development division of a major corporation. How can you get the people in your division to come up with more ideas for new products?

We are talking here about creativity, which means producing novel behavior. The work of Pryor and others suggests that if reinforcers are made contingent on producing new ideas, workers will produce new ideas.

13. How can a writing instructor get his students to write more creative stories?

This is just a different setting for the same problem posed in item 12. The teacher might read student stories aloud and be especially generous in praise when stories are creative.

14. There is some evidence that very creative people are more inclined toward mental illness. Assuming this is true, how might you account for it in terms of operant learning?

People may have a tendency to tolerate (i.e., reinforce) strange social behavior in people who are artistically or scientifically creative. It is also possible that abnormal social behavior may increase the likelihood of obtaining reinforcers for creative behavior in other spheres.

15. Why are so many gamblers inclined to be superstitious?

Superstitious behavior involves adventitious reinforcement, and to the extent that gambling involves random events, it provides ample opportunity for adventitious reinforcement. Another aspect of this problem is the fact that people are powerfully reinforced by success at controlling the environment. The gambler may therefore engage in a variety of efforts to affect gambling outcomes. The dice player, for instance, may shake the dice in a dozen different ways before getting a win; the win reinforces the most recently used method of shaking the dice.

16. Explain why people within the same family often share the same superstitious beliefs.

This gets at the notion of social transmission and the fact that many superstitions are not entirely or even primarily dependent on adventitious reinforcement.

17. Could delusions sometimes be a form of superstitious behavior?

Presumably beliefs, including delusions, can be adventitiously reinforced, and so may be superstitious. It is clear that superstitions sometimes involve delusions. For instance, the gambler who blows on his dice or says "Come 7!" while throwing the dice suffers from the delusion that such behavior affects the dice.

18. Suppose a psychiatric patient claims he is Napoleon. How could you determine whether this delusion is under the control of reinforcing consequences?

One way is to observe the patient and note the consequences of expressing the belief that he is Napoleon. It may become clear that the behavior is maintained by reinforcing consequences. Another approach is to remove all significant consequences for any Napoleonic behavior. In other words, claiming to be Napoleon or acting like Napoleon would no longer produce stares, comments or other potentially reinforcing remarks. If the behavior tends to fall off, we can conclude it is to some extent under the control of reinforcing consequences.

19. Why have the topics covered in this chapter resisted scientific analysis for so long?

Possibly the answer has to do with the fact that we had alternative explanations: Superstition was the product of innate ideas; gambling was the product of unconscious self-destructive impulses; creativity was the product of unconscious processes, etc. The explanations were not scientific, but they were intuitively appealing.

20. What mysteries of human nature not covered in this chapter might succumb to an operant analysis?

One topic was suggested in these review questions: dreams. A related problem is sleep. (No one knows exactly why people or animals sleep.) Another problem is altruistic behavior.

Key to Practice Quiz

1. In animal training, secondary reinforcement may be provided with a toy called a <u>cricket</u>.

2. Gordon Gallup provided experimental evidence of awareness in <u>chimps</u>.

3. Two strategies for achieving self-control are: <u>physical restraint/ distancing/distraction/deprivation/satiation/inform others of goals/monitor behavior</u>.

4. The study in which William Verplanck reinforced opinions is an example of an <u>ABA</u> or within-subject experiment.

5. The experiment in which pigeons pecked a banana hanging from the ceiling demonstrated that insight is the product of the history of <u>reinforcement/learning</u>.

6. Gregory Wagner and Edward Morris studied <u>superstitious</u> behavior with the help of a mechanical clown named Bobo.

7. When a behavior is maintained by coincidental reinforcement, that behavior is <u>superstitious</u>.

8. Immunity against learned helplessness may be provided by exposure to aversive stimuli that can be <u>escaped/avoided/ overcome</u>.

9. Self-injurious behavior is often maintained by attention and by <u>escape from demanding/unpleasant./aversive) situations</u>.

10. Many therapists now do a <u>functional</u> assessment before attempting to treat a behavior problem .

Chapter 7 Quiz: Operant Applications

1. The experiment in which pigeons pecked a banana hanging from the ceiling demonstrated that insight is the product of the history of _____.

2. Gordon _____ provided evidence of self-awareness in chimpanzees.

3. Mary Boyle attempted to use reinforcement to treat victims of _____.

4. Self-injurious behavior is often maintained by negative _____.

5. Richard _____ says that behavior has a tendency to drift toward its essential features.

6. Brad Alford's study of the man who thought he was followed by a witch is an example of an _____ reversal design.

7. Learned helplessness may serve as a model for human _____.

8. Lovaas and Simmons used punishment to reduce self-injurious behavior in a boy. Before treatment, this boy would hit himself at the rate of up to _____ times a minute.

9. Karen Pryor trained _____ to be more creative by reinforcing novel behavior.

10. Coincidental reinforcement plays an important role in _____ behavior.

Key to Chapter 7 Quiz

1. The experiment in which pigeons pecked a banana hanging from the ceiling demonstrated that insight is the product of the history of <u>reinforcement/learning</u>. (238-239)

2. Gordon <u>Gallup</u> provided evidence of self-awareness in chimpanzees. (223)

3. Mary Boyle attempted to use reinforcement to treat victims of <u>coma</u>. (225)

4. Self-injurious behavior is often maintained by negative <u>reinforcement</u> (256)

5. Richard <u>Herrnstein</u> says that behavior has a tendency to drift toward its essential features. (246)

6. Brad Alford's study of the man who thought he was followed by a witch is an example of an <u>ABA</u> reversal design. (252)

7. Learned helplessness may serve as a model for human <u>depression</u>. (250)

8. Lovaas and Simmons used punishment to reduce self-injurious behavior in a boy. Before treatment, this boy would hit himself at the rate of up to <u>30</u> times a minute. (255)

9. Karen Pryor trained <u>porpoises</u> to be more creative by reinforcing novel behavior. (241)

10. Coincidental reinforcement plays an important role in <u>superstitious</u> behavior. (244)

8

Vicarious Learning

Chapter Outline

Introduction
Basic Procedures
    Vicarious Pavlovian Conditioning
    Vicarious Operant Learning
Vicarious Learning versus Imitation
Generalized Imitation
Variables Affecting Vicarious Learning
    Consequences of the Model's Behavior/Consequences of the Observer's
        Behavior/Characteristics of the Model/Observer's Age/Observer's Learning
        History/Other Variables
    Box: Vicarious Learning and Human Nature
    Box: The Venus Effect
Theories of Vicarious Learning
    Bandura's Social Cognitive Theory/Miller-Dollard Reinforcement Theory
Applications of Vicarious Learning
    Foraging/Crime and Television/Therapy for Phobia
Recommended Reading
Review Questions
Practice Quiz
Query Answers

Main Points

Vicarious learning has received relatively little attention from researchers, possibly because early studies produced disappointing results. Vicarious learning means learning from observing the behavior of a model. Vicarious learning is affected by several variables, including the consequences of the observer's and model's behavior and the characteristics of the model. The two main theories of vicarious learning are those of Bandura and of Miller and Dollard. Vicarious learning plays an important role in adaptation, as illustrated by research on foraging and the influence of TV on criminal behavior. Modeling procedures have been useful in treating behavior problems, including phobia.

Class Notes

<u>Background</u>. This chapter illustrates that progress in science is not always smooth and inevitable. Further, what seems obvious to one generation may not seem so to the next.

Exercise: Where Did They Go Wrong?

It might be fun to challenge students to theorize about why Thorndike and Watson did not find observational learning in animals. Was their methodology at fault? Did bias enter into it?

Basic procedures. The discussion of vicarious Pavlovian conditioning raises considerable doubt about its existence. I would like to hear from instructors about whether this topic should be included in future editions.

Variables affecting vicarious learning. In discussing the characteristics of the model, it may be useful to mention specific public figures known to be widely imitated, such as movie stars and athletes.

Exercise: Looking Up

Some students might like to perform a simple experiment on the role of model characteristics. Two students of the same gender would serve as models, while a third would record data. One model might be dressed in rather formal business dress, while the other would be dressed casually. First one model would stare up at a roof top, as though looking at something of interest. Then, sometime later, the other model would look up at the same roof. The recorder would note the number of passersby who look up at the roof top in each condition. A variation of the experiment would involve models of different gender dressed similarly.

Theories of observational learning. In the Herbert and Harsh study, cats that observed the model on 30 trials did markedly better than those that observed the model on only 15 trials. It seems to me that neither theory of vicarious learning adequately accounts for this phenomenon. Some instructors may want to raise this problem with their class.

Applications of vicarious learning. I include the Fisher and Hinde observation of songbirds and milk cartons for two reasons: First, because it has been widely publicized, and second, because it provides an opportunity to remind students again about the limitations of anecdotal evidence.

The adverse effects on children of viewing realistic television violence for many hours over a period of years is clearly established. The question arises as to why parents permit their children to watch such programming. This issue may provide an excellent opportunity to explore the way that consequences affect behavior.

Exercise: TV Crime Debate

One thing that people can learn from television is how to commit crimes. Two groups of students might debate the following position: Television programs that show how crimes may be committed should be banned.

Key to Review Questions

1. Define the following terms in your own words:

Attentional processes: In Bandura's theory of vicarious learning, any activity by an observer that aids in the observation of relevant aspects of a model's behavior and its consequences.
Generalized imitation: The tendency to imitate modeled behavior even though the modeled behavior is not reinforced.
Motivational processes: In Bandura's theory of vicarious learning,, the expectation that a modeled behavior will be reinforced.
Motor reproductive processes: In Bandura's theory of vicarious learning, the skills required to perform modeled behavior.
Participant modeling: A procedure in which a trainer first models a behavior and then assists the observer to perform it.
Retentional processes: In Bandura's theory of vicarious learning, any activity by an observer that aids recall of modeled behavior.
Vicarious learning: Any procedure in which an organism learns by observing the behavior of another organism.

2. Why has vicarious learning received less attention than other forms of learning?

The behavior of scientists is a function of its consequences, and the consequences of the early research on vicarious learning were negative. Positive findings are generally more reinforcing than negative findings, so researchers moved into other areas.

3. If vicarious learning can lead to the widespread use of certain practices, how can one determine whether those practices are innate or learned?

One way is to preclude the opportunity for vicarious learning in given individuals and see if they display the behavior. We might, for example, incubate and rear cowbirds in a lab and see if, as adults, they put their eggs into other birds' nests. If they do, then the possibility that they learn to do so by observation is ruled out.

4. Given what you know about vicarious learning, what advice would you give a friend whose children watch four to five hours of television daily?

There are two points that might be made. First, there is evidence that the more television children watch, the more likely that they are to behave in undesirable ways. (E.g., children who watch a great deal of TV are more likely to get into trouble with the authorities.) The student might point this out and advise the friend to limit the children's access to the TV. Second, children learn by observing their parents, and many parents spend their free time watching TV. Thus, the student might advise the friend to spend free time in activities other than watching TV so that the children might imitate that behavior.

5. How could you use vicarious procedures to create a fad on a college campus?

One way to go about this would be to get popular students to engage in the behavior to be imitated. Another way would be to create an ad campaign in which people are depicted engaging in the target behavior. This item might easily become a student project.

6. How might the value of Bandura's retentional processes be tested experimentally?

It is not altogether certain that these processes are sufficiently well defined to be tested experimentally. However, learning sign language would presumably enhance the ability of chimps to symbolically represent and rehearse observed behavior. If chimps that have learned sign language are more likely to learn modeled behavior than chimps that have not learned sign language, the value of retentional processes is supported.

7. If you wanted to ensure that an observer would learn from a model, what sort of model would you choose?

This is straight forward: Models are more likely to be imitated when they are attractive, intelligent, prestigious, etc.

8. How would you determine whether snakes can learn through observation?

The trick here is to find some behavior that snakes might imitate. One way to do that would be to have a male snake find its way to and copulate with a sexually receptive female snake. The model might have to choose one of two openings in a wall to reach the female. If the observer follows the same path after any trace of odor from the model is removed, this suggests that snakes learn through observation.

9. How could you teach a child to tie her shoes *without* using modeling?

The point of this item is to make the student appreciate how commonplace modeling is and how difficult certain tasks are to learn without modeling. The answer would presumably involve shaping and chaining.

10. Studies of vicarious learning of aggression usually involve children. Why?

The preference for children may have to do with the fact that aggression learned early has important implications for adult behavior, or it may have to do with the difficulty of getting adults to display aggression in a controlled setting. Another possibility is that aggression is considerably more dangerous in adults than it is in children. But perhaps the best reason for using children is that the choice of models is easier: Children are likely to imitate just about any adult, but adults are more discriminating and finding effective models is more problematic.

11. After Marilyn Monroe died, apparently by suicide, several other people took their own lives. Explain these copycat suicides.

Students who have difficulty with this question should be asked to consider the events that followed Monroe's suicide (publicity, eulogies, adulation). Instructors may want to draw attention to similar episodes, such as the Pepsi contaminations in early 1993. A hypodermic syringe was reportedly found in a can of diet cola. This received wide publicity, and was soon followed by some 50 copycat "findings," most or all of which were fabrications.

12. Why do so many fads get started by rock groups and movie stars?

If students have trouble with this one, the instructor might ask, "When was the last time you heard of 50,000 students attending a lecture?" Rock groups and movie stars are very popular, which means they are observed and therefore might be imitated by many people. In addition, imitation of such people is more likely to be reinforced than is imitation of less popular people.

13. Design an experiment to determine the role of delayed reinforcement of a model's behavior in vicarious learning.

Note that the task is to determine the effects of delayed reinforcement of the model's behavior, not that of the observer. A group design might have children observe an adult model, with the model's target behavior reinforced immediately in one condition and after a delay in another. In a single subject design, the same children might observe models in two situations, one involving immediate reinforcement, the other involving delayed reinforcement. In either case, the dependent variable would be the tendency of the observers to imitate the model's behavior.

14. How might superstitious behavior be acquired through vicarious experiences?

Presumably, superstitious behavior would be acquired in the same way as any other modeled behavior. If the model's behavior is adventitiously reinforced, the observer should be more likely to perform the behavior.

15. What is the chief difference between the Miller-Dollard theory and Bandura's theory of vicarious learning?

In my view, the chief difference is that Miller and Dollard view observational learning as operant learning in which the model's reinforced behavior becomes a prompt for imitation. Bandura sees observational learning as a distinct kind of learning that is fundamentally cognitive.

16. According to the Miller-Dollard theory, vicarious learning is merely a form of operant learning. Describe the researchers' reasoning.

Answers should note that imitative behavior is frequently reinforced, so that a model's behavior, particularly modeled behavior that has reinforcing consequences, becomes a signal for imitation. The law of effect is operating, and learning can be accounted for in terms of the functional relationship between a response and its consequences, just as is the case in all operant learning.

17. Design a study to determine whether Kawamura's monkeys really learned to wash potatoes by observing model's.

One possibility is to train a monkey to wash potatoes, then give another monkey the opportunity to observe and the model.

18. Suppose you proved that vicarious learning ability improves markedly as children develop speech. How would Bandura account for this finding? How would Miller and Dollard account for it?

Bandura would suggest that speech enhanced the ability to perform attentional and retentional activities. Miller and Dollard might say that speech provides cues for imitative behavior.

19. How might our view of human nature differ if psychologists had never succeeded in demonstrating vicarious learning in animals?

In this case, vicarious learning would provide a basis for claiming that humans are qualitatively different from beasts.

20. If you could learn in only one way (through Pavlovian, operant, or vicarious procedures), which would you choose?

The point of this question is to get the students to think about the kinds of things people learn in each of the three ways.

Key to Practice Quiz

1. Vicarious learning can be defined as a change in behavior due to the experience of <u>observing a model</u>.

2. Research suggests that what appears to be vicarious classical conditioning may in fact be a form of <u>higher-order</u> conditioning.

3. Susan Mineka studied fear of <u>snakes</u> in <u>monkeys</u>.

4. The tendency to imitate models even when the modeled behavior is not reinforced is called <u>generalized</u> imitation.

5. Vicarious learning is affected by characteristics of the model. For example, models are more likely to be imitated when they are <u>competent/attractive/likable/prestigious</u>.

6. Viki was a <u>chimpanzee</u>.

7. Bandura's theory relies on four processes. These include <u>attentional/retentional/motivational/motor reproductive</u> (any two) processes.

8. The Miller-Dollard theory says that the tendency to observe and imitate models depends on reinforcement of the <u>observer</u>'s behavior.

9. Zing Yang Kuo found that cats were far more likely to kill rats if they had <u>seen their mothers kill rats</u>.

10. A form of treatment for phobia that combines modeling with counterconditioning is called <u>participant modeling</u>.

Chapter 8 Quiz: Vicarious Learning

1. Research suggests that what appears to be vicarious classical conditioning may in fact be a form of _____ conditioning.

2. Herbert and Harsh had cats observe a model work at a problem 15 times or _____ times.

3. In the 1960s, Otto Larsen and his coworkers found that in television programs intended for children, TV characters achieved their goals by violent or illegal acts _____ % of the time.

4. According to Miller and Dollard, vicarious learning is a form of _____ learning.

5. Fiorito and Scotto studied vicarious learning in the _____.

6. _____ imitation is the tendency to imitate models even when doing so is not reinforced.

7. The term attentional processes is associated with the theory of _____.

8. A treatment for phobia that makes use of vicarious learning is _____ modeling.

9. Carl _____ was one of the first people to demonstrate vicarious learning in animals.

10. The Rocky and Johnny study demonstrated that children would imitate the _____ behavior of adult models.

Key to Chapter 8 Quiz

1. Research suggests that what appears to be vicarious classical conditioning may in fact be a form of <u>higher-order</u> conditioning. (271)

2. Herbert and Harsh had cats observe a model work at a problem 15 times or <u>30</u> times. (273)

3. In the 1960s, Otto Larsen and his coworkers found that in television programs intended for children, TV characters achieved their goals by violent or illegal acts <u>56</u> % of the time. (293)

4. According to Miller and Dollard, vicarious learning is a form of <u>operant</u> learning. (289)

5. Fiorito and Scotto studied vicarious learning in the <u>octopus.</u> (280)

6. <u>Generalized</u> imitation is the tendency to imitate models even when doing so is not reinforced. (280)

7. The term *attentional processes* is associated with the theory of <u>Bandura</u>. (288)

8. A treatment for phobia that makes use of vicarious learning is <u>participant</u> modeling. (296)

9. Carl <u>Warden</u> was one of the first people to demonstrate vicarious learning in animals. (271)

10. The Rocky and Johnny study demonstrated that children would imitate the <u>aggressive</u> behavior of adult models. (294)

Generalization, Discrimination, and Stimulus Control

Chapter Outline

Main Points

Generalization is the tendency for behavior learned in one situation to occur in other situations. The greater the similarity of a situation to the training situation, the more likely behavior is to generalize. Generalization can be based on physical attributes or semantic attributes. Discrimination is the tendency for behavior to occur in one situation but not others. Discriminations can be established through various procedures, including errorless discrimination training. When discrimination training brings behavior under the control of discriminative stimuli, the result is called stimulus control. Two popular theories of generalization and discrimination today are Spence's theory of excitatory and inhibitory gradients and the Lashley-Wade theory. Discrimination training provides insight into concept learning, mental rotation, smoking relapse, and possibly some forms of neurosis.

Class Notes

Background. Generalization and discrimination add tremendously to the survival value of learning. The point might be made that it is precisely because environments are always changing that generalization and discrimination are so very important.

Generalization. Some students, especially those majoring in education, may ask if generalization is another name for transfer of training. Strictly speaking, transfer of training refers to the tendency for training in one skill to improve the rate of learning another skill. Generalization refers to the tendency of behavior learned in one situation to occur in other situations. The two terms are often used interchangeably, however, and the distinction has become blurred. Certainly the concepts are closely related, and it may be best not to make the distinction unless a student makes an issue of it.

Exercise: Amazing Generalizations

Have some students work on a finger maze repeatedly, with their efforts timed by other students. When they have reached a given level of mastery, they might then work at a different maze. Assuming the two mazes are equally difficult, faster mastery of the second maze may be attributed to generalization of skills learned on the first maze. A variation of this would involve giving some students mazes that closely resembled the first, while giving other students mazes that are quite different.

Discrimination. Some instructors may want to talk about the idea that reinforcement strengthens a response class, not just a specific response. A response class is defined by reinforcement. Discrimination training can be viewed as the process of defining a response class.

I have shifted in this edition from S^D and S^Δ to S^+ and S^-. Although I personally prefer the traditional terms, I have made the change because the newer terms seem to be preferred today and because they are easier to work with in printed documents.

Stimulus control. The word *control* gets us into all sorts of trouble with students, since it usually implies threats and other aversives. It should be emphasized therefore that stimulus control refers to the increased tendency to behave a certain way in one situation and a decreased tendency to behave that way in a different situation. Certainly I *can* proceed through a red light, and might under certain circumstances. But there is a definite tendency to stop at red lights, and this tendency is clearly a function of reinforcing and punishing consequences.

Exercise: Bish and Bosh

Concept learning through discrimination training can be demonstrated by presenting a series of items, some of which are Bish and some are Bosh. The items might be drawings of geometric forms. Bish items might be those that have curved lines; Bosh might be those with angles. Or the items might be common kitchen utensils. Bish might be those with some wood; Bosh those that are all metal. The instructor holds up an item, the students guess Bish or Bosh, and the instructor announces "Correct" or "Incorrect." When the students are able to identify the training items correctly, the instructor holds up a series of new items and asks if each is Bish or Bosh. The students also may be asked to write a definition of Bish and Bosh. Some students who can correctly identify the two kinds of items may not be able to identify the defining elements.

Theories of generalization and discrimination. Pavlov's theory seems hardly worth considering, but is included for its historical value and because of the benefits of studying other people's mistakes.

Some students may understand the graph illustrating excitatory and inhibitory gradients better if the figure is turned on its side. Also, students who have trouble understanding Spence's theory might get it if the two gradients are described as hot and cold fluids: The inhibitory gradient "cools" the warmer excitatory gradient.

Applications. I include transposition in the discussion of relational concepts because it seems to me that transposition is a relational concept. I do not see that it deserves a name of its own, or the extensive treatment that it is sometimes given in learning texts.

In the third edition of *Learning and Behavior* I suggested that mental rotation could be viewed as stimulus generalization, and reformulated data from Cooper and Shepard (1973) in the form of a generalization gradient. Since then Brady Phelps and Donna Reit (e.g., Reit & Phelps, 1996; Phelps & Reit, 1997) have produced original data supporting this notion.

Experimental neurosis may or may not help account for human neuroses. However, it is worth noting that Carr's work (described in Chapter 10) shows that retarded and psychotic children sometimes behave in a bizarre fashion when called on to perform tasks that are beyond them. And is that not what was demanded of Pavlov's dog?

Stimulus Control and Adaptation.

There are some excellent photographs of well-camouflaged animals that show just how difficult it is to discriminate between the animal and its natural background. (I think of the copperhead snake lying on fallen oakleaves.) The case of Biston betularia (see Chapter 1) also is relevant, since the decline of white butterflies and ascendancy of black ones reflected a change in their relative discriminability.

Key to Review Questions

1. Define the following terms:

Concept: Any class (i.e., group, category) the members of which share one or more defining features. The term may also be defined in terms of the tendency to respond in a particular way toward a particular class of stimuli.

Differential outcomes effect: The finding that discrimination training proceeds more rapidly when different behaviors produce different reinforcers.

Discrimination: The tendency for a behavior to occur in the presence of certain stimuli, but not in their absence.

Discrimination training: Any procedure for establishing a discrimination. A distinction may be made between Pavlovian and operant discrimination training.

Discriminative stimulus: In operant discrimination training, any stimulus that signals either that a behavior will be reinforced (the S^+ or S^D) or that it will not be reinforced (the S^- or S^Δ). Some instructors object to the word signals, so the term may also be defined as a stimulus that is associated with reinforcement or nonreinforcement. In Pavlovian discrimination training, discriminative stimulus refers to a CS that is associated either with the appearance of a US (the CS+) or with its absence (the CS–).

Errorless discrimination training: A form of discrimination training in which the S^- is introduced in very weak form and gradually strengthened. The usual result is that discrimination is achieved with few or no errors.

Excitatory gradient: In Spence's theory of generalization and discrimination, a generalization gradient showing an increased tendency to respond to the S^+ or CS+ and stimuli resembling them.

Experimental neuroses: Any bizarre or neurotic-like behavior induced through an experimental procedure such as discrimination training.

Generalization: The tendency for a learned behavior to occur in the presence of stimuli were not present during training. (The text deals only with stimulus generalization, not response generalization.)

Generalization gradient: Any graphic representation of generalization data.

Inhibitory gradient: In Spence's theory of generalization and discrimination, a gradient showing a decreased tendency to respond to the S^- or CS– and stimuli resembling them.

Matching to sample: A discrimination training procedure in which the task is to select from two or more comparison stimuli the one that matches a sample.

Mismatching: A variation of matching to sample in which reinforcement is available for selecting the comparison stimulus that is different from the sample.

Peak shift: The tendency following discrimination training for the peak of responding to shift away from the S^- or CS–.

S^+ A stimulus in the presence of which a behavior will be reinforced.

$S-$ A stimulus in the presence of which a behavior will not be reinforced.

Semantic generalization: Generalization based on an abstract (as opposed to a physical) property of a stimulus.

Simultaneous discrimination training: A discrimination training procedure in which the S^+ and S^- are presented at the same time.

Stimulus control: The tendency for a behavior to occur in the presence of an S⁺ but not in the presence of an S⁻.

Successive discrimination training: A discrimination training procedure in which the S⁺ and S⁻ are presented one after the other in random sequence.

2. Describe the relationship between generalization and discrimination.

Here the point is that the relationship is reciprocal: As one increases, the other necessarily decreases by the same proportion.

3. How is semantic generalization different from other examples of generalization?

Semantic generalization involves variation in responding based on differences in an abstract, rather than a physical, feature of the stimuli involved.

4. A student learns to draw human figures. How could you determine whether this learning had improved the student's ability to draw animal figures? What phenomenon would you be studying?

It is easy enough to set up an experiment, but answers should indicate the need for a measure of the student's ability to draw animal figures before and after learning to draw human figures. The phenomenon studied would be generalization.

5. There is a saying that goes, "He who has been bitten by a snake fears a rope." What phenomenon does this proverb implicitly recognize?

Generalization: people respond toward a rope as they had previously responded toward the snake. This is Pavlovian generalization, since we are talking about the pairing of a snake and a bite (or other aversive events, such as someone screaming in your ear, "SNAKE!!!!") and the behavior involved is an emotional response.

6. Mark Twain once said that a cat that gets burned on a hot stove thereafter avoids cold stoves as well as hot ones. How could you change the behavior of a cat that fits this description?

Twain is talking about generalization, and changing the behavior means establishing a discrimination. The student should propose some sort of discrimination training. Perhaps the cat could learn to discriminate on the basis of the heat radiating from the stove.

7. B. F. Skinner (1951) once taught pigeons to "read." They would peck a disk when a sign read "Peck," and would not peck when a sign read "Don't peck." Describe how Skinner might have accomplished this.

Again, the student should propose discrimination training, with Peck as the S⁺ and Don't peck as the S⁻. My hope is that some students will turn to Skinner's 1951 paper for help in answering this question.

8. Thorndike (1911) wrote that "by taking a certain well-defined position in front of [a monkey's] cage and feeding him whenever he did scratch himself I got him to always scratch himself within a few seconds after I took that position" (p. 236). Explain what sort of training is going on here. Try to identify the S^+, the S^-, the response being learned, and the reinforcer.

This is operant discrimination training with Thorndike in his defined position as the S^+, Thorndike in any other position as the S^-, the response learned is scratching in the presence of the S^+, and the reinforcer is food.

9. Diane says that in the experiment described in question 8, it is not the monkey that is undergoing discrimination training, but Thorndike. Why might she say this?

The relationship between trainer and trainee is reciprocal, with each reinforcing the behavior of the other. It could be said that the monkey reinforced Thorndike's food-giving behavior by scratching.

10. Why is generalization important to the teacher?

Very few skills that students learn in the classroom are ever used in exactly the same situation again. Students must be able to perform skills in new situations or their education is useless.

11. How would you test the hypothesis, "Experimental neurosis can be avoided through errorless discrimination training?"

This is an interesting problem, and I'm not sure it can be solved satisfactorily. The student needs to understand both the experimental neurosis procedure and errorless discrimination training. The task is to train successively finer discriminations, as in the experimental neurosis experiments, using errorless discrimination training.

12. How might you use discrimination training to make someone capable of recognizing, from facial expressions and other "body language," when people are lying?

A person might be instructed to lie when answering certain questions and tell the truth when answering others. The trainee is asked to guess in each case whether the person is lying. Correct responses are reinforced (perhaps with money). I do not know whether this would work or, if it did, whether the effects of training would generalize to other situations. It would make an interesting research project.

13. What might be the role of discrimination training in racial prejudice?

Prejudice implies discrimination training, usually at the hands of parents and other influential adults. It is interesting to note that the very term discrimination is popularly used more or less as a synonym for prejudice.

14. Some people object to the practice of using the pronoun *he* to refer to people in traditional male roles (e.g., scientists) while using *she* to refer to people in traditional female roles (e.g., nurses). Are they right to object?

Obviously this is a matter of opinion. However, traditional female positions are often lower in status than traditional male positions. (For example, teachers were traditionally women, whereas school principals were traditionally men.) If the object is to avoid discrimination training that would incline people to think that high status positions belong to men and low status positions belong to women, then there is some reason to object to the traditional use of he and she.

15. How does Spence's theory differ from Pavlov's?

Students might note that Pavlov's theory is physiological, while Spence's theory emphasizes behavioral tendencies (excitatory and inhibitory gradients).

16. A music teacher has trained students to recognize middle C on the piano. She then tests for generalization by playing other keys. Draw a hypothetical generalization gradient of the results.

The gradient should show the tendency to respond to be a regular function of the similarity of the key to middle C.

17. How could you teach a fellow student the concept of generalization?

Concepts are readily learned through discrimination training, so the question suggests a discrimination procedure.

18. What implications does research on errorless discrimination training have for the construction of educational software?

It is popularly believed, even by some educators, that we learn mainly by making mistakes. Errorless discrimination training implies that we could design educational software so that students could learn easily without making mistakes. Whether eliminating errors entirely is a desirable goal is an open question.

19. Explain why a stimulus that becomes an S^+ also becomes a secondary reinforcer.

This probably occurs because of Pavlovian conditioning: The S^+ is regularly paired with a US or well-established CS (the reinforcer).

20. Explain why a person who is red-green colorblind (that is, red and green objects look gray) is at a disadvantage compared to his or her peers.

We discriminate objects partly on the basis of color. It is therefore harder for the colorblind person to make discriminations when the colors red or green are involved. For instance, certain poisonous animals are brightly colored. This makes them easy to see and avoid. Snakes that are red or green are harder for the colorblind person to see.

1. One of the first reports of generalization came from <u>Thorndike</u> in 1898.

2. Arthur Bachrach and others got generalization of therapy in a young woman who would not <u>eat</u> .

3. Gregory Razran found greater generalization in response to words with similar <u>meanings</u> than to words with similar sounds.

4. Richard Herrnstein used discrimination training to teach the concepts "tree" and "human being" to <u>pigeons</u>.

5. The peak shift phenomenon supports the theory of generalization and discrimination proposed by <u>Spence</u>.

6. A smoker always lights a cigarette after a meal. Lighting a cigarette is under <u>stimulus control</u>.

7. Through discrimination training, we can learn to discriminate between <u>punks</u> and skinheads.

8. When generalization data are plotted on a curve, the result is a generalization <u>gradient</u>.

9. One kind of discrimination training procedure is abbreviated MTS. This stands for <u>matching to sample</u>.

10. Requiring a subject to discriminate between stimuli that are more and more alike may produce an <u>experimental neurosis</u>.

Chapter 9 Quiz: Generalization, Discrimination, Stimulus Control

1. When generalization data are plotted on a curve, the result is a generalization _____.

2. An S^+ and an S^- are both _____ stimuli.

3. A procedure that is designed to result in very few errors during training is called _____ discrimination training.

4. Robert Eisenberger and his coworkers have found that rewarding a high level of effort on one task increases the level of effort on other tasks, a phenomenon they call _____ _____.

5. The finding that providing different outcomes for different behavior improves discrimination training is known as the _____ effect.

6. The _____ theory emphasizes the importance of experience with stimuli that differ from the S^+.

7. The flatter the generalization gradient, the greater the degree of _____.

8. In _____ generalization, generalization is based on an abstract feature of the stimuli.

9. In the _____ discrimination training procedure, the discriminative stimuli alternate.

10. When a behavior occurs reliably in the presence of an S^+ and not in the presence of an S^-, the behavior is under _____.

Key to Chapter 9 Quiz

1. When generalization data are plotted on a curve, the result is a generalization <u>gradient</u>. (306)

2. An S^+ and an S^- are both <u>discriminative</u> stimuli. (314)

3. A procedure that is designed to result in very few errors during training is called <u>errorless</u> discrimination training. (319)

4. Robert Eisenberger and his coworkers have found that rewarding a high level of effort on one task increases the level of effort on other tasks, a phenomenon they call <u>learned industriousness</u>. (305)

5. The finding that providing different outcomes for different behavior improves discrimination training is known as the <u>differential outcomes</u> effect. (320)

6. The <u>Lashley-Wade</u> theory emphasizes the importance of experience with stimuli that differ from the S^+. (329)

7. The flatter the generalization gradient, the greater the degree of <u>generalization</u>. (313)

8. In <u>semantic</u> generalization, generalization is based on an abstract feature of the stimuli. (308)

9. In the <u>successive</u> discrimination training procedure, the discriminative stimuli alternate. (318)

10. When a behavior occurs reliably in the presence of an S^+ and not in the presence of an S^-, the behavior is under <u>stimulus control</u>. (322)

10

Schedules of Reinforcement

Chapter outline

Main points

Rules governing the delivery of reinforcers are called reinforcement schedules. The most important simple reinforcement schedules are FR (including continuous reinforcement, or CRF), VR, FI, and VI. Other simple schedules include FT, VT, and various differential reinforcement schedules. Schedules may be thinned by gradually stretching the ratio. An extinction schedule is one in which a response is never reinforced. Complex schedules are combinations of simple schedules. The concurrent schedule is of special interest because of its resemblance to choice situations. In such situations, organisms distribute responses in proportion to the reinforcement available, a principle known as the matching law. Schedules research has proved useful in understanding various phenomena, including gambling, economics, and malingering.

Class notes

Background. The quotation at the beginning of the chapter could be considered a reformulation of the law of effect. Schedules research is, ultimately, research on the law of effect.

Simple schedules. Continuous reinforcement and extinction are usually treated as distinct schedules, as they are here, but they may be considered the logical extremes of the possible FR schedules: CRF is FR 1; Extinction is FR ∞. This idea may be helpful to some students.

Sniffy Exercise: Schedule Effects

Have students put Sniffy's lever-pressing on a particular intermittent schedule and describe the cumulative record obtained. Then have the students switch to another schedule and note the change in the record.

It's astonishing, but bright students can fall for the gambler's logic. (E.g., "If the slot machine hasn't paid off for a long time, it's bound to pay off big any minute.") It is probably worthwhile noting that the logic comes after the behavior, as a way of explaining behavior that is actually produced by reinforcement contingencies. It might also be noted that efforts to rehabilitate compulsive gamblers rarely pay any attention to reinforcement contingencies; instead they focus on treating character flaws or attempt to argue the person out of his faulty logic.

Students sometimes conclude that reinforcement is of little value since, when you stop reinforcing the behavior, it returns to its former rate. This is, of course, what the law of effect predicts. However, stretching the ratio means that behavior often can be maintained with a very thin schedule. This makes reinforcement far more important than it would otherwise be. The box on harrassment was included to provide an example of a very persistent behavior that is difficult to account for without reference to intermittent reinforcement. Very likely the prolific science writer Isaac Asimov provides another example: working 12 hours a day, very nearly every day for years on end, in a room with the blinds drawn so as not to be distracted, and writing as fast as he could type, he managed to produce nearly 500 books by the time of his death at age 72.

Complex schedules. I wonder about the wisdom of discussing complex schedules in a first course in learning; however, the work on concurrent schedules strikes me as important because of its relevance to choice situations.

Exercise: Extinction

Play the Training Game (see Chapter 5 of this manual) to establish a behavior. Then, after reinforcing the desired response two or three times, end all reinforcement. (The instructor might provide a subtle cue to the class by, for instance, crossing his or her arms.) Once the behavior is on extinction, certain characteristic behavior may emerge: An initial increase in the variability of behavior; the appearance of emotional behavior; and resurgence of previously reinforced behavior. These products of extinction can then be discussed. It is sometimes necessary to cut the exercise short because of the emotional effects on the student whose behavior is on extinction.

Choice and the matching law. I have attempted to simplify the discussion of choice and the matching law somewhat. The thing to emphasize, it seems to me, may be that choices can be understood in terms of consequences; this makes them, theoretically at least, predictable.

Applications of Schedules. My goal here is not to analyze the topics concerned strictly in terms of schedules, but to show that schedules provide a way of tackling complex behavior problems.

Importance of reinforcement schedules. In his later years, Skinner expressed disappointment at the lack of progress in schedules research. He thought that it was a neglected area that still had much to offer. Whether he was right or not, it seems clear that schedules work has been important to an understanding of behavior.

Key to review questions

1. Define the following terms:

Chain schedule: A complex reinforcement schedule that consists of a series of simple schedules, each of which is associated with a particular stimulus, with reinforcement delivered only on completion of the last schedule in the series.

Concurrent schedule: A complex reinforcement schedule in which two or more simple schedules are available at the same time.

Cooperative schedule: A complex reinforcement schedule in which reinforcement is contingent on the behavior of two or more individuals.

CRF: A reinforcement schedule in which a behavior is reinforced each time it occurs.

Discrimination hypothesis: The proposal that the PRE occurs because it is harder to discriminate between intermittent reinforcement and extinction than between continuous reinforcement and extinction.

DRH: A form of differential reinforcement in which a behavior is reinforced only if it occurs at least a specified number of times in a given period.

Experimental economics: The use of reinforcement schedules, among other techniques, to study economic principles.

Fixed duration schedule: A reinforcement schedule in which reinforcement is contingent on the continuous performance of a behavior for a fixed period of time.

Fixed interval schedule: A reinforcement schedule in which a behavior is reinforced the first time it occurs following a specified interval since the last reinforcement.

Fixed ratio schedule: A reinforcement schedule in which every *nth* performance of a behavior is reinforced.

Fixed time schedule: A reinforcement schedule in which reinforcement is delivered independently of behavior at fixed intervals.

Frustration hypothesis: The proposal that the PRE occurs because nonreinforcement is frustrating and during intermittent reinforcement frustration becomes an S^+ for responding.

Intermittent schedule: Any of several reinforcement schedules in which a behavior is sometimes reinforced.

Matching law: The principle that, given the opportunity to respond on two or more reinforcement schedules, the rate of responding on each schedule will match the reinforcement available on each schedule.

Mixed schedule: A complex reinforcement schedule in which two or more simple schedules, neither associated with a particular stimulus, alternate.

Multiple schedule: A complex reinforcement schedule in which two or more simple schedules alternate, with each schedule associated with a particular stimulus.

Partial reinforcement effect: The tendency for a behavior to be more resistant to extinction following partial reinforcement than following continuous reinforcement. (It's probably worth noting that some people now refer to this as the PREE, the partial reinforcement extinction effect.)

Post-reinforcement pause: A pause in responding following reinforcement.

Ratio strain: Disruption of the pattern of responding due to stretching the ratio of reinforcement too abruptly or too far.

Response unit hypothesis: The idea that the PRE is due to differences in the definition of a behavior during intermittent and continuous reinforcement.

Run rate: The rate at which a behavior occurs once it has resumed following reinforcement.

Schedule effects: The distinctive rate and pattern of responding associated with a particular reinforcement schedule.

Schedule of reinforcement: A rule describing the delivery of reinforcers for a behavior.

Sequential hypothesis: The idea that the PRE occurs because the sequence of reinforced and nonreinforced behaviors during intermittent reinforcement becomes an S^+ for responding during extinction.

Stretching the ratio: The procedure of gradually increasing the number of responses required for reinforcement.

Tandem schedule: A complex reinforcement schedule that consists of a series of simple schedules, with reinforcement delivered only on completion of the last schedule in the series. The simple schedules are not associated with different stimuli.

Variable duration schedule: A reinforcement schedule in which reinforcement is contingent on the continuous performance of a behavior for a period of time, with the length of the time varying around an average.

Variable interval schedule: A reinforcement schedule in which a behavior is reinforced the first time it occurs following an interval since the last reinforcement, with the interval varying around a specified average.

Variable ratio schedule: A reinforcement schedule in which, on average, every *nth* performance of a behavior is reinforced.

Variable time schedule: A reinforcement schedule in which reinforcement is delivered at varying intervals regardless of what the organism does.

2. Give an example (not provided by the text) of a decrease in responding that indicates learning has occurred.

The point of this question (which appeared in slightly different form in Chapter 2) is to remind the student that learning does not necessarily mean an increase in responding. Examples might include eating less, drinking less, smoking less, arguing less, criticizing less, and so on.

3. John wants to teach Cindy, age five, the alphabet. He plans to reinforce correct responses with praise and small pieces of candy. What sort of schedule should he use?

The text makes the point that CRF is the most efficient schedule in the early stages of learning. However, some students may think of using praise and candy on two different schedules. Thus, John might reinforce with praise on a CRF schedule, and reinforce with candy on, say, a FD 1' schedule.

4. Mary complains that her dog jumps up on her when she gets home from school. You explain that she reinforces this behavior by petting and talking to the dog when it jumps up, but Mary replies that you must be wrong, since she "hardly ever" does this. How would you respond to Mary's comment?

The student should recognize that Mary is intermittently reinforcing the unwanted behavior, and should note that such intermittent reinforcement makes behavior very persistent.

5. Five-year-old David gives up easily in the face of frustration. How could you develop his persistence?

Frustration is typically an emotional reaction to failure, so what this means is that David gives up whenever his efforts are not immediately successful. The problem then becomes that of increasing the persistence of responding despite failure. This can be accomplished by presenting David with problems he can immediately solve, and then gradually increasing the difficulty so that reinforcement is contingent on persisting at problems for longer and longer periods. Social reinforcement, such as attention and praise, might also be provided for persistence on an intermittent basis.

6. Joyce is annoyed because some of her employees fail to take the periodic rest breaks required by the union and the state's safety regulations. Why do you suppose this happens, and what can Joyce do to correct the problem?

Students should look to the consequences of behavior for an explanation. If they do, they will probably hypothesize that there are reinforcing consequences for work through breaks. Very likely Joyce's employees are paid on an FR schedule, so taking breaks reduces their income. Joyce can alter their behavior by altering their pay schedule. For instance, she might provide pay during breaks at the rate earned immediately prior to the break.

7. Every Saturday at noon, the local fire department tests the fire signal. Is this a reinforcement schedule and, if so, what sort of schedule is it?

Not every regularly occurring event constitutes a reinforcement schedule. (The sun rises and sets, but it is not a reinforcement schedule.) Unless the student maintains that the sound of the siren, or some other consequence of the test, reinforces some specified behavior, the test probably cannot be said to be a reinforcement schedule.

8. Many people regularly check the coin return after using a public telephone even though their call went through. Explain this behavior.

Three things might be mentioned: First, we have all had the experience of receiving coins from the coin return when a call doesn't go through. Second, when the coins drop into the bank, it often sounds as though they have fallen into the coin return. Third, sometimes when we check the coin return we find coins there. This last point means that the behavior is on intermittent reinforcement and therefore persists even though the vast majority of time it is not reinforced.

9. Mr. Smith and Ms Jones both give their students new spelling words on Friday. Mr. Smith always tests his students on the following Friday. Ms Jones also tests her students once a week, but the day varies, and she does not announce the test day in advance. Whose students are more likely to study on Tuesday nights?

One reinforcement for studying is avoiding failure. The probability of reinforcement for studying on Tuesday night is greater for Ms Jones' students than for Mr. Smith's. Therefore the best bet has to be Ms Jones' students.

10. How might casino operators increase their income by "stretching the ratio"?

They might increase the *chances* of winning early on and gradually stretch the ratio. Slot machines, for example, could pay off at a 5% return (i.e., $1.05 received, on average, for each $1 wagered), then pay a zero return, then a -5% return, then -10%, and so on. This is very likely illegal.

11. Concurrent schedules are said to represent a choice situation. Why is a multiple schedule not said to represent a choice?

This item is meant to get at the fundamental difference between a concurrent schedule, in which reinforcement for two or more responses is available, and a multiple schedule, in which only one response can be reinforced. Choice implies more than one source of reinforcement.

12. Describe the similarities and differences between multiple and chain schedules.

Both involve two or more simple schedules, and in both cases schedule changes are indicated by changes in stimuli. In multiple schedules, however, reinforcement is delivered during each of the schedules, while in a chain schedule, reinforcement occurs only on completion of the last schedule.

13. Rat X's lever pressing is put on a concurrent FR 10 FR 20 schedule. Rat Y's behavior is put on a concurrent VR 10 VR 20 schedule. Which rat will select the more reinforcing schedule first?

I am not sure it is possible to answer this question except to say, "It depends." The VR 10 schedule could, for a time, provide reinforcement at a higher rate than the FR 10 schedule, and the VR 20 schedule could, for a time, provide reinforcement at a lower rate than the FR 20 schedule. If this happened, the discrepancy between VR 10 and VR 20 would be larger (more discriminable) than the difference between the FR 10 and FR 20 schedules.

14. How might you use what you know about reinforcement schedules to study the effects of the presence of observers on human performance?

One way would be to establish responding at a steady rate on a given schedule, say VR 20, and then introduce observers and see what happens to the steady rate. After a period of time, remove the observers and see if the rate returns to the previous steady rate.

15. Someone says to you, "George is a nasty fellow. It's just his nature." How could you account for George's personality in a more scientific way?

The point here is that being nasty means emitting certain kinds of behavior at a high rate. It is conceivable that this tendency is partly the result of heredity, but it is also likely that nasty behavior has had positive consequences on an intermittent schedule. George probably learned to be nasty.

16. A student tells you that studying reinforcement schedules is a waste of time. Give arguments for the opposing view.

Students might mention that schedules provide a scientific way of defining and studying personality; help account for differences in response rate; show how to make behavior resistant to extinction; provide a way of studying the effects of drugs and other variables on behavior, etc.

17. A teacher reinforces longer and longer periods of quiet behavior in her students. How can she avoid creating ratio strain?

Ratio strain is due to stretching too far or too fast. To avoid it, avoid these errors. Some students might also suggest looking for signs of ratio strain, such as disruption of the response pattern and, if it occurs, increasing the reinforcement frequency. The danger here is, of course, that unwanted behaviors will be reinforced.

18. This chapter describes schedules of reinforcement. How would schedules of punishment work? Use, as an example, a VR 10 punishment schedule.

Punishment schedules are not much studied, but they look much like reinforcement schedules except that the occurrence of a response is punished instead of reinforced. In a VR 10 punishment schedule, every tenth response, on average, would be punished. A punishment schedule, however, implies a reinforcement schedule as well, since a response is not likely to continue if there are no reinforcing consequences. Thus, we cannot study the effects of a punishment schedule for long unless the behavior is also on a reinforcement schedule.

19. Pretend you are a behavioral economist who wishes to know the effect of inflation on purchasing. Describe an experiment that will shed light on the problem.

The key here is to define inflation and purchasing in measurable ways. One way to do that would be to train a rat to press a lever for food. The rat "purchases" food with its labor, and the price of the food is the amount of labor required to obtain it. Inflating the price means increasing the amount of labor required for a given amount of food.

20. How might an understanding of schedules of reinforcement help account for the poor economic performance of communist countries?

The quotation from B. F. Skinner at the beginning of the chapter might be used here. Schedules research shows that when working hard pays off (produces reinforcement) no better than doing the absolute minimum, organisms eventually do the minimum. The Goldberg and Cheney (1984) study is relevant here. One of the major problems of any society is to find a way of reinforcing desirable behaviors at desirable rates. Communist countries seem to have failed in that effort. However, capitalistic countries have not been entirely successful at it.

Key to Practice Quiz

1. In CRF, the ratio of responses to reinforcement is <u>one</u> to <u>one</u>.

2. After a reinforcement, the response rate may fall to or near zero before increasing again. The period of infrequent responding is called a <u>post-reinforcement pause</u>.

3. One difference between FT and FI schedules is that in the <u>FT</u> schedule, reinforcement is not contingent on a behavior.

4. An excellent schedule for increasing the rate of a behavior is called differential reinforcement of <u>high rate</u>.

5. Stretching the ratio too rapidly or too far can produce <u>ratio strain</u>.

6. Of the four explanations of the PRE, the one that essentially says there is no such thing is the <u>response unit</u> hypothesis.

7. If reinforcement is contingent on the behavior of more than one organism, a <u>cooperative</u> schedule is in effect.

8. Choice involves <u>concurrent</u> schedules.

9. Compulsive gambling may be the product of a <u>variable ratio</u> schedule of reinforcement.

10. Schedule effects are sometimes very different in people than in rats and pigeons. The difference is often due to the influence of <u>instructions</u>.

Chapter 10 Quiz: Schedules of Reinforcement

1. Stretching the ratio too rapidly or too far can produce _____.

2. The best schedule for shaping new behavior is _____ .

3. A schedule in which reinforcement is contingent on the behavior of more than one subject is a _____ schedule.

4. Studies of choice involve _____ schedules.

5. _____ schedules produce cumulative records with scallops.

6. Alan Christopher studied the role of intermittent reinforcement in compulsive _____.

7. The _____ hypothesis emphasizes the role of internal cues in explaining the PRE.

8. A schedule in which a behavior is never reinforced is called an _____ schedule.

9. Ratio strain is associated with the procedure known as _____ the ratio.

10. Strictly speaking, the reinforcers provided in a fixed _____ schedule are not noncontingent.

Key to Chapter 10 Quiz

1. Stretching the ratio too rapidly or too far can produce <u>ratio strain</u>. (359)

2. The best schedule for shaping new behavior is <u>CRF/continuous reinforcement</u>. (349)

3. A schedule in which reinforcement is contingent on the behavior of more than one subject is a <u>cooperative</u> schedule. (369)

4. Studies of choice involve <u>concurrent</u> schedules. (369)

5. <u>Fixed interval</u> schedules produce cumulative records with scallops. (353)

6. Alan Christopher studied the role of intermittent reinforcement in compulsive <u>gambling</u>. (376)

7. The <u>frustration</u> hypothesis emphasizes the role of internal cues in explaining the PRE. (363)

8. A schedule in which a behavior is never reinforced is called an <u>extinction</u> schedule. (360)

9. Ratio strain is associated with the procedure known as <u>stretching</u> the ratio. (360)

10. Strictly speaking, the reinforcers provided in a fixed <u>time</u> schedule are not noncontingent. (358, n3)

11

Forgetting

Chapter outline

Main points.

Experience does not create memories; rather, it changes behavior. Forgetting refers to the deterioration of learned behavior over time. This deterioration can be measured in various ways, including free and prompted recall and recognition. Several factors affect the rate of forgetting, including the degree of learning, prior learning, subsequent learning, and changes in context. Studies of foraging provide ample evidence of the role of forgetting in survival; studies on eyewitness testimony show the role of forgetting in modern life. To reduce forgetting we can: overlearn, use mnemonics and mnemonic systems, use context cues, use prompts. Even when forgetting seems complete, some effects of learning may remain.

Class notes

<u>Background</u>. The idea that experiences are "stored away" as memories is so widespread that it is difficult to get students to consider a different approach. That is the main task of this chapter.

<u>Defining forgetting</u>. Our concern is not with a hypothetical system for storing experience, but with the decline in the effects of experience on behavior. Thus, forgetting is deterioration in *performance*, not in some hypothetical construct.

<u>Measuring forgetting</u>. The extinction method of measuring forgetting is seldom discussed in learning texts, but it is an established way of measuring forgetting and perhaps should be considered. It is a neat way of measuring forgetting in animals.

<u>Variables in forgetting</u>. This section deals with the factors that affect the rate of forgetting. Proactive and retroactive interference are usually treated together in their own section. Instead, I have considered them in discussions of prior and subsequent learning.

Applied research on forgetting. Students are likely to be amazed at the "memory capacity" of animals revealed in the foraging studies. If birds (which have peanut sized brains) can learn the locations of thousands of seed caches, what might college students achieve!

Learning to remember. It is worth noting that suggestions for reducing forgetting usually are ways of improving learning. Even the use of prompts during recall works best if the prompts were used during learning.

A final word on forgetting. This section is here to make the point that learning is not a waste of time, even when we seem to have entirely forgotten what we learned. That applies to what we learn, and later forget, about learning.

Box: Myth of Permanent Memory. Many students accept without question the notion that experiences are permanently "stored away." The bulk of the evidence supports a different view, the idea that we don't store experiences but are changed by them.

Key to review questions

1. Define the following terms:

Cue-dependent forgetting: Forgetting that results from the absence of cues that were present during training.

Delayed matching to sample: A method of measuring forgetting in which the opportunity to match a sample follows a retention interval.

Extinction method: A method of measuring forgetting by comparing the rate of extinction after a retention interval with the rate of extinction immediately after training.

Fluency: The rate of performance, typically the number correct per minute. (A measure of learning, it can also be used to measure forgetting.)

Forgetting: Deterioration in learned behavior following a period without practice.

Free recall: A method of measuring forgetting that consists of providing the opportunity to perform the learned behavior.

Gradient degradation: A method of measuring forgetting in which a behavior is tested for generalization before and after a retention interval. A flattening of the generalization gradient indicates forgetting.

Method of loci: A mnemonic system in which each item to be recalled is "placed" in a distinctive spot in an imagined scene, such as a walking path.

Mnemonic: Any technique for aiding recall.

Overlearning: The continuation of training beyond the point required to produce one errorless performance. (Some instructors may object to the language "errorless performance," since the standard for mastery may not always be zero errors. The phrase may be replaced with "satisfactory performance," though that language is problematic because of its subjectivity.)

Paired associate learning: A learning task involving pairs of words or other stimuli in which the subject is presented with the first item of a pair and is expected to produce the second item. (Some authors, especially in decades past, have considered PA learning analogous to Pavlovian conditioning, but I have always thought it is a form of operant learning. In fact, the three parts of the three-term contingency are nicely illustrated in PA learning.

Peg word system: A mnemonic system in which each of the first n integers is associated with a particular image (a "peg"), and each item to be recalled is "placed" on a peg.

Proactive interference: Forgetting caused by learning that occurred prior to the behavior in question.

Prompted recall: A method of measuring forgetting in which hints (prompts) about the behavior to be performed are provided.

Recognition: A method of measuring forgetting in which the subject is required to identify stimuli experienced earlier.

Relearning method: A method of measuring forgetting in which a behavior is learned to criterion before and after a retention interval.

Reminiscence: Improvement in performance following a retention interval.

Retention interval: The time between training and testing for forgetting.

Retroactive interference: Forgetting caused by learning that occurred subsequent to the behavior in question.

Savings method: Another name for the relearning method.

State-dependent learning: Learning that occurs during a particular physiological state (such as alcoholic intoxication) and is lost when that physiological state passes.

2. Why do some teachers ask their students to take the same seat at each class meeting, particularly at the beginning of the year?

Clearly teachers do this to make it easier to recall the students's names, but the question is why does it make it easier? The answer probably has to do with contextual cues (neighboring students, wall coverings, etc.). When students take different seats, these cues are useless.

3. John was determined to do well on the final exam in biology, so he studied from 10:00 P.M. to 2:00 A.M. each night for the 2 weeks before the test. To keep from falling asleep, he drank strong coffee.The night before the 8:00 A.M. exam, John made sure he got a good night's sleep, but he did not do nearly as well on the test as he thought he should. What explanation can you offer? Describe how you could test the accuracy of your explanation.

The most obvious suggestion is that state dependent learning is involved: John learned the material while under the influence of caffeine, and cannot recall it when that drug is absent. Another possibility involves the difference between when the material was studied (late at night) and when it was recalled (early in the morning). John's body was probably in a different physiological state when he studied than when he took the exam. Contextual cues may also be involved. John studied when it was dark, for example, and took the test when it was light. The idea that state dependent learning is involved could be tested in several ways. For instance, we might give John the exam at midnight and see if his performance improves.

4. How could you use fluency to measure forgetting?

Fluency (referred to as automaticity by educators) is often measured as the number of correct (or satisfactory) responses per minute. If, after a retention interval, there is a decline in the number correct per minute, then forgetting has occurred.

5. Freud believed that nothing we experience is ever truly forgotten. How could you prove or disprove this statement?

One of the problems with so many of Freud's ideas is that they are not susceptible to scientific test. That is the case with this proposition. If a person is unable to recall an event, Freud might argue that it is suppressed. That might be true, but it makes the proposition meaningless.

6. Hilda and Ethel work together to train a rat to press a lever. When they are satisfied that the response has been well learned, Hilda suggests that they remove the lever from the cage for a while and then reinstall it to see what happens. Ethel proposes that they leave the lever in place but disconnect the feeding mechanism. Then they begin to wonder whether they would be studying different phenomena or the same thing. What do you think?

Clearly, they would be studying different things. Hilda's suggestion is to study forgetting. Since the lever pressing response cannot be performed if the lever is not available, any deterioration in the response is forgetting. Ethel wants to leave the lever in place, and it is certain that the animal will continue to press it. This is an extinction procedure. Later failure to press the lever would reflect, not forgetting, but learning: The animal would have learned not to press the lever.

7. In paired associate learning, what is the reinforcer?

Typically, the subject answers and then sees (or hears) the correct response. When the subject responds correctly, this feedback is probably reinforcing.

8. The amount of forgetting varies directly with the length of the retention interval. Why, then, is time not a cause of forgetting?

As McGeoch said, time is not an event, so it cannot cause anything.

9. What is wrong with defining forgetting as the loss of behavior?

Sometimes learning means not doing something or doing it less often, and in such instances forgetting can mean an increase in the rate of behavior. Some students may also note that behavior that has been forgotten according to one measure may not have been forgotten if another measure is used. In this case, some forgetting has occurred, yet it cannot be said that the behavior has been entirely lost.

10. What is the defining difference between free recall and prompted recall?

The difference is the presence or absence of prompts. It could be said that even free recall involves prompts (the question, "How much are 6 and 3?" is a kind of prompt), but prompted recall involves explicit cues about the answer.

11. Which measure of learning discussed in the text is likely to detect the most subtle degrees of forgetting? How could you prove you are right?

Recognition tests probably provide the most sensitive measures of forgetting, since the cues provided can be easily graded. One way to test this hypothesis would be to have subjects learn a list of words to a given criterion, and then measure forgetting in one of three ways (free recall, prompted recall, recognition). Assuming there are no important differences in subjects, differences in recall should reflect differences in measurement.

12. What is the implication of research on overlearning for your study practices?

Students should study beyond the point at which they first master material. Some may suggest studying half again as many times as it takes to learn the material.

13. Which is more likely to be a factor in forgetting what you have learned from this course, retroactive interference or proactive interference?

I doubt if anyone knows the answer to this question. However, some students might argue that the answer depends on what courses they have had before this course and what courses they will have later. The idea is that psychology courses taken before this course will tend to produce proactive interference, while psychology courses taken afterwards will tend to produce retroactive interference.

14. What is the practical significance of the study by Greenspoon and Ranyard (1957)?

The study shows that subtle differences in context during learning and during recall affect performance. This implies, among other things, that learning under a variety of conditions (i.e., in the presence of different cues) may reduce forgetting.

15. Some psychologists maintain that spontaneous recovery is a form of forgetting. Explain this.

In spontaneous recovery, extinguished behavior reappears. Since extinction means learning not to perform an act, spontaneous recovery can be considered forgetting the behavior of not performing.

16. Mary went through a bad divorce and later found the whole experience seemed a blank; she could remember almost nothing that happened. When she went through a second divorce some years later, she found herself remembering all sorts of things about her first divorce. Explain why.

Again, the student is required to speculate. In this case, a reasonable speculation might invoke state dependent learning. The original learning presumably occurred under great stress, possibly involving sleepless nights, fatigue, and the use of coffee and possibly other stimulants or tranquilizers. Once these conditions were no longer in effect, the experiences were difficult to recall. The second divorce might have induced conditions similar to the first (stress, fatigue, etc.) and so what was learned previously would be recalled. Another idea is that certain contextual cues (lawyers, legal papers, courtrooms, etc.) that were present during the first divorce may have prompted recall when they reappeared during the second divorce.

17. Give an example of both retroactive and proactive interference from your own experience.

Obviously answers will vary greatly. The point is for the student to think about the terms and apply them to his or her own experience.

18. Humans forget a great deal. Why have they not evolved greater ability to retain what they have learned?

This calls upon ideas discussed in the first chapter. Students tend to think of evolution as progress, according to which view people should develop increasingly better ability to retain what they learn. But of course evolution is not goal-directed, and is not trying to turn out a superior product each generation. Superior recall would evolve only if it contributed to survival. To some extent it must, but there is little reason to believe that the ability to recall, for example, baseball scores or historical facts for many years has any survival value.

19. What sorts of prompts (or self probes) could you use to remember the name of the sea captain in Moby Dick?

Answers will vary, of course, but might involve going through the alphabet and testing letters or letter sounds; picturing a scene from the film or book; imagining oneself on the Pequod and calling out, "Captain....!"

20. Some people say that what happened in Nazi Germany in the 1930s and 1940s could never happen here. What have you learned about forgetting that would make you doubt the truth of this statement?

One point students might make is that you cannot recall what you have not learned. If today's students have not learned about the holocaust and the events that led to it, then they cannot be recalled. Forgetting research also demonstrates that people distort experiences, particularly those that do not fit their biases. So, if a nation becomes hostile toward a particular ethnic group, the events in Nazi Germany may be remembered, if at all, in a way that supports current biases.

Key to Practice Quiz

1. The period between training and testing for forgetting is called the <u>retention</u> interval.

2. In his studies of nonsense syllables, Ebbinghaus used the <u>relearning/savings</u> method.

3. DMTS stands for <u>delayed matching to sample</u>.

4. John McGeoch argued that <u>time</u> does not cause forgetting.

5. Practicing a skill even after it is performed without errors is called <u>overlearning</u>.

6. When experiences after training interfere with performance, the effect is called <u>retroactive</u> interference.

7. The tendency for performance to improve after training ends is called <u>reminiscence</u>.

8. The research of Elizabeth Loftus and her colleagues raises doubts about the trustworthiness of <u>eye-witness</u> testimony.

9. <u>Luria</u> is known for his study of the man who could not forget.

10. <u>Freud</u> and <u>Penfield</u> believed that experiences are permanently stored in the mind or brain.

Chapter 11 Quiz: Forgetting

1. John McGeoch argued that _____ does not cause forgetting.

2. The Clark's nutcracker can recall the location of about _____ food caches.

3. _____ was the first person to study forgetting experimentally.

4. Forgetting can be measured as a flattening of a generalization gradient, a phenomenon called gradient _____.

5. One measure of forgetting requires the subject to match a stimulus presented earlier, a procedure called _____.

6. "SF" was able to recall a series of up to _____ digits.

7. _____ is often defined as number of correct responses per minute.

8. If performance improves following a retention interval, we speak of _____.

9. In _____ interference, new learning interferes with old learning.

10. Research by Loftus on _____ undermines the view that experiences are permanently stored in the brain.

Key to Chapter 11 Quiz

1. John McGeoch argued that <u>time</u> does not cause forgetting. (398)

2. The Clark's nutcracker can recall the location of about <u>2000</u> food caches. (409)

3. <u>Ebbinghaus</u> was the first person to study forgetting experimentally. (393)

4. Forgetting can be measured as a flattening of a generalization gradient, a phenomenon called gradient <u>degradation</u>. (396)

5. One measure of forgetting requires the subject to match a stimulus presented earlier, a procedure called <u>delayed matching to sample</u>. (394)

6. "SF" was able to recall a series of up to <u>82</u> digits. (412)

7. <u>Fluency</u> is often defined as number of correct responses per minute. (399)

8. If performance improves following a retention interval, we speak of <u>reminiscence</u>. (406)

9. In <u>retroactive</u> interference, new learning interferes with old learning. (404)

10. Research by Loftus on <u>eyewitness testimony</u> undermines the view that experiences are permanently stored in the brain. (409)

12

The Limits of Learning

Chapter outline

Main points

Limits on learning are set by the physical characteristics of the learner, the fact that learned behavior is not transmitted to the next generation, innate ability, neurological damage, critical periods, and biological preparedness for learning.

Class notes

Physical characteristics. I include this section because it is sometimes the obvious things that trip us up. The first efforts to teach chimps to communicate failed because of the physical limitations of the animals, but the failure was widely interpreted to mean that chimps were incapable of learning to communicate.

Exercise: Mitten Problem

Have students solve puzzles (such as the Block Design item of the WAIS) while wearing mittens. A competition should make the task fun and persuade the students of the importance of physical characteristics to performance.

Nonheritability of learned behavior. This is another "obvious" limitation, yet McDougall's work shows that it wasn't always so obvious.

Heredity and learning ability. Some students may object to the suggestion that heredity affects learning ability, but the evidence is overwhelming that it does. Even so, the role of early learning experiences is vital, and it is worth making the point that if Einstein had been reared in a closet for his first 12 years, it is unlikely that he would have become a famous physicist. Students who are interested in this question should be urged to read *Meaningful Differences* by Betty Hart and Todd Risley (1995; for a summary, see Chance, 1997).

Neurological damage and learning. I may be accused of sermonizing, but it seems to me that students should be reminded that fetuses and young children are especially vulnerable to neurological damage from exposure to drugs, lead, and other toxins.

Critical periods. John Paul Scott's work with dogs is worth expanding on. We tend to think of puppies as quite amenable to human contact at any age, but there seems to be a critical period for this learning. Of course, the interesting question is whether there are critical periods in humans, and this might be something to have students debate.

Preparedness for learning. I wonder about the link between preparedness and critical periods. Do critical periods represent a kind of transient preparedness? This is a question that might prompt an interesting class discussion.

Key to review questions

1. Define the following terms:

   Critical period: A period in the development of an organism during which it is especially likely to learn a particular kind of behavior.
   Imprinting: The tendency of some animals, particularly birds, to follow the first moving object they see after birth, usually (but not necessarily) their mother.
   Instinctive drift: The tendency for behavior to "drift toward" a fixed action pattern.
   Preparedness: The innate tendency to learn some things with ease and other things with difficulty.
   Sign tracking: A procedure in which a stimulus is followed by a reinforcer regardless of what the organism does. The procedure often results in the "shaping" of behavior without reinforcement.

2. Sally buys a high-frequency whistle at a discount store. She attempts to train her dog to come on command using the whistle as a signal. She follows the correct training procedures but is unsuccessful. What is the likely cause of the failure?

   Since the item indicates that Sally follows the correct training procedure, it is likely that Sally's dog is unable to hear the whistle. This hypothesis might be tested by using a different sort of whistle, perhaps one with a different pitch or a higher volume.

3. Explain why it is sometimes difficult to assess the intelligence of people who suffer from infantile paralysis and similar disorders.

   Intelligence tests require the performance of various tasks. Any physical handicap that interferes with the performance of those tasks make any inference about intelligence problematic.

4. Suppose that, because of its superior vision, a falcon can learn a discrimination task faster than a person. Mary believes this means the bird is smarter than the person. What reasons might she have for this idea?

   Intelligence is often defined as learning ability. If the falcon learns faster in a particular situation, it is smarter in that situation. In the same way, a blind man is "smarter" (relative to sighted people) in a dark room than he is in a lighted room.

5. Design an experiment that would determine whether there are genetic differences in the learning abilities of men and women.

   This is extremely difficult to do because learning plays such an important role in gender differences. Students might suggest rearing children in such a way as to control gender bias. For instance, the children might be reared by androgynous parental figures. This experiment could be improved on by using fraternal twins different in sex. Learning abilities would then be tested when the children reached adulthood.

6. How might preparedness to learn be nonadaptive?

   Preparedness to learn is adaptive only if the behavior involved is adaptive. Humans may be prepared to learn to fear and hate strange people, ideas, and customs. Such xenophobia may have been adaptive in prehistoric times, when an entire clan might be wiped out by disease or betrayed if they were too eager to take in strangers. In today's international market place, the tendency to be mistrustful of outsiders may be counterproductive.

114

7. Explain the role of evolution in the findings of Garcia and Koelling.

Evolution is concerned with survival in the real world. In the real world, birds are more likely to get sick after eating a strange tasting food than after eating a food that has a distinctive color and makes a funny noise. The tendency to acquire an aversion to a food with a distinctive taste is apt to contribute to survival, and hence to propagation.

8. In what sense might it be said that autoshaping represents preparedness to acquire a superstition?

In autoshaping, there is no contingency between behavior and reinforcement, yet there is a tendency to behave as though responding produced reinforcement. This is the essence of superstitious behavior.

9. Some people believe that it is important for a human infant to have intimate contact with the mother during the first few hours after birth (rather than being hurried off to a nursery). How could you determine whether there is a critical period for the formation of an adult-infant bond?

One way would be to compare the mother-infant bond when intimate contact is permitted shortly after birth with the bond that exists when such intimacy is prevented. The bond might be measured at various ages by such things as the length of time the mother nurses the child, the child's tendency to go toward the mother when frightened, and so on.

10. Design a study to determine the effects of prenatal exposure to tobacco on subsequent learning ability.

A descriptive approach would involve comparing test performance of children whose mothers smoked during pregnancy with those who did not. Mothers would have to be matched for education and, ideally, IQ, since better educated and more intelligent mothers might be less likely to smoke during pregnancy. An experimental study could not be performed with humans, but students might design experiments with animal analogues. Pregnant rats, for example, might be systematically exposed to tobacco smoke. Their pups would then be compared on various learning tasks with pups from smoke-free mothers. An alternative would be to compare rat pups from the same mothers, with the mothers exposed to smoke during one pregnancy but not another.

11. Could variability in learning ability be useful to the survival of our species?

There might be some utility in having wide differences in learning ability. For example, extremely bright people are probably not well suited to jobs that involve long hours at simple, repetitive tasks, while duller lights find such activities challenging and interesting.

12. Suppose you had inherited everything your parents and grandparents knew. How would you be different?

Students are likely to mention racial and ethnic prejudices, accents, foreign languages spoken, cooking and other household skills, job skills, etc.

13. Identify a social problem and explain how it might be dealt with through the application of learning principles you have learned in this text.

Students might focus on racial prejudice, crime, pollution, education, exhaustion of natural resources, overpopulation, poverty, AIDS and other diseases, etc. It is hoped that the students will focus on the behavior and its consequences, rather than on preaching the need for attitude changes.

14. How would you go about creating a genius?

The anecdotal evidence of Stern and Mill is suggestive. It ought to be possible to use what is known about learning to create environments that would be nearly optimal for learning. (Again, see Hart & Risley [1995] on this point.) Some students may also suggest that a good way to begin the project would be to look for potential parents with good genetic histories.

15. A visitor to New York complained about the noise of the city. Her host replied, "Oh, you get used to it." Does this demonstrate that learning is helpful or harmful?

In one sense it is helpful, since it makes a bad situation tolerable. In another sense it is harmful, since getting used to a bad situation reduces the tendency to change or escape it. The result is that we get used to lots of bad things and go on enduring them rather than making them better.

16. How could you determine whether humans are biologically prepared to learn language?

Theoretically, we might rear a group of children without ever exposing them to any form of language. If they develop a language of their own, the hypothesis is supported. Such an experiment is impossible for ethical reasons, and it is difficult to see how the problem might be tackled otherwise.

17. Roger McIntire (1973) recommends that people be required to undergo training in child-rearing before being allowed to have children. What support for his position can you provide?

Many students find the idea of compulsory parental training repugnant, but the question forces them to consider the consequences of leaving child rearing to people who know very little about learning and behavior.

18. What would it take to make our judicial system an effective instrument for reducing crime?

One way of answering the question is to identify the features of effective punishment, in particular contingency and contiguity. Another approach would be to suggest that our judicial system might not be devoted exclusively to punishment. It might, for instance, provide benefits to citizens who have not been arrested, fined or ticketed in the previous 12 months. Punishing criminal behavior is one way of reducing it; another way is to reinforce behavior that is incompatible with criminal behavior.

19. Explain why it would be desirable to have political leaders who understand basic learning principles.

An understanding of learning principles may incline one toward a pragmatic approach to problems. It might also result in reduced reliance on punitive tactics and a corresponding increase in more effective and humane approaches, such as reinforcement.

20. What protection could the public have against the abuse of learning principles by political leaders?

The best protection people can have against abuse of learning principles is an understanding of those principles.

116

Key to Practice Quiz

1. An example of the role of physical characteristics in learning is provided by the difficulty apes had in learning <u>to speak</u>.

2. Harry and Martha Frank found that <u>wolves</u> solved certain problems better than dogs.

3. William <u>McDougall</u> mistakenly believed that learned behavior could be inherited.

4. Substances that damage neural tissues are called <u>neurotoxins</u>.

5. A <u>critical period</u> is a stage in development during which an organism is particularly likely to learn a particular behavior.

6. Soon after hatching, ducklings become <u>imprinted</u> on an object that moves, usually their mother.

7. <u>Instinctive</u> drift is the tendency of an animal to revert to innate patterns of behavior.

8. Garcia and Koelling found that when rats became sick after drinking water that was tasty and noisy, they were more likely to drink water that was <u>noisy</u> than water that was <u>tasty</u>.

9. According to Martin Seligman, all behavior falls along a continuum of <u>preparedness</u>.

10. Rhesus monkeys can acquire a fear by observing a fearful model, but Cook and Mineka found that they are more likely to acquire a fear of snakes than of <u>flowers</u>.

Chapter 12 Quiz: Limits of Learning

1. Garcia and Koelling found that when rats became sick after drinking water that was tasty and noisy, they were more likely to drink water that was _____ than water that was _____.

2. Harry and Martha Frank found that dogs did not perform as well as _____ on barrier problems.

3. Konrad Lorenz was one of the first to study _____.

4. If a behavior is likely to be learned only during a particular stage of development, we can speak of a _____ period.

5. According to Martin Seligman, all behavior may be said to fall along a continuum of _____.

6. The tendency to revert to a fixed action pattern is called instinctive _____.

7. Keller and Marian _____ are known for their article, "The Misbehavior of Organisms."

8. William _____ mistakenly believed that learned behavior could be inherited.

9. Robert Tryon studied the role of _____ in maze learning.

10. Early efforts to teach _____ to speak failed because the animals lacked the necessary vocal equipment.

Key to Chapter 12 Quiz

1. Garcia and Koelling found that when rats became sick after drinking water that was tasty and noisy, they were more likely to drink water that was <u>noisy</u> than water that was <u>tasty</u>. (438)

2. Harry and Martha Frank found that dogs did not perform as well as <u>wolves</u> on barrier problems. (430f)

3. Konrad Lorenz was one of the first to study <u>imprinting</u>. (434)

4. If a behavior is likely to be learned only during a particular stage of development, we can speak of a <u>critical</u> period. (434)

5. According to Martin Seligman, all behavior may be said to fall along a continuum of <u>preparedness</u>. (439)

6. The tendency to revert to a fixed action pattern is called instinctive <u>drift</u>. (437)

7. Keller and Marian <u>Breland</u> are known for their article, "The Misbehavior of Organisms." (436)

8. William <u>McDougall</u> mistakenly believed that learned behavior could be inherited. (429)

9. Robert Tryon studied the role of <u>heredity</u> in maze learning. (430)

10. Early efforts to teach <u>chimpanzees</u> to speak failed because the animals lacked the necessary vocal equipment. (427)

Test Bank

Note: Numbers in parentheses indicate the pages on which the answers may be found. When an answer is not specifically provided in the text, but must be inferred (typically from the chapter as a whole), the word *inferred* appears in parentheses.

There are 659 questions in this bank: 422 multiple choice, 113 true-false, 64 completion, and 60 short answer. There is some overlap in the questions, so that a given point might be asked about in a MC item and in a true-false question.

Chapter 1: Introduction: Learning to Change

<u>Multiple choice</u>
1. The author of your text evidently believes that _____.
    a. change is a good thing
    b. behavior is best accounted for by nature
    c. adaptation occurs slowly
 * d. learning is a way of adapting to change (24)
2. Variation and natural selection are the foundations of _____.
    a. genetics
 * b. evolution (4)
    c. learning
    d. adaptation
3. Darwin's theory of evolution has been around for about _____.
    a. 50 years
    b. 75 years
 * c. 150 years (2)
    d. 200 years
4. Chapter 1 includes a box called *The Face of Change*. One point the essay makes is that
    _____.
 * a. many changes in our lives are imperceptible (3)
    b. change means progress
    c. faces are recognizable even though they change
    d. learning means changing
5. *The Beak of the Finch* is primarily about the work of _____.
 * a. Peter and Rosemary Grant (7)
    b. Harry and Margaret Harlow
    c. Lee Cronk
    d. Richard Dawkins
6. The gollypod, a fictitious aquatic animal, breaks out in a cold sweat whenever exposed to the sun. This reaction is most likely _____.
 * a. a reflex (8)
    b. a fixed action pattern
    c. a general behavior trait
    d. the result of learning
7. Teenagerus Americanus, a two-legged ape indigenous to North America, breaks out in a cold sweat whenever exposed to elevator music. This reaction is most likely _____.
    a. a reflex
    b. a fixed action pattern
    c. a general behavior trait
 * d. the result of learning (24)

8. The tendency of some animals to hoard food is probably an example of _____.
   a. a reflex
   b. a fixed action pattern
 * c. a general behavior trait (13f)
   d. learned behavior
9. The quotation, "Change is the only constant," is attributed to _____.
   a. Buckminster Fuller
   b. Virgil
 * c. Lucretius (2)
   d. Einstein
10. Fixed action patterns are induced by events called _____.
    a. genes
    b. stimuli
  * c. releasers (13)
    d. reflexes
11. The chief advantage of learning over natural selection as a means of adapting to change is that learning _____.
  * a. is faster (22, 24)
    b. is more enduring
    c. is less enduring
    d. does not affect all members of a species
12. The experiments of Harlow and Harlow demonstrated that how monkeys are reared _____.
    a. has little effect on their behavior later in life
  * b. can have a profound effect on their behavior later in life (29)
    c. has no effect on adult sexual activity
    d. can improve their mental health
13. The phenomenon that is nearly the opposite of habituation is _____.
    a. habitation
    b. inhabituation
    c. stabilization
  * d. sensitization (10)
14. The person who demonstrated that the marching of tropical army ants is not intelligent behavior is _____.
  * a. Schneirla (14)
    b. Schneider
    c. Schneidman
    d. Schneirman
15. The list of alleged human fixed action patterns _____.
  * a. has gotten shorter in recent years (16)
    b. has gotten longer in recent years
    c. has remained about the same over the years
    d. is longer for pre-industrialized peoples than for those living in industrialized nations
16. One person who raised doubts about the incest taboo is _____.
    a. Grant
  * b. Freud (17)
    c. Wilson
    d. McDougall
17. In her study of baboons, Shirley Strum found that the most successful males were _____.
    a. offspring of dominant females
    b. bigger than other males
  * c. less aggressive than other males (25)
    d. the youngest

18. The brown-headed cowbird deposits its eggs in the nests of other birds.   This is most likely a
_____
    a. reflex
* b. fixed action pattern (13)
    c. general behavior trait
    d. learned behavior
19. Natural selection is often _____
    a. ahead of the times
* b. behind the times (23)
    c. up with the times
    d. under the times
20. Learning is an evolved _____
    a. selectivity
* b. modifiability (24)
    c. biology
    d. karma
21. According to David Buss, the work of Gregor Mendel _____.
    a. required mathematical skills Darwin lacked
* b. had little or no influence on Darwin's thinking (4, n2)
    c. is irrelevant to evolution
    d. was done 40 years after Darwin's death
22. According to the author of your text, the theory of evolution _____.
    a. leads inevitably to atheism
    b. leads inevitably to religious fundamentalism
    c. leads to science as religion
* d. is compatible with a belief in God (4, n3)
23.   Natural selection is illustrated by changes in the coloration of the Peppered Moth resulting
    from _____.
* a. industrial pollution (6)
    b. drought
    c. loss of habitat
    d. long term changes in the hydraulic cycle
24. Most mutations _____.
* a. are not helpful to survival (8)
    b. contribute to survival in important ways
    c. cause monsterism
    d. occur in one-celled organisms
25. Research by Keltner and Anderson suggests that _____ may protect us from injury by
    appeasing others we have offended.
    a. crying
    b. sighing
    c. yawning
* d. blushing (9,n5)
26. A reflex is _____.
    a. any very simple behavior
    b. a simple response to a simple event
* c. a relationship between an event and a simple response (8)
    d. a purely physiological phenomenon

27. There is evidence that the rate of _____ in fetuses is correlated with intellectual development after birth.
    a. mutagenesis
    b. sensitization
  * c. habituation (11, n7)
    d. FAPs
28. The rooting of pigs (for worms, larvae, and truffles) is an example of a
  * a. FAP (13)
    b. reflex
    c. general behavior trait
    d. learned behavior
29. The color _____ is a releaser for aggression in the male stickleback.
    a. green
    b. blue
    c. yellow
  * d. red (14)
30. The author of your text refers to Steven J. Gould as _____
  * a. Mr. Evolution (30)
    b. Darwin's modern bulldog
    c. the last of the evolutionists
    d. the panda guy
31. E. O. Wilson suggests that there are two FAPs in humans, the incest taboo and _____.
    a. gynocomastia
    b. beastialism
  * c. biophilia (16, n11)
    d. zoomania
32. An _____ is something an organism tries to escape or avoid.
  * a. aversive (17)
    b. adversive
    c. adhesive
    d. adenoid
33. The figure below most likely illustrates _____.
  * a. habituation (11)
    b. sensitization
    c. a FAP
    d. insurgence

34. The best title for the figure below is _____.
   a. diet and heredity
 * b. fearfulness and heredity (19)
   c. addiction and heredity
   d. aggressiveness and heredity

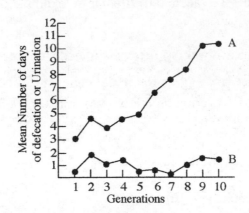

35. In the fox-breeding experiment, researchers selectively mated foxes that displayed _____ behavior.
   a. aggressive
   b. intelligent
 * c. dog-like (20)
   d. habituated

36. Lee Cronk wrote an article on how evolved behavior can prove nonadaptive when the environment changes. The article was called _____.
 * a. Old Dogs, Old Tricks (23)
   b. The Once and Future King
   c. Murder Most Fowl
   d. History Recalled

37. _____ poked fun at the human tendency to see itself as the crowning achievement of evolution.
   a. Charles Darwin
   b. Gregor Mendel
 * c. Bertrand Russell (27)
   d. Alexander Pope

38. Zing Yang Kuo found that 86% of kittens that saw their mothers kill rats later killed rats themselves. He also found that _____ of kittens that never saw their mothers kill rats later killed rats themselves.
   a. 87%
   b. 73%
   c. 65%
 * d. 45% (28)

39. Hart and Risley did a longitudinal study of the influence of the home verbal environment on children from different socioeconomic backgrounds. They found that _____
   a. children whose parents talked to them a lot later scored lower on IQ tests
 * b. children whose parents talked to them a lot later scored higher on IQ tests (30)
   c. the amount of parental talk was unrelated to later IQ scores
   d. the influence of parental language depended on parental income.

124

40. _____ refers to fixed action patterns as complex reflexes.
   a. Gregor Mendel
   b. Charles Darwin
   c. Zing Yang Kuo
 * d. Howard Rachlin (31)

True-false
41. The evolution of most species is now complete. F (inferred, but see especially p. 4)
42. Probably the reason the world seems relatively stable is that we don't live long enough to see many drastic changes. T (2)
43. Darwin founded his theory of evolution on the work of Gregor Mendel. F (4; also see n2)
44. Natural selection helps the individual adapt to changes in its environment. F (23)
45. Reflexes are generally less variable than fixed action patterns. T (10)
46. All reflexes contribute to survival. F (9, n6)
47. Darwin believed that there were no human instincts. F (15)
48. Research on the sexual orientation of sisters of lesbian women demonstrated that homosexuality is an inherited characteristic. F (20)
49. A major problem with natural selection as an adaptive mechanism is that it is slow. T (22)
50. Natural selection helps the species to adapt to change, not the individual. T (23)

Completion
51. The brown-headed cowbird puts its eggs in other birds's nests. This is an example of a fixed action pattern/instinct. (13)
52. Repeated exposure to a stimulus that evokes a reflex response results in habituation. (11)
53. The dispute over the relative importance of genetics and learning is often called the nature-nurture debate. (26)
54. The chief limitation of natural selection as a means of adapting to change is that it is slow/takes place over generations/helps the species but not the individual. (22)
55. Learning, like natural selection, is a biological mechanism for adapting to change. (24)
56. Learning is a change in behavior due to experience. (24)

Short Essay
Note: It should be possible to answer most short essay questions in 50 words or less.

57. What was Bertrand Russell's point when he noted that it is philosophers, not protozoans, who assure us that humans are superior to other animals. (27)

This question refers to the box on page 27. Russell was suggesting that judgment about the superiority of a particular species must necessarily be made from the biased perspective of the species making the judgment. Through the eyes of a baboon, the baboon might be the highest form of animal life.

58. Explain the role of mutations in evolution. (7)

The answer should indicate that mutations provide new variations which, if adaptive, will be selected.

125

59. Why is natural selection helpful to species, but not to individuals? (22-24)

This point is covered in the query on p. 22 of the text. Students should note that natural selection produces changes across generations, not within a given individual.

60. How are reflexes, fixed action patterns, and general behavior traits alike? How are they different? (8-18)

This question appears as item 13 in the list of review questions. Answers should note that all three are "hard wired" or "programmed" into the genes, and differ chiefly in the degree to which they vary and in the degree to which they are elicited by specific environmental events. For example, reflexes are less variable than inherited behavior traits, with fixed action patterns falling between the two.

61. The phrase "survival of the fittest" is often interpreted to mean that natural selection is the result of combat. What would be a more accurate interpretation of the phrase? (4)

This question is hinted at in review question number 4 about the field mouse. The "fittest" individuals are those most likely to produce young that survive and reproduce. Survival of the fittest does not mean survival of the strongest or most savage, but those most likely to reproduce themselves.

Chapter 2: The Study of Learning and Behavior

<u>Multiple choice</u>

1. Steven says that he was very nervous when he first attended college classes, but now he feels quite relaxed. Steven's loss of anxiety is most likely an example of _____
   * a. learning (36, 42)
   b. disease
   c. maturation
   d. fatigue

2. A thumbtack stuck in a bulletin board several feet away is less likely to affect your behavior than a thumbtack placed on the chair on which you are sitting. Even though both examples involve a thumbtack, the second is more likely to qualify as a _____
   * a. stimulus (40)
   b. contiguous relation
   c. contingency
   d. response

3. Harry teaches an advanced painting class. His goal is to teach students to paint more creatively. Harry will probably measure learning as a change in response _____
   * a. topography (42)
   b. intensity
   c. speed
   d. rate

4. Marjorie drives a school bus. Sometimes the kids get rather noisy. She decides to play music the kids like through speakers on the bus, but whenever the kids get too noisy she turns the music off. When they quiet down, she turns the music back on. In this way, she hopes to get the kids to make less noise. Marjorie is probably going to measure learning as a change in response _____
   a. topography
   * b. intensity (42)
   c. speed
   d. rate

5. In a cumulative record, learning is indicated by change in response _____
   a. topography
   b. amplitude
   c. speed
   * d. rate (44)

6. The figure below shows the results of an experiment comparing the effects of two teaching methods. Phyllis was taught by method A; Gertrude was taught by method B. This study is an example of _____
   * a. between-subjects design (50)
   b. within-subject design
   c. random assignment
   d. yoked control

Average performance on 10 spelling tests (20 items each) following 2 methods of instruction.

127

7. The figure below shows the results of an experiment on the effects of heat on aggressive social behavior. There is a sharp increase in the rate of aggressive behavior when the temperature goes above 90. This study is an example of _____
   a. between-subjects design
 * b. within-subject design (52)
   c. case study
   d. anecdotal evidence

Aggression and temperature. Cumulative responses in 10 rats all exposed to 3 different temperature conditions.

8. When a behavior is defined by the procedure used to measure it, the definition is said to be _____
   a. mechanistic
   b. lexicographic
   c. procedural
 * d. operational (38)

9. The kind of experiment that is most likely to require statistical analysis is a _____
 * a. between-subjects experiment (50)
   b. within-subject experiment
   c. ABA experiment
   d. descriptive study

10. The kind of study that is most likely to involve a large number of subjects is one with a _____
 * a. between-subjects design (51)
   b. within-subject design
   c. ABA design
   d. matched sample

11. In within-subject experiments, each subject's performance is compared with its performance during a _____
   a. control period
   b. random sampling period
 * c. baseline period (52)
   d. benchmark session

12. Your text views experience as _____
 * a. stimuli (40)
   b. the environment
   c. subjective events
   d. our reactions to events

13. A person who says, "Everyone knows that...." is referring to _____
 * a. anecdotal evidence (47)
   b. case study evidence
   c. descriptive research evidence
   d. experimental research evidence

14. Using an ABA research design is rather like using a _____
    a. vacuum cleaner
    b. fountain pen
  * c. light switch (53)
    d. barber's chair
15. Experiments done in natural settings are called _____
    a. natural experiments
    b. spontaneous experiments
    c. unplanned experiments
  * d. field experiments (55)
16. _____ wrote, "My business is to teach my aspirations to conform themselves to fact, not to try and make facts harmonize with my aspirations."
    a. Charles Darwin
    b. B. F. Skinner
    c. Brian Weiss
  * d. T. H. Huxley (35)
17. _____ called learning the "great problem in all human psychology."
    a. Ivan Pavlov
  * b. John B. Watson (35, n1)
    c. Bertrand Russell
    d. Lucretius
18. A _____ explanation is one in which the evidence for the explanation of an event is the event itself.
    a. scientific
  * b. circular (36)
    c. logical
    d. redundant
19. Your text defines behavior as anything an organism does that can be _____.
  * a. measured (37)
    b. tested
    c. inferred
    d. accounted for
20. The figure below shows learning as a change in _____.
    a. intensity
    b. frequency
  * c. topography (42)
    d. redundancy

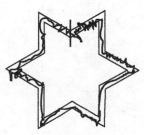

    Trial 1   Trial 15

21. The figure below shows learning as a change in _____.
 * a. intensity (42)
   b. frequency
   c. topography
   d. speed

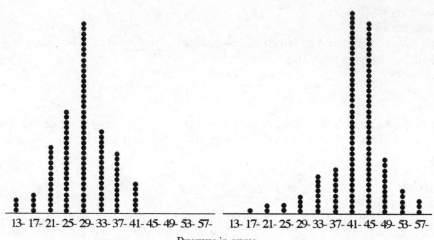

13- 17- 21- 25- 29- 33- 37- 41- 45- 49- 53- 57-   13- 17- 21- 25- 29- 33- 37- 41- 45- 49- 53- 57-

Pressures in grams

22. A teacher who looks for an increase in the number of correct performances per minute is using _____ as a measure of learning.
   a. topography
   b. speed
   c. rate
 * d. fluency (46)

23. In the cumulative record below, the rate of behavior is _____.
   a. increasing
 * b. decreasing (46)
   c. stable
   d. fluctuating wildly

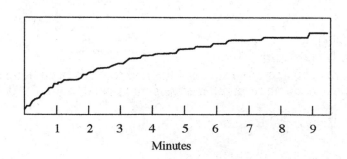

1   2   3   4   5   6   7   8   9

Minutes

130

24. Fluency is also known as _____.
   a. rate
 * b. automaticity (46, n13)
   c. cumulative rate
   d. frequency
25. Any variable an experimenter manipulates is a/an _____ variable.
   a. autonomous
   b. dependent
 * c. independent (50)
   d. synchronous
26. Any variable that is allowed to vary freely is a/an _____.
   a. autonomous
 * b. dependent (50)
   c. independent
   d. synchronous
27. In group-design experiments, researchers often use _____ to reduce differences among
   participants.
   a. clones
   b. statistics
   c. DNA matching
 * d. matched sampling (51)
28. Experimental research on behavior is often said to be artificial. To compensate for this
   problem, researchers do _____ .
 * a. field experiments (55)
   b. open-ended research
   c. follow-up studies
   d. free sampling research
29. Balster and colleagues suggest that inhumane treatment of research animals is _____.
   a. not good PR
   b. expensive, in the long run
 * c. bad science (59)
   d. likely to result in litigation
30. A computer simulation that is useful for teaching certain principles of learning is called

   _____.
   a. MacAnimal
   b. Animal Trainer
 * c. Sniffy the Virtual Rat (59)
   d. Howard the Holographic Hog
31. One problem with computer simulations as a substitute for animal research is that

   _____
   a. they are terribly expensive
   b. they take years to develop
   c. "bugs" in the software distort the findings
 * d. no one knows what behavior to program until the research has been done (59f)
32. One highly readable little book on research methods mentioned in your text is called

   _____.
   a. The Idiot's Guide to Behavioral Research
   b. Research Made Simple
 * c. Psychological Research: An Introduction (62)
   d. Random Designs

33. Any event that is capable of affecting behavior is called a _____.
   a. natural event
 * b. stimulus (40)
   c. instigator
   d. releaser
34. The person who suggested that to learn how nature works, we must "sit down before fact as a little child," and "be prepared to give up every preconceived notion" was _____
 * a. T. H. Huxley (35)
   b. E. L. Thorndike
   c. Charles Darwin
   d. John B. Watson
35. The school of thought that rejects scientific method and claims that science is just a debate about an unknowable reality is called _____
   a. Intellectualism
   b. Realism
   c. Sufism
 * d. Constructivism (36, n2)

True-false
36. As far as the study of learning is concerned, experience refers primarily to events that take place inside the person. F (40, n6)
37. All changes in behavior are examples of learning. F (41)
38. Learning researchers note that results with humans usually parallel those with animals. T (57)
39. B. F. Skinner was the first person to record data cumulatively. F (45, n11)
40. A cumulative record shows the total number of responses that have occurred in a given period of time as well as the rate at which they occurred. T (45)
41. Your text views learning as a change in the brain that is represented in behavior. F (37)
42. The natural science approach emphasizes physical events. T (35)
43. Learning always involves the acquisition of new behaviors. F (36)
44. It is sometimes difficult to say whether an event is behavior or physiology. T (37, n5)
45. Learning research focuses on changes in behavior because we cannot reliably measure learning as changes in physiology. F (40)
46. The word stimulus always refers to events in an organisms surroundings. F (40, n6)
47. *Speed* and *rate* are different terms for the same measure of learning. F (45, n10)

Completion
48. A stimulus is an environmental event that is capable of affecting behavior. (40)
49. Latency is one measure of learning. Two others are changes in errors/topography/intensity/speed/frequency/fluency. (Any two) (41-46)
50. Learning is a change in behavior due to experience. (36)
51. One thing researchers can control better with animal subjects than with human subjects is genetic history/environmental history/learning experiences. (56)
52. Response latency refers to the time that passes before a response occurs. (44)

53. Discuss the various ways of measuring learning. (41-46)

Answers should name and describe topography, errors, intensity, speed, latency, rate, and perhaps fluency.

54. Explain how a cumulative recorder works. (45-46)

An inked pen leaves a line on a moving sheet of paper. Each response causes the pen to move at right angles to the direction of the paper, so that the rate of responding is reflected in the slope of the line.

55. Explain the difference between within-subject and between-subjects experiments. (50-54)

In between-subjects experiments, two or more groups of subjects perform under different conditions and the performance of the groups is compared. In within-subject experiments, each subject performs under different conditions; the performance of a subject in one condition is compared with the performance of that subject in another condition.

56. Explain why random assignment of subjects is unnecessary in ABA experiments. (52-54)

Random assignment is meant to control for inter-subject variability. Each subject is compared against himself or herself, so inter-subject variability is eliminated.

57. Discuss the ethics of using animals for research on learning. (56-60)

Answers may note that some people argue that humans have no more right to use animals for research than animals have to use humans. This argument implies that it is wrong to use animals for farm work, for entertainment, and even for household pets. If those uses are allowed, why not research? Another argument says that animal research is unethical because computer simulations render it unnecessary. But computers can be programmed to simulate behavior only after we know how the organism behaves.

Chapter 3: Pavlovian Procedures

<u>Multiple choice</u>
1. Ivan Pavlov is best known for his research on the _____
* a. psychic reflex (68)
  b. partition complex
  c. operant response
  d. digestive process
2. What fascinated Pavlov most about his salivating dogs was that _____
  a. the behavior of the dogs never changed
  b. the behavior of the dogs changed erratically
* c. the dogs began to salivate before receiving food (68)
  d. some dogs salivated and others did not
3. Pavlov is best described as _____
  a. the father of learning research
  b. the father of modern psychology
  c. an American from Russia
* d. an experimenter from head to foot (69)
4. The notation that best describes the Pavlovian procedure is _____
  a. S-->R
  b. CS-->UR
  c. CS-->CR
* d. CS-->US (72)
5. John, "Mr. Anxiety," finally musters up the courage to ask the beautiful and popular Carole to go to the movies. She finds the idea so ridiculous that she laughs out loud the instant he has gotten the question out. John's face turns the color of a steamed lobster. In classical conditioning terms, John's experience is an example of _____
* a. trace conditioning (79)
  b. delayed conditioning
  c. simultaneous conditioning
  d. backward conditioning
6. A week later John (see item 5) bumps into Carole on campus, feels his face turn red and recalls with embarrassment their earlier encounter. Carole has become a _____
* a. CS for blushing (72)
  b. US for blushing
  c. CR to John
  d. good candidate for training as a career diplomat
7. Oafish Bill (John's twin brother) has heard nothing of John's unfortunate encounter with Carole (see item 5), and he decides to ask her out. Just as he approaches her she bursts into laughter, apparently in response to a joke someone just told. Bill immediately pops the question and she politely declines, having decided to join a convent at the end of the semester. A week later Bill bumps into Carole on campus but feels no particular embarrassment. The pairing of Bill's request for a date and Carole's laughter is most likely an example of _____
  a. trace conditioning
  b. delayed conditioning
  c. simultaneous conditioning
* d. backward conditioning (80)

8. Of the following, the one that does not belong with the others is _____
   a. latent inhibition
   b. overshadowing
   c. blocking
 * d. higher-order conditioning (74-76)
9. Each time a buzzer sounds, a puff of air makes a rabbit blink. Soon the rabbit blinks when it hears the buzzer. George believes that this means the buzzer takes the place of the air puff. George is an advocate of _____
 * a. stimulus substitution theory (96)
   b. exchange theory
   c. preparatory response theory
   d. stimulus-response theory
10. Doris disagrees with George (see item 9). She believes that the rabbit's response to the buzzer prepares it for the puff of air. Doris is an advocate of _____
   a. stimulus substitution theory
   b. exchange theory
 * c. preparatory response theory (97)
   d. stimulus-response theory
11. Two students, Edward and Edwina, serve as subjects in a conditioning experiment. The CS is a buzzer; the US is a mild electric shock; the UR is a change in electrical conductivity called the Galvanic Skin Response. Both subjects undergo 50 trials, but the experimenter feels sorry for Edwina so periodically he lets her off without a shock. The results will indicate that _____
 * a. the CR is stronger in Edward (81, 88)
   b. the CR is stronger in Edwina
   c. there is no difference in the CRs produced by Edward and Edwina
   d. Edward salivates at sight of Edwina
12. In studying "psychic secretions," Pavlov focused his attention on the _____
   a. dog's thoughts and feelings
 * b. events in the dog's environment (70)
   c. genetic history of the dog
   d. behavior of the dog before and after feeding
13. Pavlov called reflexes present at birth _____
   a. innate
 * b. unconditional (70)
   c. unconditioned
   d. fixed
14. Pavlov became interested in psychic reflexes around _____
   a. 1870
 * b. 1900 (67)
   c. 1920
   d. 1927
15. An experimenter presents a flash of light and a bell simultaneously followed by food. Conditioning proceeds satisfactorily, but when the experimenter presents the light and bell separately, he finds that the bell is an effective CS, but the light is not. The experimenter has demonstrated _____
   a. counterconditioning
   b. latent inhibition
   c. blocking
 * d. overshadowing (84)

16. Pavlov said that the salivary glands behaved as though they had _____
    a. reason
    b. an instinct
 * c. intelligence (68)
    d. free will
17. Pavlov's main interest initially was _____
    a. psychology
    b. learning
 * c. physiology (67)
    d. the philosophy of mind
18. The word *reflex* is a synonym for _____
    a. conditional response
    b. conditional reflex
    c. unconditional response
 * d. unconditional reflex (70)
19. Of the following conditioning procedures, the one that is least like the others is _____
    a. trace
    b. delayed
    c. simultaneous
 * d. backward (80)
20. When exposure to a stimulus prior to pairing with a US interferes with conditioning, the phenomenon is called _____
 * a. latent inhibition (86)
    b. overshadowing
    c. blocking
    d. higher-order conditioning
21. The time between conditioning trials is called the _____
    a. inter-stimulus interval
 * b. inter-trial interval (89)
    c. contiguity gap
    d. trace period
22. Braun and Geiselhart found that eyelid conditioning generally proceeded slowly with _____
    a. infants
    b. children
    c. young adults
 * d. older adults (89)
23. If, following conditioning, a CS is repeatedly presented without the US, the procedure is called _____
    a. higher-order conditioning
    b. latent inhibition
 * c. extinction (91)
    d. preconditioning
24. Spontaneous recovery is associated with _____
    a. higher-order conditioning
    b. latent inhibition
 * c. extinction (92)
    d. preconditioning
25. The researcher who might have become known as the American Pavlov was
    a. William James
    b. John B. Watson
 * c. Edwin Twitmyer (94)
    d. Alfred Gedunk

136

26. _____ said that Pavlov was one of the greatest geniuses of all time.
 * a. H. G. Wells (69)
   b. G. B. Shaw
   c. C. P. Snow
   d. I. M. Guessin
27. Pavlov was born in _____.
   a. Lithuania
 * b. Russia (69)
   c. Sweden
   d. Poland
28. The author of your text uses the terms *unconditional reflex* and *conditional reflex*, but he notes that most authors use the terms _____ and _____ reflexes.
   a. innate and learned
   b. natural and contrived
 * c. conditioned and unconditioned (71, n4)
   d. individual and species
29. Pavlovian conditioning is also called _____ conditioning.
 * a. classical (72)
   b. simple
   c. basic
   d. unconscious
30. J. M. Graham and Claude Desjardins established the odor of _____ as a CS for sexual arousal in rats.
 * a. wintergreen (73)
   b. mint
   c. licorice
   d. sulfur
31. The experiment in which a dog learned to salivate at the sight of a black square after it had been paired with a CS for salivating is an example of _____ conditioning.
   a. second-tier
 * b. higher-order (74f)
   c. signal
   d. second-signal
32. The experiments of Staats and Staats with nonsense syllables are examples of _____ conditioning.
   a. second-tier
 * b. higher-order (75)
   c. signal
   d. second-signal
33. One way to determine if conditioning has occurred is to present the CS alone. Each such presentation is called a/an _____ trial.
   a. extinction
   b. experimental
 * c. test (77)
   d. pseudo-
34. The rate of conditioning is affected by the degree to which the US is _____ the occurrence of the CS.
   a. bi-pendant on
   b. contracted to
 * c. contingent on (81)
   d. ipsilateral to

35. In Pavlovian conditioning, contiguity usually refers to the _____.
* a. time between CS and US (83)
    b. interval between CS-US trials
    c. space between CS and US
    d. interval between training sessions

36. A _____ stimulus is one that consists of two or more stimuli presented simultaneously.
    a. conjugal
    b. complex
    c. concordant
* d. compound (84)

37. In general, the more intense a US, the _____.
* a. faster conditioning proceeds (85 figure 3-5)
    b. slower conditioning proceeds
    c. more intense the CS
    d. less intense the CS

38. In so far as the rate of learning is concerned, the most important pairings of the CS and US are those that come _____.
* a. at the beginning of training (88)
    b. in the middle of training
    c. toward the end of training
    d. at the very end of training

39. Recent research suggests that poor conditioning in elderly people may signal the early stages of _____.
    a. Parkinson's Disease
* b. dementia (89, n11)
    c. brain cancer
    d. terminal illness

40. In the figure below, the data point at the extreme right illustrates _____.
    a. extinction
    b. a lack of conditioning
* c. spontaneous recovery (93, fig 3-12)
    d. blocking

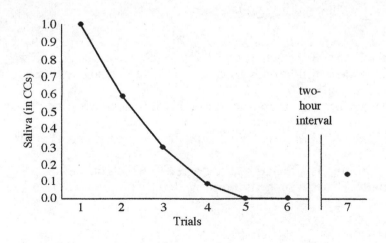

41. Pavlov won the Nobel Prize for his research on conditioning. F (69)
42. Pavlov's work paved the way for Darwin's theory of evolution. F (67, 69)
43. One way to test for the effects of conditioning is to use test trials. T (76)
44. If a CS is presented several times alone, and is then repeatedly paired with a US, conditioning proceeds more rapidly than if the CS had never been presented alone. F (86)
45. In contrast to Thomas Edison, Pavlov worked on his own. F (68, n1)

Completion
46. Conditional reflexes are so named because they <u>depend on many conditions</u>. (70)
47. Each pairing of a CS and US is one <u>trial</u>. (72)
48. In <u>delayed</u> conditioning the CS and US overlap. (79)
49. A CS that consists of two or more stimuli is called a <u>compound</u> stimulus. (84)
50. If two stimuli are paired and then one becomes a CS, the other will become a CS more rapidly than it otherwise would have, a phenomenon called sensory <u>preconditioning</u>. (88)

Short essay
51. Pavlov reported that repeatedly pairing a mild acid and a particular odor, in that order, failed to produce a CR. The experimenter then got a CR by presenting an odor followed by the mild acid. This time, however, he used a different odor. Explain why he used a different odor. (80)

Repeated presentation of the first odor probably caused latent inhibition. Had the experimenter used that odor again, learning would have been slow. (This question might lead to a useful discussion of research methods. For instance, it is possible that the second odor was merely a better stimulus for use as a CS.)

52. Explain the differences among trace, delay, simultaneous, and backward procedures. (78-81)

Answers should identify the differences in CS-US presentation.

53. Explain why Pavlovian conditioning is not really a simple form of learning. (78-91)

Most students will probably discuss some of the variables that affect conditioning, but some may discuss the distinction between standard and higher-order conditioning or focus on the subtleties of the conditioning procedures.

54. Explain why Pavlov became interested in psychic reflexes. (67-70)

Answers should mention that Pavlov was puzzled when dogs began to salivate before receiving food.

55. How has the study of Pavlovian conditioning altered your view of human nature? (inferred)

This is basically review question 20. Students might point out that Pavlov's work means that certain kinds of behavior can be attributed to specific kinds of experiences. Further, this realization gives us some power since it means that we can produce certain kinds of behavior by providing certain experiences.

Chapter 4: Pavlovian Applications

Multiple choice

1. Blue jays usually do not eat Monarch butterflies. This is an example of a/an _____
* a. conditioned taste aversion (122)
   b. fixed action pattern
   c. unconditional response
   d. conditioned emotional response
2. Little Albert has grown up and sees a therapist for treatment of his fear of laboratory rats and other white, furry things. The therapist is most likely to treat him by repeatedly pairing a piece of white fur with a _____
   a. loud noise
   b. piece of brown fur
   c. blast of air in his eye
* d. short piece of Albert's favorite music (109)
3. Senatorial candidate Smith's popularity increased dramatically after he was seen on television shaking hands with a very popular public figure. This is probably an example of_____
   a. preconditioning
* b. emotional conditioning (122)
   c. masochistic behavior
   d. backward conditioning
4. The studies of Carolyn and Arthur Staats demonstrating that words paired with pleasant words become pleasant are examples of_____
   a. first-order conditioning
   b. tertiary conditioning
* c. higher-order conditioning (115)
   d. oral conditioning
5. If a person sneezes after coming close to a realistic-looking artificial flower, you can be pretty sure that he or she is_____
   a. allergic to plastic
* b. allergic to pollen (127)
   c. faking
   d. nearsighted
6. The most recent variation of counterconditioning involves_____
   a. programmed texts
   b. psychoactive drugs
* c. virtual reality (109)
   d. sleep conditioning
7. The research that is most helpful to an understanding of racial prejudice is probably that of _____
   a. Watson and Rayner
   b. Garcia
   c. Pavlov
* d. Staats and Staats (111-115)
8. The CS and US in the Garcia, et al. experiment were_____
* a. flavored water and radiation (122)
   b. bell and food
   c. food and bell
   d. light and loud buzzer

9. In treating Peter's fear of rabbits, Jones used a procedure called_____
    a. systemic fear reduction
    b. pseudoconditioning
  * c. counterconditioning (109)
    d. restitution therapy
10. In _____ therapy, a stimulus that elicits an inappropriate response is paired with an aversive stimulus such as shock or an emetic drug.
    a. counter-
    b. adversive
  * c. aversion (120)
    d. shock
11. Research shows that when women receiving chemotherapy return to the hospital, they show _____
    a. increased immune functioning
  * b. decreased immune functioning (127f)
    c. no change in immune functioning
    d. incidental conditional responses
12. The use of euphemisms is best explained by the work of _____
    a. Watson
    b. Jones
  * c. Staats and Staats (inferred, but see box on p. 118)
    d. Pavlov
13. The Watson and Rayner experiment with Little Albert involved the procedure known as _____
    a. trace conditioning
  * b. delayed conditioning (107)
    c. simultaneous conditioning
    d. backward conditioning
14. The CS and US in the Little Albert experiment were a _____
  * a. rat and loud sound (107)
    b. rabbit and loud sound
    c. rabbit and slap
    d. rabbit and shock
15. People are most likely to come to tolerate painful and humiliating events if these events consistently _____
  * a. precede positive events (119)
    b. occur simultaneously with positive events
    c. follow positive events
    d. occur by themselves over a long period
16. Conditioned suppression is used as a measure of _____
    a. anger
    b. love
    c. hate
  * d. fear (112f)
17. Elnora Stuart and colleagues paired slides of pleasant scenes with_____
    a. hair tonic
    b. shampoo
  * c. toothpaste (116)
    d. milk
18. Pedophilia is sometimes treated with a form of counterconditioning called _____
    a. sexual reorientation
    b. surrogate training
    c. sexual inhibition therapy
  * d. aversion therapy (121)

19. The person whose name is most strongly associated with research on establishing taste aversions to control sheep killing by coyotes is _____
    a. John Locke
  * b. Carl Gustavson (125)
    c. Michael Russell
    d. Ivan Pavlov
20. *Conditioned Reflexes and Psychiatry* was written by _____
  * a. Ivan Pavlov (130)
    b. Mary Cover Jones
    c. John Watson and Rosalie Rayner
    d. Joseph Wolpe
21. Barbara Rothbaum and colleagues used virtual reality exposure therapy to treat a fear of _____.
    a. snakes
    b. dogs
    c. spiders
  * d. flying (110)
22. The term used to refer to sexual behavior disapproved of by society is _____.
    a. teraforms
    b. hedomanias
  * c. paraphilias (118)
    d. dysentias
23. Pavlov found that when he paired painful stimuli with food, the dog came to show no distress at the painful stimuli. This experiment may help explain _____ behavior in humans.
    a. aggressive
    b. exhibitionistic
    c. sadistic
  * d. masochistic (119f)
24. Barry Maletzky treated exhibitionists by having them imagine that they were about to perform the inappropriate behavior, and then _____.
    a. sounding a loud horn
    b. showing them a photograph of a bloody scene
    c. giving them a mild electric shock
  * d. exposing them to an unpleasant odor (120f)
25. A follow up of exhibitionists treated by Barry Maletzky with a variation of aversion therapy showed that those who had undergone treatment *involuntarily* _____.
  * a. improved as much as voluntary patients (121)
    b. improved, but not as much as voluntary patients
    c. improved during treatment, but soon reverted to their old ways
    d. did not improve
26. Garcia's interest in the role of learning in taste aversions may have begun when he became sick after eating _____.
    a. chocolate
  * b. licorice (122)
    c. strawberries
    d. a hot dog
27. The phenomenon of _____ suggests that we should be more likely to develop aversions to novel foods than to familiar ones.
    a. overshadowing
    b. blocking
  * c. latent inhibition (124)
    d. counterconditioning

28. _____ wrote: "The inborn reflexes by themselves are inadequate to ensure the continued existence of the organism...."
   a. Carl Gustavson
   b. John Garcia
 * c. Ivan Pavlov (130)
   d. Joseph Wolpe
29. The CS in the Little Albert experiment was a _____
   a. rabbit
 * b. rat (107)
   c. teddy bear
   d. mouse
30. The first person to use counterconditioning to treat a phobia was probably_____
   a. Rosalie Rayner
   b. Carl Rogers
 * c. Mary Cover Jones (109)
   d. John B. Watson

True-false
   31. Studies of taste aversion demonstrate that conditioning can occur despite a long inter-stimulus interval. T (123)
   32. If an aversive stimulus, such as a noxious odor, regularly precedes a pleasant stimulus, such as a tasty meal, the former stimulus may lose much of its unpleasant quality. T (119)
   33. Pavlovian conditioning is an adaptive mechanism but can nevertheless result in the acquisition of maladaptive behavior. T (inferred)
   34. Peter's fear, like Albert's, was the result of conditioning by a researcher.   F (109)
   35. Pavlovian conditioning accounts for negative emotions, but not for positive ones. F (115)

Completion
   36. Prejudice is an example of a CER, or conditioned emotional response. (111)
   37. Blue jays acquire a taste aversion for monarch butterflies. (124)
   38. The CS in the Little Albert study was a white rat. (107)
   39. Mary Cover Jones cured Peter's fear of rabbits. (109)
   40. Pedophilia may be partly the result of the pairing of children (or pictures of them) and sexual stimulation. (120)

Short essay
   41. Describe how a person might learn to be embarrassed by the word *strawberry*. (inferred, but see box on p. 118)

   The key is to pair the word strawberry *repeatedly with a stimulus that causes embarrassment. The chief difficulty is to identify such a stimulus, since what will embarrass one person may not affect another.*

   42. Summarize Garcia's work on taste aversion. Explain how his work differed from most studies of Pavlovian conditioning. (122f)

   In addition to describing the basic procedure, answers should mention that there were fewer CS-US pairings, and that the gap between CS and US was considerably longer than usual.

43. Describe the work of Watson and Rayner with Little Albert. (107)

   Students should mention the presentation of a rat followed by the sound of a steel bar being struck with a hammer.

44. How might you use Pavlovian conditioning to produce a boost in the body's immune system in response to a CS? (127f)

   The CS would be paired with a stimulus that triggers the immune response.

45. Describe how you might have cured Little Albert's phobia. (109)

   Answers should describe a counterconditioning procedure, possibly like that Jones used in treating Peter's phobia.

Chapter 5: Operant Procedures: Reinforcement

Multiple choice
1. E. L. Thorndike's studies of learning started as an attempt to understand _____
    a. operant conditioning
    b. the psychic reflex
 * c. animal intelligence (134)
    d. maze learning
2. In one of Thorndike's puzzle boxes, a door would fall open when a cat stepped on a treadle, thus allowing the cat to reach food outside the box. Eventually the cat would step on the treadle as soon as it was put into the box. Thorndike concluded that _____
    a. the reasoning ability of cats is quite remarkable
 * b. treadle stepping increased because it had a "satisfying effect" (136)
    c. the treadle is a CS for stepping
    d. learning meant connecting the treadle with freedom and food
3. The law of effect says that _____
    a. satisfying consequences are more powerful than annoying consequences
 * b. behavior is a function of its consequences (137)
    c. how an organism perceives events is more important than the events themselves
    d. effective behavior drives out ineffective behavior
4. Operant learning may also be referred to as _____
    a. trial-and-error learning
    b. effects learning
    c. non-Pavlovian conditioning
 * d. instrumental learning (139)
5. Thorndike made important contributions to all of the following fields except _____
    a. educational psychology
    b. animal learning
 * c. social psychology (140)
    d. psychological testing
6. The notation that best describes reinforcement is _____
 * a. B--->S^R (142)
    b. B---S^P
    c. B--->S^R--->S^P
    d. S--->R
7. According to the one-process theory of avoidance, the avoidance response is reinforced by _____
    a. escape from the CS
 * b. a reduction in the number of aversive events (182f)
    c. positive reinforcers that follow aversive events
    d. non-contingent aversives
8. The training procedure Thorndike used in his famous experiments with cats is best described as _____
    a. free operant
 * b. discrete trial (144)
    c. trial-and-error
    d. field research

9. Mary's grandmother, Pearl, is from the Old Country. Although she knows some English, she continues to speak her native tongue. Pearl can't go anywhere without a member of the family because she can't communicate with people about prices, directions, bus routes, etc. Pearl's resistance to learning English is most likely the result of _____
   a. a lack of intelligence
   b. age. Studies show that after the age of 60 learning a second language is nearly impossible.
   c. the length of time she has spent speaking her native language
 * d. the benefits she receives for not speaking English (inferred)
10. Mary decides to try to modify Pearl's behavior (see item 9). She and the rest of the family refuse to respond to any comment or request by Pearl that they know she is capable of expressing in English. For example, if during dinner she says, "Pass the potatoes" in English, she gets potatoes; if she says it in her native language she gets ignored. The procedure being used to change Pearl's behavior is _____
 * a. positive reinforcement (142)
   b. negative reinforcement
   c. adventitious reinforcement
   d. punishment
11. When Mary planned her little experiment (see item 10), she decided she wanted to be able to tell whether the procedure was working. Consequently, before beginning the procedure, Mary _____
   a. ignored all comments from her grandmother for a week before she began to apply the training procedure
   b. asked her grandmother how she felt about speaking English
 * c. kept a record of the number of times her grandmother spoke English spontaneously (inferred)
   d. repeatedly criticized her grandmother for not speaking English
12. The free operant procedure is most associated with _____
 * a. Skinner (145)
   b. Thorndike
   c. Pavlov
   d. Watson
13. Studies of delayed reinforcement document the importance of _____
 * a. B-S contiguity (160)
   b. B-S contingency
   c. inter-trial interval
   d. deprivation level
14. The level of deprivation is less important when the reinforcer used is a/an _____ reinforcer.
   a. primary
 * b. secondary (165)
   c. unexpected
   d. intrinsic
15. Sylvia believes that the reinforcement properties of an event depend on the extent to which it provides access to high probability behavior. Sylvia is most likely an advocate of _____ theory.
   a. drive-reduction
 * b. relative value (174)
   c. response deprivation
   d. random guess

16. Charles Catania identified three characteristics that define reinforcement. These include all of the following except _____
    a. a behavior must have a consequence
  * b. the consequence of the behavior must be positive (141)
    c. a behavior must increase in strength
    d. the increase in strength must be the result of the behavior's consequence

17. The one thing that all reinforcers have in common is that they _____
  * a. strengthen behavior (141-143)
    b. are positive
    c. feel good
    d. provide feedback

18. Skinner describes some of his most important research in _____
    a. *Verbal Behavior*
  * b. *The Behavior of Organisms* (144, inferred)
    c. *Particulars of My Life*
    d. *Animal Intelligence*

19. The author of your text calls Skinner the _____
    a. Newton of psychology
    b. Thorndike of free operant work
    c. discoverer of reinforcement
  * d. Darwin of behavior science (145)

20. All of the following are useful tips for shaping behavior except _____
    a. reinforce small steps
    b. reinforce immediately
    c. provide small reinforcers
  * d. never back up (155)

21. The Watson and Rayner experiment with Little Albert may have involved operant as well as Pavlovian learning because the loud noise _____
  * a. occurred as Albert reached for the rat (148)
    b. occurred while Albert was eating
    c. did not bother Albert initially
    d. was aversive

22. The number of operant procedures indicated in the contingency square is _____
    a. two
  * b. four (141)
    c. six
    d. nine

23. The opposite of a conditioned reinforcer is a _____
    a. tertiary reinforcer
    b. secondary reinforcer
  * c. primary reinforcer (149)
    d. generalized reinforcer

24. Donald Zimmerman found that a buzzer became a positive reinforcer after it was repeatedly paired with _____
    a. food
  * b. water (150)
    c. escape from shock
    d. morphine

25. Shaping is the reinforcement of successive _____
    a. responses
    b. elements of a chain
  * c. approximations of a desired behavior (152)
    d. increases in the intensity or topography of a behavior
26. The first step in building a behavior chain is to do a _____
    a. response analysis
  * b. task analysis (157)
    c. elemental analysis
    d. factor analysis
27. Skinner built a behavior chain in Plyny. Plyny was a _____
  * a. rat (156)
    b. pigeon
    c. dog
    d. philosophy student
28. Schlinger and Blakely found that the reinforcing power of a delayed reinforcer could be increased by _____
    a. increasing the size of the reinforcer
  * b. preceding the reinforcer with a stimulus (162)
    c. providing a different kind of reinforcer
    d. following the reinforcer with a stimulus
29. Peter Dews did research with a subject he called Charles. Charles was a/an _____.
    a. seal
    b. squid
  * c. octopus (166)
    d. porpoise
30. The reappearance of previously effective behavior during extinction is called _____.
    a. spontaneous recovery
    b. recovery
  * c. resurgence (169)
    d. fulfillment
31. Williams found that the greater the number of reinforcements before extinction, the _____
  * a. greater the number of responses during extinction (170)
    b. faster the rate of extinction
    c. stronger the response during extinction
    d. greater the frustration during extinction
32. Premack's name is most logically associated with _____
    a. drive reduction theory
  * b. relative value theory (174)
    c. response deprivation theory
    d. equilibrium theory
33. The Premack principle says that reinforcement involves _____
    a. a reduction in drive
    b. an increase in the potency of a behavior
  * c. a relation between behaviors (175)
    d. a satisfying state of affairs
34. Negative reinforcement is also called _____
    a. punishment
    b. aversive training
  * c. escape training (143)
    d. reward training

35. The distinctive characteristic of the Sidman avoidance procedure is that _____
     a. the aversive event is signaled
  * b. the aversive is not signaled (181)
     c. the aversive event is signaled twice
     d. there is no aversive event
36. Positive reinforcement is sometimes called _____.
     a. escape training
     b. positive training
     c. satisfier training
  * d. reward training (142)
37. Thorndike complained that _____ evidence provided a "supernormal psychology of animals."
  * a. anecdotal (134)
     b. case study
     c. informal experimental
     d. intuitive
38. Thorndike plotted the results of his puzzle box experiments as graphs. The resulting curves show a _____ with succeeding trials.
  * a. decrease in time (136)
     b. decrease in errors
     c. change in topography
     d. increase in the rate of behavior
39. Alan Neuringer demonstrated that with reinforcement, _____ could learn to behave randomly.
     a. preschoolers
     b. cats
     c. rats
  * d. pigeons (137, n5)
40. John Nevin has suggested that reinforcement gives behavior _____.
     a. redundancy
  * b. momentum (137)
     c. resilience
     d. complexity
41. Operant learning is sometimes called _____ learning.
     a. free
     b. higher-order
  * c. instrumental (138)
     d. reward
42. _____ gave Skinner's experimental chamber the name, "Skinner box."
     a. Fred Keller
     b. E. L. Thorndike
     c. John Watson
  * d. Clark Hull (138, n8)
43. Thorndike's 1898 dissertation describes experiments with cats, chicks, and _____.
     a. mice
     b. rats
     c. monkeys
  * d. dogs (153)
44. Thorndike emphasized that we learn mainly from _____.
     a. errors
     b. repeated trials
  * c. success (147, n15)
     d. social experiences

45. Skinner drew a parallel between reinforcement and _____.
 * a. natural selection (147, n15)
   b. history
   c. gravity
   d. momentum
46. Secondary reinforcers are also called _____ reinforcers.
   a. transient
 * b. conditioned (149)
   c. second-order
   d. acquired
47. Money is a good example of a _____ reinforcer.
   a. primary
   b. tertiary
 * c. generalized (151)
   d. transient
48. Often the initial effect of an extinction procedure is an increase in the behavior called a/an
   extinction _____.
   a. rebound
   b. resurgence
 * c. burst (167)
   d. flyer
49. The best title for the figure below is _____.
   a. Motivation and Line Drawing
 * b. The Effect of Practice without Reinforcement (173)
   c. Trial and Error Learning
   d. Improvement in Line Drawing with Practice

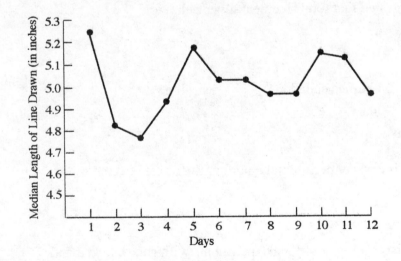

50. According to _____ theory, schoolchildren are eager to go to recess because they have
   been deprived of the opportunity to exercise.
   a. drive-reduction
   b. relative value
 * c. response deprivation (176f)
   d. stimulus substitution

150

51. Thorndike speculated that reinforcement strengthened bonds between neurons, a view that many cognitive scientists have now embraced and called _____.
   a. bonding theory
 * b. connectionism (137, n6)
   c. neurogenesis
   d. neuroconnectionism
52. Resurgence may help account for _____
   a. PMS
   b. rationalization
 * c. regression (169)
   d. reaction formation
53. John Nevin has applied the concept of behavioral momentum to _____.
   a. baseball
   b. football
 * c. basketball (137, n7)
   d. the stock market
54. The figure below from your text illustrates _____
 * a. shaping   (152, figure 5-6)
   b. chaining
   c. random behavior
   d. secondary reinforcement

55. Robinson and Bradley found that religious cult leaders sometimes use _____ to reinforce participation in and loyalty to the cult.
   a. chaining
   b. sexual favors
 * c. "love bombing" (153, n 17)
   d. psychotropic drug

True-false
   56. Negative reinforcement increases the strength of a behavior. T (142)
   57. Positive reinforcement increases the strength of a behavior. T (142)
   58. Backward chaining begins with the reinforcement of the last behavior in the chain. T (158)
   59. Studies demonstrate that operant learning is as effective with involuntary behavior, such as the salivary reflex, as it is with voluntary behavior. F (164f)
   60. Operant learning probably always involves Pavlovian conditioning as well. T (149)
   61. A general assumption of behavioral research is that any feature of a behavior may be strengthened by reinforcement, so long as reinforcement can be made contingent on that feature. T (137)

62. Operant learning sometimes occurs without any sign of awareness of the relation between behavior and its consequence. T (141, n12)
63. In shaping, it is sometimes a good idea to back up-- i.e., to reinforce earlier approximations of the desired behavior. T (135)
64. One effect of the extinction procedure is an increase in the variability of behavior. T (167)
65. The more effort a behavior requires, the fewer times the behavior will be performed during extinction. T (170)
66. Reprimands, restraint, captivity, and electrical shocks can be reinforcers. T (142)
67. According to Skinner, people are rewarded, but behavior is reinforced. T (142, n13)
68. According to your author, a general assumption of behavioral research is that any aspect of behavior may be reinforced, so long as a reinforcer can be made contingent on that feature. T (137, n5)
69. People can learn to behave randomly provided that reinforcers are made contingent on random acts. T (137, n5)
70. John Nevin has applied the concept of behavioral momentum to basketball. T (137, n7)
71. Another term for operant is instrumental. T (139)
72. The concept of reinforcement assumes an awareness between a behavior and its reinforcing consequence. F (141, n12)
73. Efforts to reinforce the contraction of individual muscle fibers have failed. F (141, n 12)
74. To say that a reinforcer increases the strength of a behavior means only that it has certain measurable effects on the behavior. T (141, n11)
75. One tip for successful shaping of behavior is to provide large reinforcers. F (154)
76. The author of your text probably believes that most childhood tantrums are due to unintentional shaping by adults. T (154)
77. Otters train their young using procedures that resemble shaping. T (155)
78. Chaining is a useful procedure for shaping behavior in laboratory animals, but it does not appear to be important in wildlife. F (156)
79. In operant learning, the word contingency usually refers to the degree of correlation between a behavior and a consequence. T (159)
80. With reinforcement, it is easy for a person to lower his blood pressure. F (164f)

Completion
81. Clark Hull's name is associated with the drive-reduction theory of reinforcement. (172)
82. Reinforcers such as praise, positive feedback, and smiles are called secondary/conditioned reinforcers. (149)
83. The Premack principle states that high probability behavior reinforces low probability behavior. (175)
84. In negative reinforcement a response is followed by the withdrawal of, or reduction in the intensity of, an aversive stimulus. (142)
85. The experimental chamber developed by Skinner is now often called a Skinner box. (138, n8)

Short essay
86. What are the differences between classical conditioning and instrumental learning? (147-9)

Classical conditioning involves stimulus-contingent stimuli and reflexive behavior; instrumental learning involves response-contingent stimuli and "voluntary" behavior.

87. What is the chief problem with the two-process theory of avoidance? (179-82)

Answers should probably focus on the fact that the avoidance response continues even when the CS is no longer aversive.

88. How does the Sidman avoidance procedure differ from other avoidance procedures? (181f)

Answers should note the absence of any stimulus preceding the shock or other aversive.

89. Describe how you would use shaping to train a pigeon to hop on one foot. (152-5)

Answers should suggest reinforcement of successive approximations, such as lifting one foot, holding the foot above the floor, etc.

90. Compare Premack's relative value theory with the response deprivation theory of Timberlake and Allison. (174-77)

Students should note that both define reinforcers as responses, but that Premack says reinforcers are defined by their probability relative to other responses while Timberlake and Allison define reinforcers by their level of deprivation relative to their baseline rate.

Chapter 6: Operant Procedures: Punishment

<u>Multiple choice</u>
1. Harriet hears a noise in the kitchen and investigates. She finds the cookie jar in pieces on the floor and 5-year-old Willy standing nearby. Harriet knows what happened, but asks Willy anyway. Willy admits that he roke the jar while trying to get cookies. Harriet gives Willy a spanking. Willy is most likely to learn from this experience that _____
   * a. it doesn't pay to tell the truth (193-195)
   b. cookies are scary
   c. his mother doesn't like him
   d. the kitchen is an unsafe place for little boys
2. All of the following enhance the effectiveness of punishment except _____
   a. using strong punishers
   b. withholding reinforcement of the punished behavior
   c. punishing immediately
   * d. increasing the reinforcer deprivation level (199f)
3. Of the following procedures, the one that reinforces behavior that *cannot* be performed at the same time as the unwanted behavior is _____
   a. DRZ
   * b. DRI (212)
   c. DRL
   d. DRA
4. Murray Sidman's book on aversive control, including punishment, is called _____
   * a. Coercion and Its Fallout (215)
   b. Aversive Control Today
   c. The Punitive Society
   d. The End of Punishment
5. The word *positive* in *positive punishment* refers to the fact that _____
   * a. something is added (191)
   b. something positive is removed
   c. the results are positive
   d. the procedure is used with good intentions
6. Generally speaking, the more intense a punisher, the _____
   a. less it suppresses behavior
   * b. more it suppresses behavior (197)
   c. more important it is to have the response on extinction
   d. less important the reinforcement history
7. David Camp and colleagues found that, compared to a two-second delay in punishment, a 30-second delay resulted in _____
   a. slightly greater response suppression
   b. slightly less response suppression
   * c. about half as much response suppression (195)
   d. about twice as much response suppression
8. The use of corporal punishment in the schools is approved by about _____
   * a. 50% of Americans (189, n1)
   b. 60% of Americans
   c. 70% of Americans
   d. 80% of Americans

9. Of the following, the person who most approved of the use of punishment was probably
_____
   a. Skinner
   b. Thorndike
   c. Franklin
 * d. Machiavelli (189)
10. Each time Charles, who has a lisp, says "Mithithippi" or the like, his wife, Evelyn, yells, "Idiot!" However, there is no evidence that Evelyn's efforts to reduce the frequency of such mispronunciations have been effective. We can therefore conclude that _____
   a. Charles's behavior is being positively reinforced
 * b. Charles's behavior has not been punished (190)
   c. Evelyn's efforts to punish Charles's behavior have actually reinforced it
   d. Charles is lisping deliberately to annoy Evelyn
11. Positive punishment is most often confused with _____
   a. negative punishment
 * b. negative reinforcement (192)
   c. aversion therapy
   d. counterconditioning
12. When disciplining their son, Jacob, Mr. and Ms Grinch begin with an extremely mild form of punishment and gradually increase its strength if the offenses continue. This procedure is likely to result in _____
   a. violent outbursts from Jacob
   b. confusing Jacob
 * c. the use of excessively strong aversives (198f)
   d. a rapid suppression of the unwanted behavior
13. Farmer Gable had a problem with motorcyclists riding across his meadow land, tearing up sod and frightening his cattle. He installed barbed wire fencing in the area and no longer had a problem. Gable's approach is best described as an example of _____
 * a. response prevention (209)
   b. extinction
   c. differential reinforcement
   d. punishment
14. When a student repeatedly behaves in an inappropriate way, probably the teacher's first step should be to _____
   a. have the child tested by the school psychologist
   b. develop a plan for applying punishment
   c. use differential reinforcement of incompatible behavior
 * d. try to discover what is reinforcing the behavior (199f)
15. Any event that follows a behavior and makes that behavior less likely to occur is called a
_____
   a. positive reinforcer
   b. negative reinforcer
 * c. punisher (188)
   d. punishment
16. If Charles Catania's thinking about reinforcement is applied to punishment, we can say that all of the following are true of punishment except _____
   a. a behavior must have a consequence
 * b. the consequence of the behavior must be negative (190)
   c. a behavior must decrease in strength
   d. the decrease in strength must be the result of the behavior's consequence

17. Disadvantages of extinction include all of the following except _____
    a. emotional outbursts
    b. slowness
    c. the reinforcers maintaining the behavior cannot always be eliminated
  * d. the behavior will persist without reinforcement (210f)
18. Differential reinforcement is best used in combination with _____
    a. punishment
    b. negative reinforcement
  * c. extinction (213)
    d. response prevention
19. Research has shown that abnormal behavior is often _____
    a. the result of unconscious urges
  * b. an inappropriate way of obtaining appropriate reinforcers (200, 213)
    c. due to the misuse of punishment
    d. an effort to punish others
20. Some studies have suggested that _____, the procedure of providing reinforcers
    regardless of what the person does, may actually reduce the frequency of undesirable behavior.
    a. extinction
    b. DRI
    c. DRO
  * d. NCR (213f)
21. John gives his dog, Alfie (a yap hound), a bit of food whenever it goes 30 seconds without
    barking. Gradually, John increases the amount of quiet time required to earn food until finally
    the dog will go for hours without a yap. The procedure John used is best described as

    _____.
    a. extinction
    b. differential reinforcement of alternative behavior
  * c. differential reinforcement of zero responding (212)
    d. non contingent reinforcement
22. The chief problem with extinction as a way of reducing the frequency of potentially harmful
    behavior is that _____.
  * a. it is slow (211)
    b. the results are not durable
    c. it is not covered by medical insurance
    d. ultimately, it makes the problem worse
23. Negative punishment is also sometimes called _____ training.
    a. escape
  * b. penalty (191)
    c. withdrawal
    d. subtraction
24. If a rat receives a shock each time it presses a lever, but not otherwise, we can say that

    _____.
    a. the rate of lever pressing will decrease, then increase
    b. the shock will reduce the frequency of lever pressing
  * c. shock is contingent on lever pressing (194)
    d. lever pressing and shock are contiguous
25. Delaying delivery of a punisher is most likely to _____.
  * a. reduce its effectiveness (195-196)
    b. increase its effectiveness
    c. have no impact on its effectiveness
    d. have variable and unpredictable effects on its effectiveness

26. The two-process theory of punishment assumes that punishment involves _____.
   a. positive and negative reinforcement
 * b. Pavlovian and operant learning (203)
   c. positive and negative punishment
   d. reward training and escape training
27. The one-process theory of punishment goes back to _____.
 * a. Thorndike (204)
   b. Watson
   c. Skinner
   d. Pavlov
28. The first formal studies of punishment were probably done by _____ .
 * a. Thorndike (216)
   b. Watson
   c. Rosalie Rayner
   d. Pavlov
29. Punishers are defined by _____.
   a. society at large
   b. experts in the field
 * c. their effects on behavior (190)
   d. their intensity
30. David Rosenhan and his students found that in psychiatric hospitals, appropriate behavior in patients tended to be _____
   a. punished
   b. negatively reinforced
 * c. ignored (200)
   d. positively reinforced

True-false
31. Punishers, like reinforcers, are defined by their effect on behavior. T (190)
32. One way to make punishment more effective is to provide an alternative means of obtaining reinforcement. T (200)
33. An early theory of punishment proposed that response suppression occurred because aversives disrupt ongoing behavior. T (202)
34. Extinction is often the best treatment when the unwanted behavior is potentially injurious. F (211)
35. Although punishment can have negative side effects, there is evidence that it can also have positive side effects. T (205)
36. In using punishment, it is best to begin with a weak punisher and gradually increase its strength as needed. F (198f)
37. Frequent use of weak punishers is more effective than occasional use of intense punishers. F (198, n7)
38. Abnormal behavior often persists despite aversive consequences because it also produces reinforcing consequences. T (200)
39. When using punishment to suppress an undesirable behavior, it is important to provide alternative means of obtaining the reinforcers that have maintained that behavior. T (200)
40. Positive punishment necessarily involves aversives. T (191, n5)
41. The term punishment, as used by behavior scientists, has nothing to do with retribution. T (190, n4)

Completion

42. When aversive events occur independently of behavior they are called <u>non contingent</u>. (193-195)
43. Positive and negative punishment have in common that they both <u>weaken/reduce the frequency of</u> behavior. (192)
44. The one process in the one-process theory of punishment is <u>operant learning</u>. (204)
45. The main difference between positive and negative punishment is that in negative punishment a stimulus is <u>removed/reduced/subtracted</u>. (191)
46. One problem with punishment is the tendency to imitate the use of punishment. Two other problems are <u>escape/aggression/apathy/abuse</u>. (206-208)

Short essay

47. It is common practice to begin punishment with a very weak punisher and gradually increase the intensity of the punisher until one finds an effective level of intensity. Is this a good idea? Why or why not? (198f)

    Students should note that this procedure often leads to an escalation of the level of punisher intensity. The result may be the use of far stronger punishers than necessary.

48. How is the effectiveness of punishment affected by the availability of reinforcement? (199f)

    Answers might focus on the availability of reinforcement for the punished behavior or on the availability of reinforcement for alternative behaviors.

49. What is the fundamental difference between the two-process and one-process theories of punishment? (203F)

    Students should reply that two-process theory assumes that both Pavlovian and operant learning are involved, while one-process theory relies entirely on operant learning.

50. Briefly discuss the problems associated with punishment. (206-209)

    Answers should mention at least four of the following: escape, aggression, abuse, apathy, and imitation of the punisher. Students might also discuss ethical problems and public opposition.

51. You have a ten-year-old child who mistreats the family dog. Describe two ways of dealing with this problem without using punishment. (209-214)

    Answers should apply two of the alternatives to punishment mentioned in the text: response prevention, extinction, differential reinforcement. For instance, response prevention might take the form of giving the dog away or keeping it out of the child's reach.

Chapter 7: Operant Applications

<u>Multiple choice</u>
  1. Self awareness means _____
    a. our attitudes about ourselves
  * b. observation of our behavior (222)
    c. self esteem
    d. awareness of the self
  2. Gordon Gallup provided evidence of self awareness in _____
    a. humans
  * b. chimps (223)
    c. pigeons
    d. rats
  3. In Mary Boyle's work with coma victims, the reinforcer was _____
    a. food
    b. massage
    c. soothing words
  * d. music (225)
  4. Joel Greenspoon's work on the reinforcement of verbal behavior showed that _____
  * a. what people say depends in part on the reactions of other people to what is said (231)
    b. it is hard to get people to express opinions
    c. people will stick to a topic if not interrupted
    d. the history of reinforcement affects the frequency of verbal behavior, but not its content
  5. Research suggests that self-injurious behavior _____
  * a. is often negatively reinforced (256)
    b. is intrinsically reinforcing
    c. is usually the result of a death wish
    d. must be punished to be stopped
  6. In the treatment of long-standing self-injurious behavior, punishment is often _____
    a. ineffective
  * b. effective (255f)
    c. effective, but the results are short-lived
    d. effective, but a new form of undesirable behavior typically appears
  7. Probably the best way of increasing the creativity of stories in an English class is to _____
  * a. praise particularly original stories (241)
    b. read all the stories to the class
    c. ask a professional writer to talk to the class
    d. create stress, since creative people are generally unhappy
  8. Herrnstein says that behavior is likely to drift toward its essential features. He means by this
    that only behavior that is _____
    a. essential is learned
  * b. required for reinforcement is likely to persist (246)
    c. superstitious will produce reinforcement
    d. modified is essential
  9. According to B. F. Skinner, we develop self-awareness largely through _____
    a. trial-and-error learning
    b. imitation of others
    c. seeing our images reflected in mirrors
  * d. the comments of other people (224)

10. The purpose of Gordon Gallup's mirror study was to determine whether chimps _____
   * a. showed evidence of self-awareness (223)
   b. experienced the same illusions as people
   c. had the ability to imagine
   d. could be induced to hallucinate
11. Insightful problem solving is best viewed as an example of _____
   a. unconscious processes
   b. trial-and-error learning
   c. Pavlovian conditioning
   * d. operant learning (235)
12. Jack is a homeless man who lives on the streets of New York City. One cold January night he takes up a position outside a fancy restaurant and starts shouting, "God has ordered an equestrian invasion of Long Island." The restaurant owner calls the police and they take Jack to a hospital, where he spends a quiet night. The next morning a doctor examines Jack and tells him he is well enough to be discharged. Jack immediately begins shouting about the equestrian invasion of Long Island. You tentatively conclude that _____
   * a. Jack's hallucinations are products of reinforcement (252f)
   b. Jack will stop hallucinating when he is placed on medication
   c. Jack is smart
   d. attention from the hospital staff is reinforcing bizarre behavior
13. Robert Epstein's banana experiment demonstrated that insight _____
   a. is a mysterious process that defies explanation
   b. occurs in people but not in animals
   c. accounts for the solution to problems
   * d. depends on an organism's learning history (238)
14. John gets into fights on a regular basis, always with formidable opponents. He has often been injured in these fights and knows that he runs the risk of sustaining serious brain damage or other permanent injuries, yet he continues to fight. John is a very successful professional boxer. This example illustrates that bizarre behavior _____
   a. can be a good way of making a living for those willing to take the risks
   b. is incomprehensible
   * c. is less puzzling when the reinforcers maintaining it are known (252f)
   d. is sometimes a good solution to the problems people face
15. Brad Alford's study of the man who thought he was followed by a witch is an example of _____
   a. anecdotal evidence
   b. the case study method
   c. a group design experiment
   * d. an ABA design experiment (252)
16. Martin Seligman has argued that learned helplessness can provide a model for _____
   a. mania
   b. schizophrenia
   * c. depression (250)
   d. anorexia nervosa
17. Montrose Wolf and his colleagues found that self-injurious behavior in disturbed children was often precipitated by _____
   a. parental visits
   b. free time
   c. punishment
   * d. teacher requests (256)

160

18. Lovaas and Simmons used punishment to reduce self-injurious behavior in a boy. Before treatment, this boy would hit himself at a rate of up to _____
    a. 5 times a minute
    b. 10 times a minute
    c. 20 times a minute
  * d. 30 times a minute (255)
19. The story of Ulysses and the Sirens illustrates the self-control technique known as _____
    a. distancing
    b. distraction
  * c. physical restraint (227)
    d. deprivation
20. Lying is probably often the result of _____
    a. punishment
    b. a lack of insight
  * c. negative reinforcement (234)
    d. positive reinforcement
21. Willpower is not a good explanation of behavior because _____
    a. you cannot see willpower
    b. you cannot measure willpower
    c. not everyone has willpower
  * d. the evidence for willpower is usually the behavior it is supposed to explain (225f)
22. Stuart Vyse's book on superstition is called _____
    a. *Quest for Truth*
    b. *The Science of Mystery*
  * c. *Believing in Magic* (260)
    d. *Self-Deception*
23. Each of the following is a self-control technique except _____.
    a. deprivation
    b. distancing
    c. distraction
  * d. distortion (227f)
24. The self-control technique of counting the number of times a behavior occurs is called _____.
  * a. monitoring (228)
    b. recording
    c. tabulating
    d. data-cording
25. In his experiments on verbal behavior, William Verplanck reinforced expressions of opinion using _____ as reinforcers.
    a. M&Ms
    b. effusive praise
    c. music
  * d. paraphrases and expressions of agreement (231)
26. Verplanck's opinion experiment used a/an _____ design.
    a. group
  * b. ABA (231)
    c. between subjects
    d. crossover

27. Herbert Quay found evidence that the topics discussed by _____ may be influenced by reinforcement.
* a. psychotherapy clients (232)
  b. clergy
  c. politicians
  d. talk show guests
28. Robert Lanza and colleagues demonstrated that _____ will lie when lying produces reinforcers.
  a. mice
  b. rats
* c. pigeons (234)
  d. cats
29. In her work with porpoises, Karen Pryor gradually realized that what she had to do to get novel behavior from the animals was to _____.
* a. reinforce novel behavior (241)
  b. punish repetitive behavior
  c. shape the novel behavior she wanted
  d. provide noncontingent reinforcement
30. Some studies show that offering rewards reduces creativity. Research by Robert Eisenberger and others suggests that this is because in these studies _____.
  a. creativity was measured differently
  b. the rewards were too weak
* c. the rewards were not contingent on creative behavior (243)
  d. the participants were too young to do creative work
31. Perhaps the first person to demonstrate learned helplessness experimentally was _____.
* a. Thorndike (250, n16)
  b. Pavlov
  c. Watson
  d. Seligman
32. Studies of learned helplessness use the _____ procedure.
  a. reward training
* b. escape training (250)
  c. positive punishment
  d. negative punishment
33. Because aberrant behavior in people is so often the result of reinforcement from the natural environment, many therapists now routinely do a _____ before beginning treatment.
  a. psychological assessment
  b. natural contingencies assessment
* c. functional assessment (256, n20)
  d. motivational analysis
34. Koichi Ono got superstitious behavior in university students by providing points noncontingently at regular intervals. One student ended up repeatedly _____
* a. jumping to touch the ceiling (246)
  b. pounding on the table with a shoe
  c. moving his head from side to side like a pendulum clock
  d. shifting her weight from one foot to the other
35. One idea for preventing learned helplessness is _____ training.
  a. self-esteem
  b. inoculation
* c. immunization (251)
  d. reality

162

36. Your text describes the use of _____ to get a bull elephant to cooperate with having his feet trimmed.
    a. physical restraint
  * b. shaping (220)
    c. chaining
    d. episodic training
37. Verbal behavior is governed by the _____.
    a. mind
    b. PMLA
  * c. law of effect (230)
    d. principle of reciprocal reinforcement

True-false
38. Kohler thought that insight was achieved suddenly, but other work suggests that it is achieved gradually. T (235f)
39. Awareness of the reinforcement contingency in force seems to be required for verbal learning to occur. F (233)
40. Creative behavior is a function of its consequences. T (241)
41. Coincidental reinforcement seems to play an important role in superstitious behavior. T (244)
42. Only humans and the great apes show evidence of self-awareness. F (224)
43. Reinforcement reduces creativity because creativity requires new forms of behavior. F (242)
44. Extinction increases variability in behavior, and this may be a way of increasing creativity. T (243f)
45. The author of your text suggests that certain ineffective medical practices, such as bloodletting, were superstitious behaviors maintained by coincidental reinforcement. T (248, n15)

Completion
46. We become good at observing our own behavior because such observations have reinforcing consequences. (223)
47. According to Skinner, we use language because it produces reinforcing consequences/has benefits/etc. (230)
48. The solution to a problem is behavior that produces reinforcement/reinforcers (235)
49. Karen Pryor demonstrated that she could reinforce novel behavior. Her subjects were porpoises. (240f)
50. Coincidental reinforcement plays an important role in superstitious behavior/superstition. (244f)

Short essay
51. What are the implications for psychotherapy of Quay's work on family recollections? (232)

Quay's work suggests that the tendency of client's to dwell on childhood experiences may be the result of subtle forms of reinforcement for talking about those experiences. More broadly, the research suggests that much of the content of psychotherapy may be the product of reinforcement.

52. Why is insight not an adequate *explanation* of problem solving? (235-239)

This is review question 10; it is also the point of the query on page 234. Although people say they solve problems "through insight" in fact the term simply describes the fact that a solution has been arrived at, apparently (but not actually) without benefit of reinforcement.

53. How could you use operant procedures to improve the adoption rate of orphans aged five to twelve? (221)

The box on page 220 suggests improving the rate of adoption of dogs in animal shelters by shaping behaviors that make the animals more appealing. The same kinds of procedures might prove effective with orphans.

54. Mary-Lou, aged 3 years, still does not speak. Medical examination reveals that she is in perfect health. Testing shows that she has normal intelligence. Her parents do not abuse her; in fact, they spoil her shamelessly. What is the most likely explanation for Mary-Lou's failure to speak? (230f)

"They spoil her shamelessly" provides an important hint. Since the usual alternative explanations have been ruled out, it is likely that there is no contingency between speaking and reinforcers. If nonverbal behavior (squeals, facial expressions, etc.) works well, there is no need to learn to speak.

55. Describe the basic laboratory procedure for establishing superstitious behavior. Explain why it is usually difficult to specify in advance what superstitious behavior will result. (244)

Students should mention coincidental reinforcement of behavior. They may mention reinforcement at timed intervals. Since there is no contingency between a particular behavior and reinforcing consequences, there is no way that the outcome can be predicted.

Chapter 8: Vicarious Learning

<u>Multiple choice</u>
1. The earliest studies of observational learning were performed by _____
    a. Ivan Pavlov
  * b. E. L. Thorndike (265)
    c. John B. Watson
    d. Carl Warden
2. The first studies of vicarious learning _____
    a. proved beyond doubt that animals learn by observing models
    b. proved that only higher animals learn by observing models
    c. suggested that some animals can learn by observing models under special circumstances
  * d. failed to find evidence of vicarious learning in animals (266)
3. In Bandura's theory of vicarious learning, steps taken during observation to improve later recall of a model's behavior are called _____
    a. mnemonic processes
    b. cognitive processes
  * c. retentional processes (288)
    d. memorial processes
4. Learning is a change in behavior due to experience. In vicarious learning, the experience consists of _____
  * a. observing a model (266)
    b. imitating a model
    c. vicariously participating in events in one's environment
    d. sharing the experiences of another person or animal
5. The Miller-Dollard theory of vicarious learning emphasizes the _____
    a. consequences of the model's behavior
  * b. consequences of the observer's behavior (289f)
    c. cognitive activity of the model
    d. cognitive activity of the observer
6. Your text includes a humorous passage on the Venus Effect. The serious point of the passage is that _____.
  * a. emotional arousal can affect learning (286)
    b. monkeys have very strong sex drives
    c. monkeys are not careful observers
    d. monkeys learn better when the model is an attractive model of the opposite sex.
7. The Sherry and Galef experiment with milk bottles suggests that _____
    a. chickadees learn very well through observation
    b. chickadees can't learn through observation
  * c. many of the birds that seem to have learned through observation haven't (292)
    d. most birds don't like milk
8. Whether children imitate an aggressive model depends largely on _____
    a. the nature of the aggressive behavior
  * b. whether the model's behavior is reinforced or punished (276f)
    c. whether the child is encouraged to imitate the model
    d. the relationship between the child and the model

9. You hear on the radio that Smash, the most popular rock video performer in Germany, has killed himself. He left a note ("Goodbye, cruel world"). You predict that _____
   a. Germans will riot in the streets
   b. Germans will pass laws against rock video
   c. the sale of rock video cassettes will decline markedly in Germany
 * d. there will be a rash of suicides or suicidal gestures among German rock video fans (285)

10. Jill is an impressionable 17-year-old college freshman with average academic skills. She lives in the college dorms with two roommates. One of them, Martha, is bright, attractive, popular, rich, and a local celebrity because of her singing; she seldom studies. Jill's other roommate, Ann, is also bright, but has only a few friends, wears inexpensive clothes, and plays the tuba poorly; she studies all the time. On the basis of what you know about vicarious learning, you predict that Jill will _____
   a. major in music
   b. major in psychology
 * c. flunk out (283f)
   d. transfer to a different college

11. You demonstrate how to make a paper airplane to two boys, Fred and Ted. Fred and Ted are the same age, have the same IQs, live in the same middle class neighborhood and in fact are exactly alike in all respects save one: You have shown Ted how to make several other kinds of toys in the past. You predict that _____
 * a. Ted's paper plane will be better than Fred's (285, 287)
   b. Fred's paper plane will be better than Ted's
   c. Fred will show more interest in your demonstration than Ted will
   d. there will be no difference in their paper planes

12. According to the views of Miller and Dollard, vicarious learning
   a. should vary across age groups _____
   b. takes place before the observer makes any imitative act
 * c. is really a form of operant learning (289f)
   d. requires attentional and retentional processes

13. In the Rocky and Johnny study, after viewing the videotape children were more _____
   a. likely to lie
 * b. aggressive (294)
   c. sympathetic
   d. likely to solve problems

14. Of the following terms, the one most associated with Bandura's theory is _____
   a. covert modeling
   b. symbolic observation
 * c. retentional processes (288)
   d. simulation training

15. Fisher and Harris found that observers learned more when a model _____
 * a. frowned and shook her head (283)
   b. showed no emotional reaction
   c. vacillated between happy and sad
   d. avoided looking at the observer

16. Presley and Riopelle studied vicarious avoidance learning in monkeys. They found that _____
 * a. the slowest learning observer did as well as the fastest learning model (274)
   b. there was not much difference in the performance of observers and models
   c. the observers were no match for the models
   d. observers did not attend to the model

166

17. Fiorito and Scotto studied vicarious learning in the _____
    a. squid
    b. whale
  * c. octopus (280)
    d. jellyfish
18. The tendency to imitate modeled behavior even when doing so is not reinforced is called
_____
    a. superstitious imitation
    b. neurotic imitation
  * c. generalized imitation (280)
    d. habitual imitation
19. Judith Fisher and Mary Harris found that if a model wore an eye patch, observers learned
_____
    a. less from the model's behavior
  * b. more from the model's behavior (283)
    c. about the same amount from the model's behavior
    d. only about the eye patch
20. Those who are most likely to learn from observing a model are probably _____
    a. young children
    b. older children
  * c. adults (285)
    d. very old adults
21. Vicarious learning may be defined as _____.
    a. imitation of a model's behavior
    b. a change in an observer's behavior
  * c. a change in behavior due to observing a model (266)
    d. a variation of operant learning
22. Mineka and Cook found that of six captive monkeys that observed their parents react fearfully
    at the sight of a snake, _____ of the six then showed fear of snakes.
    a. 0
    b. 3
  * c. 5 (270)
    d. 6
23. Herbert and Harsh compared the behavior of cats that had observed a model perform an act
    30 times with cats that had observed only 15 performances. They found that _____.
    a. the extra 15 observances made no difference
    b. the first 15 observations had a greater impact than the next 15
  * c. cats that observed 30 performances did substantially better than those that observed 15
    (273)
    d. cats that observed 15 performances actually did better than those that observed 30
24. The influence of literary models on behavior was seen in the 18th century with the publication
    of _____.
  * a. *The Sorrows of Young Werther* (285)
    b. *Swan Song*
    c. *Death of the Knight*
    d. *This Is Not the Answer*
25. A form of treatment for phobia that makes use of observational learning is called _____.
    a. virtual exposure therapy
    b. observational desensitization
  * c. participant modeling (296)
    d. vicarious sensitization

26. The Herbert and Harsh study found that cats that had observed a model perform 30 times did better than those that had observed a model perform 15 times. T (273)
27. If an observer watches a well-trained model perform a response, the procedure is not really observational learning. F (274)
28. Vicarious learning leads inevitably to imitation. F (279)
29. Herbert and Harsh demonstrated vicarious learning in cats. T (273)
30. Carl Warden was one of the first researchers to demonstrate vicarious operant learning in animals. T (271)
31. Cook and Mineka showed that though monkeys can learn by observing live monkeys, they do not learn from watching videotaped monkeys. F (270f)
32. When a character on a British soap opera called Eastlanders took a drug overdose to get attention, cases of self-poisoning increased at certain hospitals. T (285)

Completion
33. Bandura says that observational learning involves four processes. One of these is attentional/retentional/motor reproductive/motivational. (287f)
34. Mineka and Cook found that monkeys could acquire a fear of snakes vicariously. (270f)
35. Research suggests that what appears to be vicarious classical conditioning may in fact be a form of higher-order conditioning. (270)
36. Berger found that one important variable affecting vicarious learning in humans is the status of the model. (283)
37. A treatment for phobia that makes use of vicarious learning is called participant modeling. (296)

Short essay
38. Why has observational learning received less attention than other forms of learning? (265f)

Answers should probably point to the early failures of Thorndike and Watson.

39. You hold the patent on a special beard-trimming razor, so it is to your advantage if beards are popular. How would you use modeling to increase the popularity of beards? (inferred)

Answers should indicate that students recognize the importance of modeling and model characteristics.

40. Design an experiment to determine the role of delayed reinforcement of a model's behavior in vicarious learning. (inferred)

This is review question 13. A group design might have children observe an adult model, with the model's target behavior reinforced immediately in one condition and after a delay in another. In a single case design, the same children might observe models in two situations, one involving immediate reinforcement, the other involving delayed reinforcement. In either study, the dependent variable would be the tendency of the observers to imitate the target behavior.

41. How might a person acquire superstitious behavior through observing a model? Give an example. (276)

Superstitious behavior is presumably no different from other behavior as far as observational learning is concerned. If a model's superstitious behavior is repeatedly reinforced, it is likely to be imitated by an observer.

42. Does the Venn and Short experiment with Mickey Mouse and Donald Duck toys demonstrate vicarious Pavlovian conditioning? Explain why or why not. (268-270)

It does not. The essential point is that when the model's interacted with the toys, the toys were never paired with a frightening US. It was the pairing of the toy and the model's reaction that apparently produced the change in the observers' behavior. Thus, the experiment demonstrates that what appears to be vicarious conditioning may in fact be ordinary conditioning.

Chapter 9: Generalization, Discrimination, and Stimulus Control

<u>Multiple choice</u>
1. When Little Joey, now six months old, cries, Martha can tell what he needs even before she goes to him. Martha's skill is an example of _____
   a. generalization
      *   b. discrimination (313, 315)
   c. semantic generalization
   d. errorless discrimination training
2. Howard studied hard for his math test and found that what he learned helped him on his physics test. Howard benefited from _____
   * a. generalization (306)
   b. discrimination
   c. transposition
   d. semantic generalization
3. The figures below illustrate various generalization gradients. The greatest degree of generalization is depicted by figure _____
   a. 1
   * b. 2 (314)
   c. 3
   d. 4

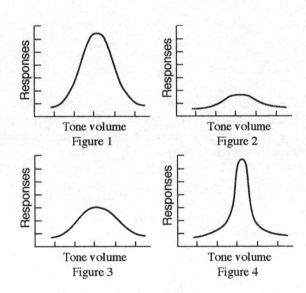

Tone volume
Figure 1

Tone volume
Figure 2

Tone volume
Figure 3

Tone volume
Figure 4

4. Look again at the figures in item 3. The one that shows the greatest degree of discrimination is figure _____
   a. 1
   b. 2
   c. 3
   * d. 4 (314)

5. In errorless discrimination training, _____
   a. training continues until the animal or person makes no errors
   b. subjects look on as well-trained models perform the response to be learned
   c. generalization soon reappears
 * d. the S⁻ is introduced in very weak form (319)
6. A dog learns to salivate at the sound of a soft buzzer, but not at the sound of a loud buzzer. After training, the dog is presented with buzzers of various volumes. You predict that the dog will salivate most in response to a buzzer that is _____
   a. identical to the CS+
 * b. slightly softer than the CS+ (328)
   c. slightly louder than the CS+
   d. slightly louder than the CS-
7. Jill trains her dog, Bowser, to come to her when she snaps her fingers. She snaps her fingers, then gives the dog a bit of food when it approaches. Finger snapping is a/an _____
 * a. S⁺ (314f)
   b. S⁻
   c. transposed stimulus
   d. concept
8. Robert Eisenberger found that rewarding a high level of effort on one task increases the level of effort on other tasks. This illustrates _____
   a. discrimination
 * b. generalization (305)
   c. motivational transfer
   d. a motivational paradox
9. The finding of Eisenberger and others concerning effort (see item 8) is called _____
   a. learned helplessness
   b. motivational transfer
 * c. learned industriousness (305)
   d. increased potentiation
10. Bill conducts an experiment in which he pairs the word *psychologist* with words such as *nasty*, *evil*, and *corrupt*. Later Bill asks his subjects to give their opinion of various professions by rating them on a scale from very positive to very negative. Of the following professions, _____ will probably receive the lowest rating.
   a. mathematician
   b. accountant
   c. biologist
 * d. social worker (310)
11. The hypothetical finding in item item 10 is called _____
   a. discriminant function
   b. abstract transfer
   c. transportation
 * d. semantic generalization (308)
12. Steven, a drug abuser, is released from a clinic. He is free of drugs, and has sworn never to take drugs again. He returns to his old neighborhood. You predict that within six months, Steven will _____
   a. have moved to a new neighborhood
   b. have new friends and be free of drugs
 * c. be abusing drugs again (322f)
   d. have committed suicide

13. Harriet gives a monkey a choice between two blocks of wood, one rough and the other smooth. If the animal selects the rough block, it receives a raisin; if it picks the smooth one, it receives nothing. When the animal regularly picks the rough block, Harriet gives the animal a choice between the rough block of wood and a new block of wood that is even rougher than the first. You predict that the monkey will _____
 * a. pick the new, very rough block (334)
   b. pick the old, somewhat rough block
   c. pick neither block
   d. show signs of developing an experimental neurosis
14. Judy gives a monkey a choice between a sphere and various other three-dimensional shapes. Each time the animal selects the sphere, it receives a grape; if it selects the other object, it receives nothing. Judy is engaged in _____
   a. transposition training
   b. a peak shift experiment
 * c. concept training (332)
   d. generalization training
15. Frederick believes that discrimination training produces inhibitory as well as excitatory gradients of generalization. Frederick is most likely an advocate of the theory of generalization and discrimination proposed by _____
   a. Pavlov
 * b. Spence (327)
   c. Lashley and Wade
   d. Herrnstein
16. Frederica believes that generalization occurs because of a lack of experience with stimuli that differ from the S^+. Frederica is probably most comfortable with the theory of generalization and discrimination proposed by _____
   a. Pavlov
   b. Spence
 * c. Lashley and Wade (329f)
   d. Herrnstein
17. You test Mary's drawing ability by having her draw fruit, animals, landscapes, and houses. Mary then takes a drawing class in which she learns to draw human figures. You decide to test Mary again to see if her drawing ability has improved. You predict that if she shows any improvement at all it will be at drawing _____
   a. fruit
 * b. animals (304)
   c. landscapes
   d. houses
18. Robert Allan trained pigeons to peck pictures containing human figures. He found that birds _____
   a. refused to peck at a high rate
   b. pecked open areas free of human figures
 * c. pecked the human figures (335)
   d. pecked the pictures at random points
19. According to your text, mental rotation data are best viewed as evidence of _____
 * a. generalization (336)
   b. discrimination
   c. cognitive processing
   d. peak shift

20. If a person smokes a pack of cigarettes a day, in a year cigarette smoking is reinforced _____
  a. 730 times
  b. 7,300 times
  * c. 73,000 times (337)
  d. nearly a million times
21. Providing different consequences for different responses can enhance discrimination training. This finding is called the _____
  * a. differential outcomes effect (320)
  b. differential reinforcement effect
  c. discriminated avoidance effect
  d. stimulus control effect
22. The kind of generalization discussed in your text is _____
  a. response generalization
  * b. stimulus generalization (306, n1)
  c. reciprocal generalization
  d. discriminated generalization
23. In their study, Dweck and Repucci had teachers give students unsolvable problems, and then problems that could be solved. The result was that the students _____.
  a. solved the second set of problems more easily than expected
  b. solved the second set of problems, but more slowly than expected
  * c. failed to solve the problems in the second set (306)
  d. decided to unionize
24. In the Dweck and Repucci study, teachers asked students to work on unsolvable problems, and then on problems that could be solved. They failed to solve the second set of problems, but were able to solve similar problems when the problems were presented _____.
  a. orally
  * b. by a different teacher (306)
  c. the next day
  d. in a different room
25. In a classic study, Guttman and Kalish trained pigeons to peck a disk of a particular color, and then gave them the opportunity to peck _____.
  * a. disks of various colors (307)
  b. disks of various shapes
  c. disks of various sizes
  d. objects other than disks
26. When generalization is based on abstract rather than physical features, it is called _____ generalization.
  a. abstract
  b. meaningful
  * c. semantic (308)
  d. cognitive
27. Honig and Slivka trained pigeons to peck disks of various colors. After this they began shocking the birds when they pecked a disk of a particular color. This _____.
  a. reduced pecking on that disk, but not disks of other colors
  * b. reduced pecking on that and other disks (312)
  c. had no effect on the rate of pecking
  d. reduced pecking on that disk, but *increased* pecking on other disks

28. An _____ is a stimulus that indicates that a particular behavior will be reinforced.
   a. S^Δ
   b. S^0
   c. S^-
 * d. S^+ (314)

29. Jennifer O'Donnell suggests that a stimulus that indicates a behavior will be punished should be designated by _____.
   a. S^D
 * b. S^{Dp} (316, n5)
   c. S^P
   d. S_p

30. In _____, the task is to select from two or more alternatives the stimulus that matches a standard.
 * a. matching to sample (318)
   b. stimulus selection
   c. mismatching
   d. discriminating

31. In _____, the task is to select from two or more alternatives the stimulus that is *different from* a standard.
   a. matching to nonsample
 * b. oddity matching (318)
   c. error matching
   d. difference matching

32. In _____ discrimination training, the S^+ and S^- are presented at the same time.
   a. synchronized
   b. randomized
 * c. simultaneous (318)
   d. identical

33. The person whose name is most associated with errorless discrimination training is _____
   a. Carl Cheney
   b. Patrick Stewart
 * c. Herbert Terrace (319)
   d. Robert Eisenberger

34. When a behavior reliably occurs in the presence of an S^+ but not in the presence of an S^-, we can say the behavior is _____
 * a. under stimulus control (322)
   b. fully discriminated
   c. respondent
   d. fully operant

35. An S^+ is analogous to a _____
   a. S^Δ
 * b. CS^+ (314, n4)
   c. S^P
   d. S_p

174

36. The effects of reinforcement generalize, but the effects of extinction and punishment do not. F (312)
37. The flatter the generalization curve, the greater the degree of generalization. T (313)
38. Generalization implies that those who must speak to a large crowd in a hot auditorium should practice before a few friends in a small, air conditioned room. F (305)
39. Pigeons that have learned to peck a disk when two lights of the same color come on, and not when the lights differ, can be said to have learned a concept. T (332)
40. Herrnstein and others trained pigeons to respond to images of people. The researchers did this by pinpointing a single defining feature (such as hair) on which the birds could discriminate humans from other objects. F (332)
41. During World War II, thousands of American citizens of Japanese descent were imprisoned in this country though their only "crime" was that they resembled the enemy. T (311)
42. The effects of reinforcement generalize, but not the effects of extinction and punishment. F (312)
43. With discrimination training, pigeons have learned to discriminate between paintings by Manet and Picasso, even when the pictures were ones they had never seen before. T (316)
44. Spence's theory anticipated the discovery of the peak shift phenomenon. T (328)
45. When we speak of concepts we are speaking of discriminations. T (332)

Completion
46. The CS+ of Pavlovian discrimination training is analogous to the S^+ of operant discrimination training. (315, n4)
47. Sometimes a response generalizes on the basis of the meaning of a stimulus. This is called semantic generalization. (308)
48. In errorless discrimination training an S^- is introduced in a form so weak that the organism does not respond to it. (319)
49. In the successive discrimination training procedure, the discriminative stimuli alternate. (318)
50. Oddity matching is a form of MTS in which reinforcement is contingent on selecting a stimulus that is different from the sample, (318)

Short essay
51. Explain why a person who is red-green colorblind (that is, red and green objects look gray) is at a disadvantage compared to his or her peers. (inferred)

This is review question 20. Answers should note that we discriminate objects partly on the basis of color. It is therefore harder for the colorblind person to make discriminations when the colors red or green are involved. Snakes that are red or green are harder for the colorblind person to see.

52. How could a speech teacher encourage oratorical skills to generalize outside of the classroom? (309)

Students might suggest making training situations similar to situations that will occur outside the classroom. Or they might propose conducting the class in real world settings. (E.g., have a party and ask members of the class to make impromptu remarks.)

53. Discuss the DOE and its implications for discrimination training. (320-322)

Students should define the DOE. It implies that in certain situations trainers should provide different outcomes for different responses.

54. Describe the role that semantic generalization may play in prejudices. (310f)

The work of Staats and Staats and of Lacey and his colleagues should be cited, at least implicitly.

55. Discuss whether stimulus control is a good thing. (322-325)

Answers should note that stimulus control is good or bad to the extent that the behavior involved is appropriate to the situation.

Chapter 10: Schedules of Reinforcement

Multiple choice

1. John spent his summer picking cantaloupes for a farmer. The farmer paid John a certain amount for every basket of cantaloupes picked. John worked on a _____
* * a. fixed ratio schedule (349)
   b. variable ratio schedule
   c. fixed interval schedule
   d. variable interval schedule

2. Harry spent his summer in the city panhandling. Every day he would sit on the sidewalk, put a cardboard sign in front of him that said, "Please help," and place his hat on the sidewalk upside down. Then he would wait. Every now and then someone would put money into his hat. Harry's reinforcement schedule is best described as a _____
   a. fixed ratio schedule
   b. variable ratio schedule
   c. fixed interval schedule
* * d. variable time schedule (358)

3. Bill spends his summer in the city panhandling. Every day he takes a position on a busy corner and accosts passersby saying, "Can you spare some change?" Most people ignore him, but every now and then someone gives him money. Bill's reinforcement schedule is best described as a _____
   a. fixed ratio schedule
* * b. variable ratio schedule (351)
   c. fixed interval schedule
   d. variable interval schedule

4. The schedule to use if you want to produce the most rapid learning of new behavior is _____
* * a. CRF (349)
   b. FR 2
   c. FI 3"
   d. VI 3"

5. George trains a pigeon to peck a disk by reinforcing each disk peck. Once the response is learned, George begins to cut back on the reinforcers. At first he reinforces every other response, then every third response, every fifth response, every tenth response, and so on. George is using a procedure called _____
   a. ratio tuning
   b. reinforcement decimation
   c. intermittent reinforcement
* * d. stretching the ratio (359)

6. Things are going pretty well for George (see item 5) until he jumps from reinforcing every tenth response to reinforcing every 50th response. At this point, the pigeon responds erratically and nearly stops responding entirely. George's pigeon is suffering from _____
* * a. ratio strain (360)
   b. ratiocination
   c. satiation
   d. reinforcer deprivation

7. A schedule in which reinforcement is contingent on the behavior of more than one subject is a _____
   a. multiple schedule
   b. mixed schedule
   c. tandem schedule
* * d. cooperative schedule (369)

8. Stanley wants to determine which of two reinforcement schedules is more attractive to rats. He trains a rat to press a lever for food, and then puts the rat into an experimental chamber containing two levers. Pressing one lever produces reinforcement on an FR 10 schedule; pressing the other lever produces reinforcement on an FI 10" schedule. Lever pressing is on a _____
  - a. multiple schedule
  - b. chain schedule
* c. concurrent schedule (369)
  - d. redundant schedule

9. Shirley trains a rat to press a lever and then reinforces lever presses on an FR 10 schedule when a red light is on, and an FI 10" schedule when a green light is on. In this case, lever pressing is on a _____
* a. multiple schedule (367)
  - b. chain schedule
  - c. concurrent schedule
  - d. redundant schedule

10. Studies of choice involve _____
  - a. multiple schedules
  - b. chain schedules
* c. concurrent schedules (369)
  - d. redundant schedules

11. A pigeon is confronted with two disks, one green, the other red. The bird receives food on a VI 20" schedule when it pecks the green disk, and on a VI 10" schedule when it pecks the red one. You predict that the bird will peck _____
  - a. one disk about as often as at the other
  - b. the green disk almost exclusively
  - c. the green disk about twice as often as the red disk
* d. the red disk about twice as often as the green disk (370)

12. The principle that allows you to predict the behavior of the pigeon in item 11 is called the _____
  - a. law of effect
* b. matching law (371)
  - c. Premack principle
  - d. differential outcomes effect

13. The study of psychiatric patients by Battalio and Kagel illustrates the use of reinforcement schedules in the field of _____
* a. experimental economics (377)
  - b. ergonomics
  - c. psychopathology
  - d. schedule science

14. The study of reinforcement schedules suggests that the behavior we call stick-to-itiveness is largely the product of _____
  - a. genetics
  - b. prenatal influences
  - c. character
* d. reinforcement history (380)

15. The schedule that is *not* an intermittent schedule is _____
* a. FR 1 (349)
  - b. FR 5
  - c. VR 1
  - d. VI 1"

16. A reduction in response rate following reinforcement is called a _____
  * a. postreinforcement pause (350)
    b. scallop
    c. latency
    d. rest stop
17. The rate at which a response occurs, once the subject begins performing it, is called the _____
    a. clock rate
    b. walk rate
  * c. run rate (351)
    d. performance rate
18. Your text reports the case of a man who apparently made hundreds of harassing phone calls. The man's behavior was most likley on a/an _____
    a. FR schedule
  * b. VR schedule (352)
    c. FI schedule
    d. VI schedule
19. The schedule that is likely to produce a cumulative record with scallops is the _____
    a. FR schedule
    b. VR schedule
  * c. FI schedule (353)
    d. VI schedule
20. A schedule that does *not* require the performance of a particular behavior is the _____
  * a. FT schedule (358)
    b. FD schedule
    c. FI schedule
    d. FR schedule
21. Of the following, the schedule that is most likely to produce a superstitious behavior is the _____
    a. FD
    b. VD
    c. DRH
  * d. VT (358)
22. One explanation for the PRE implies that the effect is really an illusion. This is the _____
    a. discrimination hypothesis
    b. frustration hypothesis
    c. sequential hypothesis
  * d. response unit hypothesis (366)
23. A chain schedule is most like a _____ schedule.
    a. multiple schedule
    b. mixed schedule
    c. cooperative
  * d. tandem schedule (368)
24. Alan Christopher studied the effects of reinforcement schedule on _____
  * a. compulsive gambling (376)
    b. experimental neurosis
    c. malingering
    d. drug effects

25. A classic work on reinforcement schedules is by _____ .
    a. Darwin
    b. Herrnstein
  * c. Ferster and Skinner (383)
    d. Abercrombe and Fitch
26. A given reinforcement schedule tends to produce a distinctive pattern and rate of performance. These are called schedule _____.
    a. patterns
    b. profiles
  * c. effects (348)
    d. matrixes
27. There are two basic kinds of schedules, simple and _____.
  * a. complex (346 and inferred)
    b. compound
    c. open
    d. operant
28. CRF is synonymous with _____.
    a. EXT
  * b. FR 1 (349)
    c. CRT
    d. FI 1
29. When reinforcement is contingent on continuous performance of an activity, a _____ reinforcement schedule is in force.
  * a. duration (356)
    b. interval
    c. time
    d. ratio
30. In schedules research, VD stands for _____.
    a. video displayed
    b. verbal dependent
    c. variable dependency
  * d. variable duration (356)
31. The schedule that most closely resembles noncontingent reinforcement is _____.
    a. FD
  * b. FT (358)
    c. FI
    d. DRL
32. Stretching the ratio is also sometimes called _____ .
  * a. thinning the schedule (359, n5)
    b. reducing the ratio
    c. raising the pitch
    d. waltzing Matilda
33. The explanation of the PRE that puts greatest emphasis on internal cues is the _____ hypothesis.
    a. discrimination
  * b. frustration (363)
    c. sequential hypothesis
    d. response unit hypothesis

34. In one form of the matching law, B_A stands for the behavior under consideration and B_0 represents _____.
   a. reinforcement for B_A
   b. the baseline rate of B_A
 * c. all behaviors other than B_A
   d. all behavior that is over expectation

35. The experiment with college students by Kassinove and Schare suggests that a few "near misses" now and then _____ gambling persistence.
   a. decrease
 * b. increase (377)
   c. have no effect on

36. Goldberg and Cheney demonstrated that rats will malinger if other rats will work harder. They did this using a _____ schedule.
   a. multiple
   b. concurrent
 * c. cooperative (379)
   d. mixed

37. The Goldberg and Cheney study found that malingering occurred even though _____.
   a. malingering produced shock
   b. malingering rats received extra incentives for working
   c. nonmalingering rats received more food for working
 * d. malingering reduced the amount of reinforcement received by the malingerer (379)

38. Of the following explanations, the one that is most satisfactory from the standpoint of science is _____
   a. Mary bites her nails because she has masochistic tendencies
   b. John never sticks to a diet because he lacks will power
   c. Susan is very poor in art because she lacks creativity
 * d. Harry has stick-to-itiveness because his parents praised him for sticking with projects (380, 381. Notice that in d, stick-to-itiveness merely names a behavior, it is not used to explain the behavior.)

39. _____ is an excellent schedule for increasing the rate at which a behavior occurs.
   a. CRF
   b. DRL
   c. DRO
 * d. DRH (357; 386)

40. People sometimes behave differently from animals on a given schedule. This is most likely because _____.
   a. animals are less variable than people
 * b. people receive instructions about what they are to do (381)
   c. people deliberately do something different to demonstrate that they are not rats
   d. people are more complicated than animals

True-false

41. Although important, the matching law is restricted to a narrow range of species, responses, reinforcers, and reinforcement schedules. F (374)

42. In VI schedules, the reinforcer occurs periodically regardless of what the organism does. F (354f)

43. One everyday example of a VR schedule is the lottery. T (353)

44. In a multiple schedule, the organism is forced to choose between two or more reinforcement schedules. F (367)

45. When a response is placed on extinction, there is often an increase in emotional behavior. T (360)
46. When food is the reinforcer, it is possible to stretch the ratio to the point at which an animal expends more energy than it receives. T (360, n6)
47. One difference between FT and FI schedules is that in FT schedules, reinforcement is not contingent on a behavior. T (358)

Completion
48. The rule describing the delivery of reinforcement is called a schedule of reinforcement. (348)
49. CRF stands for continuous reinforcement. (349)
50. The explanation of the PRE that puts greatest emphasis on internal cues is the frustration hypothesis. (363)
51. The morale of the Eager Beavers baseball team has remained high even though it has won fewer games each year for the last three seasons. This is most likely the result of the phenomenon known as stretching the ratio. (359)
52. In CRF, the ratio of reinforcers to responses is 1 to 1; in FR 1, the ratio is 1 to 1. (349)
53. Choice involves concurrent schedules. (369)
54. When behavior is on an FR schedule, animals often discontinue working briefly following reinforcement. These periods are called post-reinforcement pauses. (350)
55. The term schedule effects refers to the pattern and rate of performance produced by a particular reinforcement schedule. (348)

Short essay
56. Explain why fatigue is not a good explanation for postreinforcement pauses. (350)

Answers should note that more demanding (fatiguing) schedules do not necessarily produce longer pauses than less demanding schedules. Students might also argue that the fatigue explanation is circular.

57. A teacher has a student who gives up at the first sign of difficulty. How can the teacher increase the child's persistence? (359)

This is essentially the same question as review question 5. Answers should make use of stretching the ratio.

58. A rat's lever pressing is on a concurrent VI 5" VI 15" schedule. Describe the rat's behavior. (371)

Students should indicate that for every lever press on the VI 15" schedule, there will be about three responses on the VI 5" schedule.

59. How might you use what you know about reinforcement schedules to study the effects of air temperature on behavior? (inferred, but see especially p. 382)

Answers should indicate an understanding of the value of schedule-induced steady rates to study the effects of independent variables, such as air temperature.

60. Why is the study of reinforcement schedules important? (380-383)

This is review question 16, rephrased. Students might discuss the use of schedules in defining and studying personality characteristics such as laziness, the effects of drugs and other variables on behavior, and their use in studying extinction effects and other basic phenomena.

Chapter 11: Forgetting

<u>Multiple choice</u>

1. Jack and Jill go up a hill to fetch a pail of water. Jack falls down and breaks his crown and Jill thinks he may have suffered a concussion. To test his memory, she asks him if he remembers what happened. Jill is measuring forgetting by the method known as _____
   a. relearning
   b. extinction
 * c. free recall (392)
   d. prompted recall
2. It turns out that Jack (see item 1) can't remember anything that happened from the time he and Jill started up the hill. Jill takes Jack up the hill again and finds that he remembers seeing the well before. Jill is measuring forgetting by using _____
   a. relearning
   b. extinction
   c. free recall
 * d. prompted recall (392)
3. One measure of forgetting is called delayed matching to sample. This procedures could be considered a form of_____
   a. relearning
   b. extinction
   c. free recall
 * d. prompted recall (392f)
4. Clark's nutcrackers apparently recall the location of something like _____ food caches.
   a. 100
   b. 1,000
 * c. 2,000 (409)
   d. 20,000
5. Forgetting is the deterioration of _____ .
 * a. performance (390)
   b. memory
   c. mental processes
   d. neurological tissue
6. To measure forgetting, Ebbinghaus used the _____ .
 * a. relearning method (393)
   b. extinction
   c. free recall
   d. prompted recall
7. The first person to demonstrate the relationship between forgetting and degree of learning was probably_____ .
   a. Krueger
 * b. Ebbinghaus (393)
   c. Underwood
   d. Dunlap
8. The Chase and Simon study comparing chess masters and ordinary players showed that when chess pieces were arranged in random order, _____ .
   a. chess masters forgot less
   b. ordinary players forgot less
 * c. chess masters and ordinary players forgot about the same amount (401)
   d. chess masters learned more and forgot more

9. Forgetting can be measured as a flattening of the generalization gradient, a procedure called gradient_____
   a. leveling
 * b. degradation (396)
   c. reduction
   d. deterioration
10. The work of Levine and Murphy suggests that people are more likely to forget what they read if they _____
   a. agree with it
 * b. disagree with it (402)
   c. are ambivalent about it
   d. wrote it
11. A study of immobilized cockroaches showed the importance of _____ in forgetting.
   a. sleep
   b. state dependent learning
   c. proactive interference
 * d. retroactive interference (403)
12. According to McGeoch, one reason we forget is because we_____
 * a. keep on learning (404)
   b. sleep
   c. lose brain cells
   d. fail to use mnemonics
13. Forgetting can be studied by requiring the subject to match a stimulus presented earlier, a procedure called _____
 * a. DMTS (394)
   b. MTSD
   c. MTS
   d. the extinction method
14. Kamil and Balda found that Clark's nutcrackers could recall the location of food caches for up to _____
   a. 6 hours
   b. 6 days
   c. 6 weeks
 * d. 6 months (409)
15. Ericsson and Chase found that "SF" could recall series of up to _____ digits.
   a. 7
   b.18
   c. 56
 * d. 82 (412)
16. The first person to argue that the passage of time does not *cause* forgetting was probably

   _____
   a. Ebbinghaus
 * b. McGeoch (398)
   c. Steinmetz
   d. Underwood
17. Degree of learning can be measured as the number of correct responses per minute. This is called_____
   a. rate
   b. speed
 * c. fluency (399)
   d. right-ratio

18. Meaningful material is forgotten less readily than nonsense material. This shows the importance of _____
   a. insight
 * b. previous learning (400)
   c. subsequent learning
   d. understanding
19. When what we learned on Monday interferes with our ability to recall what we learned the following Tuesday, we speak of _____
 * a. proactive interference (401)
   b. retroactive interference
   c. overlearning
   d. the training effect
20. Perkins and Weyant found that maze running performance suffered when rats ran a maze that differed from the one used in training. This suggests that remembering involves _____
 * a. generalization (405)
   b. extinction
   c. reinforcement
   d. shaping
21. Performance sometimes improves following a retention interval, a phenomenon known as_____
   a. facilitation
   b. enhancement
   c. recovery
 * d. reminiscence (406)
22. Loftus found that eyewitness reports are influenced by the words used to ask about the event. In one experiment, she found that use of the word "smashed" produced higher estimates of car speed than use of the word_____
   a. struck
   b. banged
   c. crashed
 * d. hit (410)
23. The "man who couldn't forget" was studied by_____
   a. Freud
 * b. Luria (419)
   c. Ebbinghaus
   d. Underwood
24. A system for learning with flash cards is known by the acronym_____
   a. FLASH
   b. SPDLN
 * c. SAFMEDS (413)
   d. IDANO
25. One mnemonic system is called_____
   a. luria
   b. raptor
   c. FLASH
 * d. peg-word (416)
26. According to the author of your text, the history of memory has been a story of _____.
 * a. metaphors (389)
   b. anagrams
   c. experiments
   d. scientific analysis

185

27. John Donahoe and David Marrs trained a pigeon in a discrimination task. They found that the bird discriminated correctly after a retention interval of _____.
   a. 6 months
   b. 2 years
   c. 8 years
 * d. 12 years (392)

28. According to the author of your text, the popular belief that experiences are permanently stored in the brain is due largely to the influence of _____.
   a. E. L. Thorndike and B. F. Skinner
   b. John Watson and Rosalie Rayner
 * c. Sigmund Freud and Wilder Penfield (394)
   d. Hermann Ebbinghaus and Sigmund Freud

29. When measuring forgetting using the extinction method, the behavior studied is _____
   a. put on extinction before the retention interval
 * b. put on extinction after the retention interval (395)
   c. alternately extinguished and retrained
   d. completely extinguished before training begins

30. In _____ learning, two stimuli, A and B, are presented, and the task is then to recall B when presented with A.
   a. AB
   b. ABA
 * c. paired associate (401)
   d. conjoined stimulus

31. Sir Frederick Barlett's classic study of forgetting used the story, _____.
   a. The Tortoise and the Hare
 * b. The War of the Ghosts (402)
   c. The Man in the Gray Flannel Suit
   d. Lassie Come Home

32. When forgetting occurs because the environment during recall is different from the environment during training, it is said to be _____.
 * a. cue-dependent (405)
   b. environment triggered
   c. stimulus triggered
   d. venue triggered

33. According to your author, the role of environmental cues in forgetting can be likened to

   _____.
 * a. stimulus control (405, n11)
   b. gradient degradation
   c. peak shift
   d. resistance training

34. The names of the Great Lakes can be recalled with help of the acronym, _____.
   a. HURON
 * b. HOMES (414)
   c. HOUSE
   d. MOUSE

35. Imagination inflation is probably an example of _____
   a. overlearning
   b. cue-dependent forgetting
 * c. retroactive interference (404)
   d. proactive interference

36. The name Benton Underwood is associated with paired associate learning. T (404)
37. The "savings method" is one way of measuring forgetting. T (393)
38. The length of the retention interval is unrelated to the degree of forgetting. F (397)
39. The Jenkins and Dallenback study of forgetting after sleep suggests that forgetting is a function of learning. T (403)
40. Marjory memorized her part in the school play thoroughly in her apartment, but found that she couldn't remember her lines at rehearsal. Her trouble is consistent with the effects of context cues. T (405)
41. The degree of confidence a person has in a recollection is an excellent measure of its accuracy. F (398, n7)
42. Merely imagining an event sometimes convinces people the event took place, a phenomenon called imagination inflation. T (404, n10)
43. Forgetting is a deterioration in learned performance following a period without practice. T (390)

Completion

44. The period between the end of training and the test for forgetting is called the retention interval. (392)
45. When performance varies with an organism's physiological state, it is said to be state-dependent. (407)
46. When the task is to identify stimuli to which the subject was exposed earlier, the measure of forgetting used is called recognition. (393)
46. Bob is introduced to Matilda at a party. A few minutes later he is introduced to Harriet. When he meets Matilda again, he can't recall her name. This is most likely an example of retroactive interference. (404)
48. Studies of interference often involve learning pairs of words. This procedure is called paired_associate learning. (401)

Short essay

49. What did Harry Bahrick's study of Spanish reveal about the relationship between learning and forgetting? (399f)

    It showed that the greater the degree of original learning (e.g., the better Spanish was learned), the less forgetting there was years later.

50. Compare extinction and forgetting. (390)

    Answers should note that both involve a reduction in the rate of a response, and they should identify the differences in procedures.

51. Some people say that what happened in Nazi Germany in the 1930s and 1940s could never happen here. What have you learned about forgetting that would make you doubt the truth of this statement? (inferred)

    Forgetting implies repetition of past errors, and people do forget. Perhaps another point to be made is that we cannot forget what we have not learned. If we have not learned tolerance, we may behave as abominably toward minority groups as the Nazis did.

52. Describe Krueger's study of overlearning and its findings. (398f)

The key points are that subjects learned lists of words to three different criteria (zero overlearning, 50% overlearning overlearning, and 100% overlearning), and that they forgot less following overlearning.

53. What did Bartlett's *War of the Ghosts* study reveal about forgetting? (402)

It showed that people tended to recall the story in a way that was more meaningful to them, thus demonstrating the influence of previous learning.

Chapter 12: The Limits of Learning

<u>Multiple Choice</u>

1. Armadillos curl up into a ball when attacked. Reginald teaches an armadillo to curl up into a ball when a buzzer sounds. Reginald is making use of the phenomenon known as _____
   a. intelligence
   b. critical periods
   c. overadaptability
   * d. preparedness (439)

2. The psychologist who mistakenly believed that learned behavior could be inherited was _____
   a. McArthur
   b. McConnell
   * c. McDougall (429)
   d. McEdwards

3. Robert Tryon's work demonstrates the role of heredity in _____
   * a. maze learning (430)
   b. preparedness
   c. critical periods
   d. contingency traps

4. Sign tracking is also called _____.
   a. sign monitoring
   b. autotracking
   * c. autoshaping (439, n3)
   d. autotrack

5. While walking in the woods, Larry happens to stumble across a nest of turkey eggs just as they are hatching. Larry watches the chicks as they emerge from their eggs and begin walking about. As he leaves the nest area, Larry finds the young birds are determined to go with him. Larry's new friends are victims of _____
   a. instinctive drift
   * b. imprinting (434)
   c. the nonhereditability of learning
   d. low intelligence

6. John has difficulty training a raccoon to pick up coins and put them in a bank. It is most likely that _____
   a. the raccoon lacks the intelligence to learn this task
   * b. the raccoon was contraprepared to learn this task (439)
   c. this task had to be learned during a critical period
   d. raccoons lack the ability for insightful problem solving

7. Skinner's efforts to teach pigeons to play ping pong demonstrate that the inability to learn a skill may sometimes be overcome by_____
   * a. making allowances for physical limitations (427)
   b. breaking the task into small parts
   c. lots of patient training
   d. surgical procedures

8. Efforts to teach chimpanzees to talk probably failed because_____
   a. the researchers did not use the proper reinforcement procedures
   b. chimps have their own language which they would not give up
   c. the researchers did not begin instruction when the chimps were very young
   * d. chimps lack the biological structures for speech (427)

9. Louise goes to an outdoor rock concert at which she tries pizza for the first time, and listens to a new rock group. During the course of the concert she becomes nauseated. You predict that she will become nauseated the next time she _____
   a. attends an outdoor rock concert
   b. hears the same rock group perform
 * c. eats pizza (438)
   d. eats dinner while listening to music
10. Frances puts a hungry rat into an experimental chamber. Whenever the rat presses a lever, food falls into a tray. In about 30 minutes, the rat is pressing the lever steadily. Frances returns the rat to the training cage for one hour a day every day until the rat produces young. Frances then trains one of this rat's offspring in the same manner as its mother and repeats this procedure for generation after generation. You predict that when the the twelfth generation rat is put into the training cage, it will press the lever steadily in about_____
    a. 7 minutes
    b.10 minutes
    c. 20 minutes
  * d. 30 minutes (429)
11. Identical twins separated at or soon after birth and reared apart typically have _____
  * a. similar IQs (431f)
    b. very different IQs
    c. IQs no more alike than those of unrelated people
    d. unusually low IQs
12. Keller and Marion Breland are known for their article, _____
    a. Prepared to Learn
  * b. The Misbehavior of Organisms (436)
    c. Learning at an Early Age
    d. Animal Farm
13. Kendler, et al. found evidence that phobias _____
    a. are more common among women than men
    b. must be learned early
  * c. have a genetic component (442)
    d. are related to learning ability
14. Learning is of vital importance because so many problems that face society involve_____
  * a. behavior (442f)
    b. heredity
    c. criminal impulses
    d. unconscious motivation
15. The person who suggests that humans may be biologically prepared to learn a language is_____
    a. Harlow
  * b. Lenneberg (440)
    c. Breland
    d. Koelling
16. Harry and Martha Frank found that on barrier problems dogs did not perform as well as _____
  * a. wolves (430f)
    b. coyotes
    c. foxes
    d. otters

190

17. Substances that damage the nervous system are called _____
   a. trace elements
 * b. neurotoxins (432)
   c. CNS inhibitors
   d. cortical blockers
18. "The Ape in Our House" was written by _____
   a. A. Gardner
   b. Kellogg and Kellogg
 * c. C. Hayes (444)
   d. Lemarck
19. Allen and Beatrice Gardner taught a chimpanzee to _____
 * a. use sign language (426)
   b. speak
   c. read and write
   d. communicate with geometric forms
20. In their study of conditioning, Garcia and Koelling paired water with radiation. They found
   that the rats later avoided _____
   a. water with a distinct odor
 * b. water with a distinct taste (438)
   c. water that was bright and noisy
   d. any kind of water

True-false
21. Joseph Wolpe has raised doubts about the idea that people are prepared to acquire certain
   phobias. T (442)
22. Learning does not always mean progress. T (441)
23. An animal that can learn to perform one trick is sure to learn another trick of similar
   complexity. F (436)
24. Fixed action patterns and other innate behavioral tendencies affect the course of learning. T
   (436-442)
25. The tendency to revert to a fixed action pattern is called instinctive drift. T (437)

Completion
26. Researchers have found that organisms differ in their readiness to learn certain tasks. Martin
   Seligman called this tendency the continuum of preparedness. (439)
27. Lorenz was one of the first to study imprinting. (434)
28. When a species is likely to learn a response, we say it is prepared to learn. When it is unlikely
   to learn a response, we say it is contraprepared to learn. (439)
29. The idea that an enriched environment in childhood can produce high intelligence is supported
   by the case of Mill/Stern. (433)
30. Experiments in which young monkeys were reared in isolation from their mothers illustrates
   the importance of critical periods for social development. (435)

31. A man who had been stricken by polio as a child spent years in an institution for the mentally retarded even though he was quite bright. Explain how his intelligence could have been misjudged. (426f)

Intelligence is measured by the way people act on the environment. Casual judgments of intelligence are based on social interactions, especially the person's use of language. Intelligence tests usually require the person to speak, manipulate objects, and write. People with physical limitations are at a disadvantage when their intelligence is being evaluated, since their ability to act on the environment is limited.

32. Suppose learning were passed on from generation to generation. How would your relationship with your parents be different? (428–430)

Answers will vary greatly. Students might note that children would know many personal things about their parents and this might undermine parental authority, or it might bring parents and children closer together.

33. Design an experiment that would determine whether there are genetic differences in the learning abilities of men and women. (430f)

This is review question 5. As noted there, this is a difficult task. Students might suggest identifying who have been reared by androgynous parental figures. This experiment could be improved on by using fraternal twins different in sex. Learning abilities would then be tested when the children reached adulthood.

34. How might preparedness to learn be nonadaptive? (436–442)

This is review question 6. Answers should make the point that preparedness to learn is adaptive only if the behavior involved is adaptive. Humans may be prepared to learn to fear and hate people who differ from themselves. Such xenophobia could have been adaptive in prehistoric times, when an entire clan might be wiped out by disease or assault if they were too eager to take in strangers. In today's international market place, the tendency to be mistrustful of outsiders may be counterproductive.

35. Does learning inevitably mean progress? Why or why not? (inferred, but see the box on p. 441)

Students might argue that since learning is an adaptive mechanism, anything one learns must have some adaptive value, at least in the short run. Most students will probably take the view (suggested in the box on p. 441) that we can learn to behave in ways that are destructive to society and ourselves.

References

Alloway, T., Wilson, G., Graham, J., & Krames, L. (2000). *Sniffy the virtual rat: Pro version.* Belmont, CA: Wadsworth.

Barry, D. (1992, February 19). What commercials would look like if they were realistic. *The Statesman*, pp.4-5.

Blakeslee, S. (2002, February 19). Highjacking the brain circuits. NYTimes.com.

Burch, M., & Bailey, J. (2000, October). Ethics for Animal Trainers. Animaltrainermagazine.com/article4.htm.

Chance, P. (2003). *Learning and behavior* (5th ed). Belmont, CA: Wadsworth.

Chance, P. (1998). *First course in applied behavior analysis.* Pacific Grove, CA: Brooks/Cole.

Chance, P. (1997, March). Speaking of differences. *Phi Delta Kappan*, pp. 506-507.

Chance, P. (1992, November). The rewards of learning. *Phi Delta Kappan*, pp. 200-207.

Cooley, C. H. (1902). *Human nature and the social order.* New York: Scribner's.

Cooper, L. A., & Shepard, R. N. (1973). Chronometric studies of the rotation of mental images. In W. G. Chase (Ed.), *Visual information processing.* New York: Academic.

Cronk, L. (1992, January/February). Old dogs, old tricks. *The Sciences*, pp.13-15.

Dawkins, R. (1987). *The blind watchmaker.* New York: Norton.

Epstein, R., Kirshnit, C., Lanza, R., & Rubin, L. (1984). Insight in the pigeon: Antecedents and determinants of an intelligent performance. *Nature*, 308, 61-62.

Eysenck, H. J. (1965). *Fact and fiction in psychology.* Baltimore: Penquin.

Fancher, R. (1992, March/April). (Letter to the Editor). *The Sciences*, p.4.

Friedman, S. (2000, May). The help at hand. *Psitta Scene*, 8-9.

Goldberg, S. G., & Cheney, C. D. (1984). Effects of chronic shock on cooperation: A potential model of learned chronic pain behavior. *Psychological Reports*, 55, 899-906.

Greenspoon, J. & Ranyard, R. (1957). Stimulus conditions and retroactive inhibition. *Journal of Experimental Psychology*, 53, 55-59.

Hart, B., & Risley, T. R. (1995). *Meaningful differences in the everyday experience of young American children.* Baltimore: Paul Brookes.

Johnson, K. R. & Layng, T. V. J. (1992). Breaking the structuralist barrier: Literacy and numeracy with fluency. *American Psychologist*, 47, 1475-1490.

King, J. (2002). *Hate Crime: The Story of a Dragging in Jasper, Texas.* New York: Pantheon.

Lanza, R. P., Starr, J., & Skinner, B. F. (1982). "Lying" in the pigeon. *Journal of the Experimental Analysis of Behavior*, 38, 201-203.

Markowitz, H. (1982). *Behavioral enrichment in the zoo.* New York: Van Nostrand Reinhold.

McIntire, R. W. (1973, October). Parenthood training or mandatory birth control: Take your choice. *Psychology Today*, p.34.

Newberg, A., D'Aquili, E., & Rause, V. (2001). *Why God won't go away: Science and the biology of belief.* New York: Ballantine.

Noonan, P. (1990). *What I saw at the revolution: A political life in the Reagan era.* New York: Random House.

Papini, M. R. & Bitterman, M. E. (1990). The role of contingency in classical conditioning. *Psychological Review*, 97, 396-403.

Pavlov, I. (1927). *Conditioned reflexes.* (G. V. Anrep, Ed. and Trans.). London: Oxford University Press.

Phelps, B. J., & Reit, D. J. (1997). The steepening of generalization gradients from "mentally rotated" stimuli. Paper presented at he 23rd annual convention of the Association for Behavior Analysis, Chicago, IL.

Pryor, K. (1999). *Don't shoot the dog: The new art of teaching and training* (2nd. ed.). New York: Bantam.

193

Pryor, K. , Haag, R., & O'Reilly, J. (1969). The creative porpoise: Training for novel behvior. *Journal of the Experimental Analysis of Behavior*, 12, 653-661.

Rachlin, H. (1976). *Behavior and learning*. San Francisco: Freeman.

Reit, D. J., & Phelps, B. J. (1996). *Mental rotation reconceptualized as stimulus generalization*. Paper presented at the 22nd annual convention of the Association for Behavior Analysis, San Francisco, CA.

Seligman, M. E. P. (1991). *Learned optimism*. New York: Knopf.

Shermer, M. (2001, December). God on the Brain. *Psychology Today*, pp. 72-73.

Skinner, B. F. (1951). How to teach animals. *Scientific American*, 185, 26-29.

Thompson, R. F. (2000). Habituation. In A. E. Kazdin (Ed.), *Encyclopedia of Psychology* (pp. 47-50). New York: Oxford University Press.

Thompson, T. M. (undated). How to train an elephant to ride a tricycle.Animaltrainermagazine.com/article2.htm.

Thorndike, E. L. (1898). Animal intelligence. *Psychological Review Monographs*, 2(8).

Thorndike, E. L. (1911). *Animal intelligence: Experimental studies*. New York: Hafner.

Van Buren, A. (1995, March 15). Good behavior must be taught early, *The* (Wilmington, DE) *News Journal*, p. D4.

Appendix

* Figures are intended for use as transparencies. Numbers in parentheses indicate most relevant chapters in *L&B*.

Key Words

The key words below, arranged by chapter, should prove useful in finding information on InfoTrac.

In using InfoTrac, you have the option of searching by Subject Guide or Key Words. Often the two searches yield very similar results. However, if there are many related items, subject searches will provide subcategories, whereas key word searches give you a list of articles. Subject search categories are very useful when there are many articles on a topic. For example, when I searched key words for *operant conditioning*, I got 75 items; when I searched subjects, I got 73 items in 16 categories, including moral and ethical aspects (one article), therapeutic use (two articles), and research (36 articles). Subject searching is also helpful when a word has several distinct meanings. For example, the word *reinforcement* is used in very different ways in the context of behavior research, engineering, and the military. Do a key word search and you will have to sift through the irrelevant articles for those of interest; do a subject search and they will be organized according to their different uses. Thus, subject searching is an easy way to narrow your search and eliminate many irrelevant items. The advantage of key word searching is that it takes you directly to the article or articles. If you choose your terms carefully and narrow your search, this can save you time.

Many key words are possible besides those listed here, but obvious terms are not always effective. The word *forgetting*, for instance, produced little, but *memory* proved fruitful; *fixed action patterns* turned up nothing, but *instincts* got results. I have listed only those terms that yielded either many articles or a few articles that I thought might be particularly useful to students or instructors.

1. Introduction: Learning to Change
   evolution
   evolution and religion
   evolution and the Bible
   genes and behavior
   mutations
   natural selection

2. The Study of Learning and Behavior
   animal rights
   learning and measurement
   operational definitions

3. Pavlovian Conditioning
   classical conditioning
   classical conditioning and awareness
   Ivan Pavlov
   Pavlovian conditioning

4. Pavlovian Applications
   aversion therapy
   conditioned taste aversion
   prejudice and learning
   virtual reality therapy

5. Operant Reinforcement
       operant behavior
       operant conditioning
       reinforcement
       reinforcer

6. Operant Punishment
       problems with punishment
       punishment
       punishment alternatives

7. Operant Applications
       animals, training of
       learned helplessness
       learned industriousness
       problem solving
       rewards and punishment in education
       self-destructive behavior
       self-perception

8. Vicarious Learning
       imitation
       observational learning

9. Generalization, Discrimination, and Stimulus Control
       discrimination learning
       discrimination training
       stimulus control
       stimulus generalization

10. Schedules of Reinforcement
       choice
       compulsive gambling
       experimental economics
       extinction
       malingering
       partial reinforcement effect
       reinforcement schedules

11. Forgetting
       eyewitness testimony
       memory
       mnemonics
       state-dependent learning

12. The Limits of Learning
       critical periods
       heredity
       instinct and learning
       learning ability
       neurotoxic agents

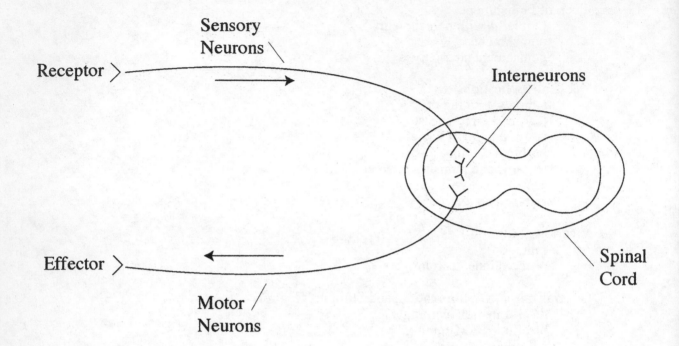

Reflex arc. This schematic shows the "wiring" of a simple reflex: A stimulus contacts receptor tissues(e.g., pain receptors) which transmit electro-chemical impulses to sensory neurons which in turn transmit impulses to the spinal cord. At the spinal cord, impulses travel via interneurons to motor neurons, which transmit impulses to effector tissues (muscles or glands). In the spinal cord, some neurons (not depicted) carry impulses to the brain, where they may or may not result in awareness of the stimulus.

Topographic learning. Figures such as this star can be used in several ways to demonstrate and experience learning. One possibility is to put the figure on an overhead projector and trace within its lines with a laser pointer. This procedure can be modified so that one person attempts to trace the image while blindfolded while another calls out instructions ("Turn right fifteen degrees," "Go straight"). Both exericses will give some appreciation of the role of immediate feedback in learning, but neither produces a record of learning. An alternative is to conceal the figure from view and have a student attempt to trace within its lines while looking at a reflection of the figure in a mirror. If the learner makes several attempts using a clean copy of the image each time and numbering each attempt, he or she will have a clear record of progress.

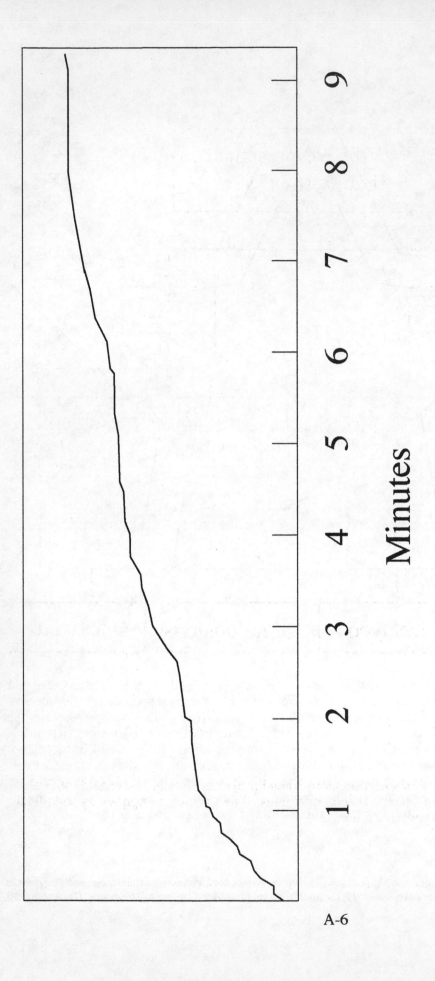

Minutes

Cumulative record. An increase in response rate is reflected in a slope that gets steeper, a decrease in response rate is reflected in a slope that gets shallower, and no responding is reflected in a flat line.

A-6

This material was prepared by Paul Chance and Diane Chance. It may be reproduced for noncommercial classroom use provided this credit line appears on all copies. Any other use of this material is strictly prohibited. Copyright © Wadsworth Publishing, 2003.

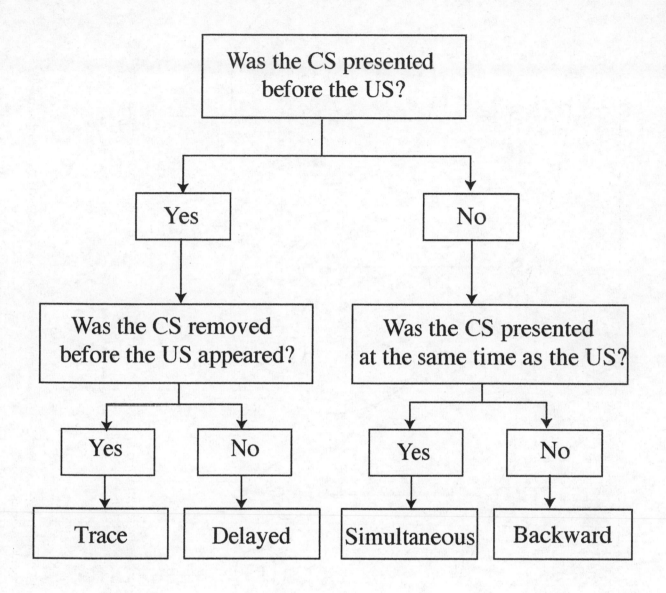

Pavlovian flowchart. Use this flowchart on an overhead projector to help students identify the kind of conditioning procedure used in several examples. The examples might be hypothetical or taken from *Learning and Behavior* (5th ed).

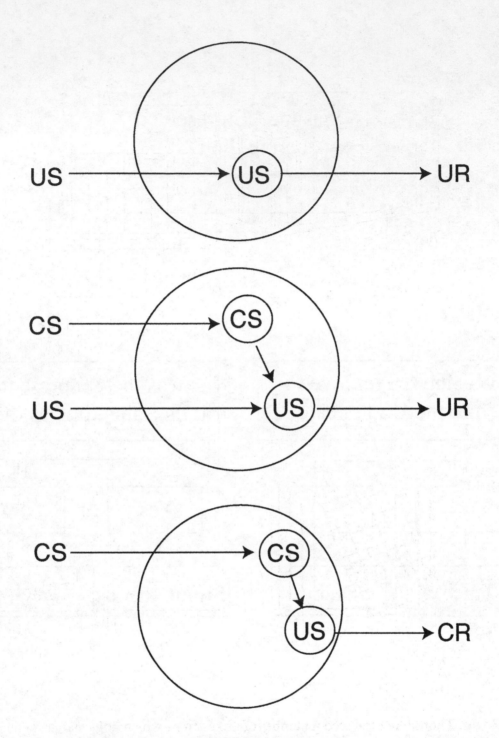

Stimulus substitution theory. Pavlov assumed that the US stimulated a particular part of the brain, and that this triggered the UR. He theorized that pairing the CS and US causes a new connection to form between the CS area and the US area, so that presenting the CS indirectly stimulates the US area of the brain, producing a CR.

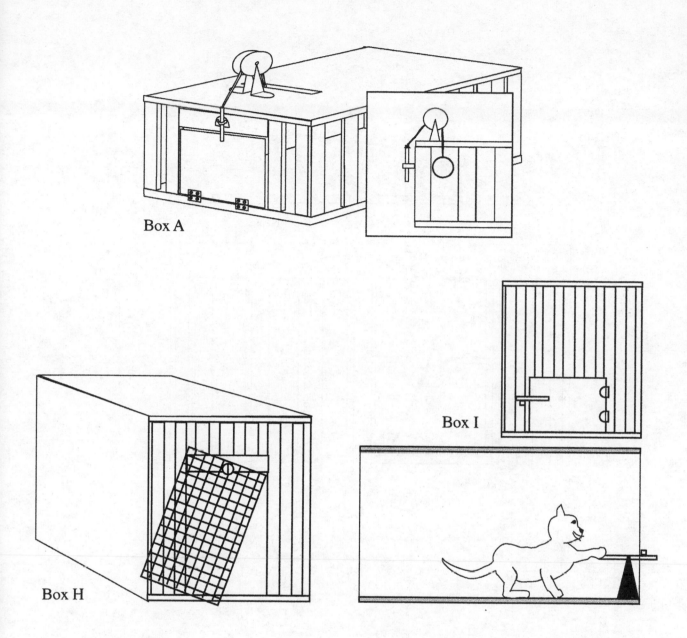

Box A

Box I

Box H

Puzzle Boxes. Thorndike produced a number of boxes from which dogs and cats could escape by acting on some part of their environment. In most cases a simple act would open a door. In A, pulling on a loop released a slide bolt so that a door fell open, allowing the animal to escape and reach food. In H, the door could be pushed to the right or left. In I the door opened when the animal pressed a lever.

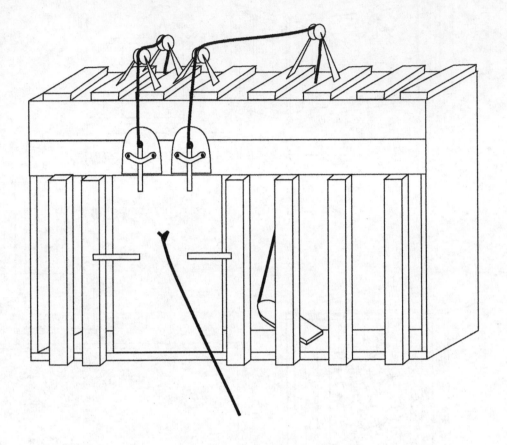

This is box K, the only one Thorndike depicted in his 1898 dissertation. To escape the box and obtain a bit of fish, the cat had to step on a treadle, pull on a string, and push a bar up or down. Progress was slow on box K. Thorndike, (1898).

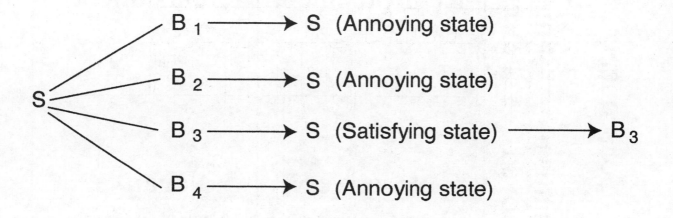

Illustrated Law of effect. Thorndike noticed that an animal in a given situation (S) typically does many things (B1,2,3...), most of which are ineffective. Only those acts that produced a "satisfying state of affairs" persisted.

Strength of Behavior

	Increases	Decreases
Stimulus is Presented	Positive Reinforcement	Positive Punishment
Stimulus is Removed	Negative Reinforcement	Negative Punishment

Consequence

Contingency square. There are four operant procedures; two strengthen behavior, two weaken it.

Strength of Behavior

	Increases	Decreases
Stimulus is Presented	Reward Training	Punishment
Stimulus is Removed	Escape Training	Penalty

Consequence

Contingency square with alternate terms. Operant reinforcement and punishment procedures go by many names. Positive reinforcement is often called reward training (or learning); negative reinforcement is also known as escape training (or learning); positive punishment is often just called punishment; negative punishment sometimes goes by the name penalty training.

Strength of Behavior

	Increases	Decreases
Stimulus is Presented		
Stimulus is Removed		

Consequence

Contingency square practice sheet.

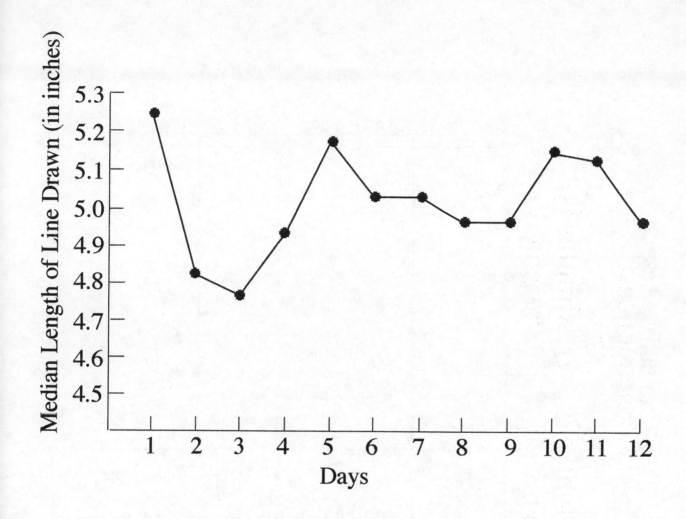

Practice without reinforcement. Thorndike saw no improvement in ability to draw a four-inch line after repeated attempts while blindfolded. Compiled from data in Thorndike, 1931/1968.

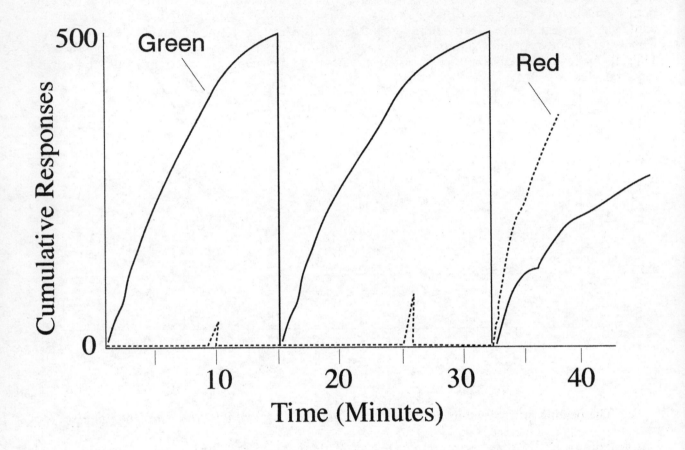

Resurgence. If a bird is trained to peck a green disk and this behavior is then put on extinction, another behavior that had at one time been reinforced (pecking a red disk) will reemerge, a phenomenon called resurgence. Hypothetical data.

The Reflex Arc

A reflex is a relation between a specific event and a simple response to that event. Reflexes are mediated by a relatively simple set of interconnected units called the reflex arc. The familiar patellar reflex, better known as the knee jerk reflex, provides a convenient example.

A sharp blow to the patellar tendon, just beneath the kneecap, causes the foot to swing forward. What happens is this: The blow excites receptors at the tendon. This electrochemical excitation is transferred to nearby sensory neurons (nerve cells) which carry the impulse to the spinal cord, where interneurons are activated. The interneurons carry the impulse to motor neurons, which convey the excitation to muscles in the leg. The muscles contract, pulling the leg forward. Thus, the reflex arc consists of receptors, sensory neurons, interneurons, motor neurons, and effectors (muscles or glands).

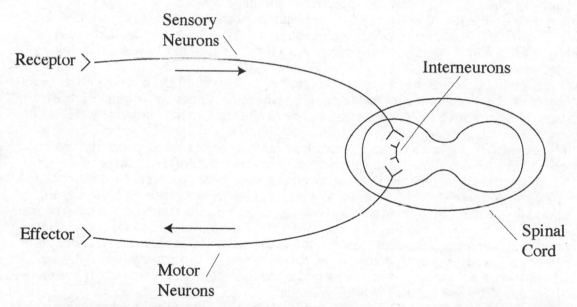

The patellar reflex is an example of a spinal reflex. In spinal reflexes, when the impulse from a stimulus reaches the spinal cord neurons in the cord may carry the signal to the brain, perhaps reaching the cortex and prompting us to look at, listen to, or otherwise attend to the stimulus. At this point we are likely to say that we notice or become aware of the event. Note, however, that in this case the impulse that activates effector tissues does not emanate from the brain, but from the spinal cord. In the patellar reflex, we do not jerk our foot forward *after* realizing that we have been hit; rather, we notice the blow and move our foot at about the same time.

Other reflexes involve higher brain centers. Watching a horror film may raise blood pressure and induce sweating, and reading a bawdy novel may produce erection of the penis in men and mucous secretion of vaginal glands in women. Learning clearly plays an important role in these and similar reflexes, but, as Ivan Pavlov showed, it can also have a powerful effect on simpler reflexes, such as the knee jerk.

Are Rewards Bad?
by Paul Chance

Are rewards bad? Many people think so. The view is especially popular among educators, but many parents and some people in the business world also believe that rewards are detrimental.

The idea has been around for a very long time. It received it's first great impetus from the 18th century French philosopher, Jean-Jaques Rousseau. Rousseau believed that education should be "natural," meaning that the child should explore on his own; any effort by a teacher to reward certain kinds of behavior would, according to Rousseau, interfere with learning.

A. S. Neill established a school based on Rousseau's ideas. At Summerhill, students were their own teachers, and rewards were not allowed. Over the past 40 years Neill's book, *Summerhill*, has been required reading in college education classes, so thousands of today's teachers have been taught that, in Neill's words, "Rewards are superfluous and negative."

In the 1990s, journalist Alfie Kohn joined the battle against rewards with his book, *Punished by Rewards: The Trouble with Gold Stars, Incentive Plans, A's, Praise, and Other Bribes*. As his title suggests, Kohn is opposed to any use of any kind of reward in any setting, including childrearing, education, and business.

The chief complaint against rewards is that they are demotivating. "To offer a prize for doing a deed," wrote Neill, "is tantamount to declaring that the deed is not worth doing for its own sake." In other words, reward a child for reading and he or she is thereafter sure to spend less time reading.

Is the charge true? Do rewards really undermine interest in the rewarded activity? More than a hundred studies have addressed this question (for reviews from different perspectives, see Chance, 1992; Deci and Ryan, 1985; Dickinson, 1989; Eisenberger & Cameron, 1996; Lepper and Greene, 1978). Most of these studies follow a set pattern: (1) participants (usually children) are given the opportunity to participate in an activity without rewards; (2) they are then asked to continue participating in the activity in exchange for a reward; (3) some time later, they are once again given the opportunity to participate in the activity without rewards. The results also typically follow a set pattern: when a reward is promised, there is increased interest in the activity (usually measured in terms of time spent on it), but later, when no reward is available, the participants show less interest in the activity than they had before they were rewarded.

An experiment by Mark Lepper and colleagues (1973) will illustrate. Lepper and his co-workers watched nursery school children play with various toys, including felt tip pens of various colors and paper to draw on. The researchers noted how much the children drew with the pens. After this, the researchers promised some children a "Good Player Award" if they would draw more pictures; the researchers also asked the other children to draw more, but said nothing to them about an award. Two weeks later, the researchers returned to the school, provided the children with felt tip pens and paper, and watched to see how much they drew. They found that children who had received an award spent only half as much time drawing as they had originally. The children who had not worked for an award showed no decline in interest in drawing.

It appears, then, that under certain cirumstances rewarding an activity can undermine interest in that activity. In interpreting this literature, however, two facts must be taken into account: First, most of the studies involve tangible rewards-- things like food, a toy, money. Second, the rewards are held out as incentives; in essence, the experimenter says to the participant, "If you do X, I will give you Y." Thus, the worst that these studies allow us to say about rewards is that *tangible* rewards used *as incentives* can undermine interest in the rewarded activity.

But even tangible rewards used as incentives are not always bad. An example is provided by a study involving high-risk, low-income adolescents and young adults in Lafayette Parish, Louisiana (Hotard & Cortez, 1987). The students were paid $3.40 an hour to participate in a summer program of academic instruction and job training. Students in this program gained an average of 1.2 grade levels in reading and 1.5 grade levels in math in just *eight weeks*. And since these students had little or no interest in reading and math to begin with, there is not much reason to be concerned about rewards undermining their interest in these subjects. (This point has been made even by some critics of reward; see, for example, Greene & Lepper, 1974).

There have been many programs like that in Louisiana Parish, and so far as I know there is not one that has found that at-risk students have become less interested in school or sufferred any other negative consequences as a result of the rewards offered.

But even if tangible incentives always undermined interest in an activity, that would not justify a blanket condemnation of rewards since not all rewards are tangible, and not all rewards are used as incentives.

There is, for example, no evidence that positive feedback about a performance does any harm. Nor are social rewards (e.g., praise, smiles, high fives, and hugs) detrimental when they are provided spontaneously for good work. On the contrary, there is ample research evidence that positive feedback and social rewards can be extremely beneficial. One of the benefits is an *increase* in interest in the rewarded activity. Even the researchers who have been critical of rewards have supported the use of positive feedback and intangible rewards for achievements (Amabile, 1983; Deci and Ryan, 1985; Lepper and Greene, 1978).

Are rewards bad? They can cause problems if used improperly. Any parent or teacher who has promised children a treat if they would stop misbehaving should have learned that. But when rewards are used properly, they can be a powerful motivational and instructional tool. It is quite possible to use rewards effectively without doing harm. Here are a few rules of thumb that will help:

Rewarding Guidelines

1. Whenever possible use intangible rewards. Don't provide a toy if a compliment will do.

2. Whenever possible, avoid using rewards as incentives. Instead of saying, "If you do X, I'll give you Y," wait for the behavior (or for something approximating the behavior) and then provide the reward without having promised it.

3. Reward at a high rate in the early stages of learning, and gradually reduce the frequency of rewards as learning progresses.

4. Reward only behavior that you want repeated. If you don't want a child to whine and complain, don't provide rewards to quiet her when she whines and complains.

5. Remember that what is an effective reward for one person may not be effective for another. Praise, recognition, approval, status, awards, and free time are usually rewarding, but not everyone marches to the same drummer.

6. Reward success, and set standards so that success is achieveable.

7. Bring attention to the intrinsic rewards the activity itself offers. Point out, for eample, the fun to be had from word play in poetry, or the fun of discovering something from a hands-on experiment.

References

Amabile, T. (1983). *The social psychology of creativity*. New York: Springer-Verlag.
Chance, P. (1992, November). The rewards of learning. *Phi Delta Kappan*, 200-207.
Deci, E. L., & Ryan, Rm M. (1985). *Intrinsic motivation and self-determination in human behavior*. New York: Plenum.

Dickinson, A. M. (1989). The detrimental effects of extrinsic reinforcement on 'inrinsic motivation.' *The Behavior Analyst*, 12, 1-15.

Eisenberger, R., & Cameron, J. (1996). Detrimental effects of reward: Reality or myth? *American Psychologist*, 51, 115-166.

Eisenberger, R., & Cameron, J. (1998). Reward, intrinsic interest, and creativity: New findings. *American Psychologist*, 53, 676-679.

Greene, D., & Lepper, M. R. (1974, September). Intrinsic motivation: How to turn play into work. *Psychology Today*, pp. 49-54

Hotard, S. & Cortez, M. J. (1987, August). *Evaluation of Lafayette Parish Job Training Summer Remedial Program: Report presented to the Lafayette Parish School Board and Lafayette Parish Job Training Department of Lafayette Parish government.*

Kohn, A. (1993). *Punished by rewards: The trouble with gold stars, incentive plans, A's, praise, and other bribes.* Boston, MA: Houghton-Mifflin.

Lepper, M. R., & Greene, D. (Eds.) (1978). *The hidden costs of reward: New perspectives on the psychology of human motivation.* Hillsdale, NJ: Erlbaum.

Lepper, M. R., Greene, D., & Nisbett, R. E. (1973). Undermining children's intrinsic interest with extrinsic rewards. *Journal of Personality and Social Psychology*, 28, 129-137.

Neill, A. S. (1960/1985). *Summerhill: A radical approach to child rearing.* New York: Pocket Books.

Rousseau, J.-J. (1762/1979) Emile: or on education. (Allan Bloom, trans.) New York: Basic.

Is Punishment Therapeutic?

Aristotle said that punishment is a kind of medicine. Punishment, including slaps, shocks, and other forms of physical punishment, is sometimes used in the treatment of behavior problems, especially self-injury and violence. Is punishment a legitimate form of therapy?

The fact that punishment may cause discomfort should not, in itself, exclude it from consideration. After all, who has not felt discomfort at the hands of a dentist? Many common medical procedures, including surgery, radiation, and chemotherapy, cause considerable discomfort, but no one denies that they are legitimate forms of therapy.

Even so, the therapeutic use of punishment, especially physical punishment, is controversial. Some people who would not hesitate to have a dentist perform a root canal to save a child's tooth would not dream of letting a therapist slap that child's buttock to stop self-injurious behavior. Many of these people believe that "therapeutic punishment" is an oxymoron and should be outlawed. Other people feel just as strongly that banning punishment would deprive some people of the most effective treatment available.

Professional therapists are also divided on the use of punishment (Jacobson, 1989). Therapists generally agree, however, that if physical punishment is used, it should be only under certain conditions:

> When the behavior to be controlled poses a risk to the client or others or
>   materially interferes with the client's rehabilitation
> When other, less aversive procedures have failed to control the problem
> When administered by competent staff
> When the results of its use are carefully monitored
> When the client or responsible adult has given written consent

Adherence to such guidelines may prevent abuse, but it does little to quiet the debate over therapeutic punishment. That debate tends to become overrun with emotion, with opponents of punishment accusing advocates of being sadistic, and advocates accusing opponents of killing with kindness.

There is no question that the proper use of punishment can alleviate suffering. The real question is whether it is ever justified. In answering that question, our goal should be to put the rancor aside and consider what is in the best interest of the individual who needs help.

Learning to See Again

One day a normal, healthy 14-year-old girl choked on some candy, and suddenly she was neither normal nor healthy. Because of the incident, she suffered brain damage that slowed her learning, interfered with her speech, and made it impossible for her to walk. It also left her blind.

Learning principles have proved remarkably useful in the rehabilitation of people suffering from brain damage (Chance, 1986), but could such principles help a person regain her sight? Kay Merrill and Donald Kewman (1986) think so.

Their client was not wholly blind. Her eyes reacted to light, and she could correctly identify the color of notebook-sized objects such as her hospital chart cover. But she was unable to point to the features of a person's face and did not react normally when an object was thrust toward her eyes. Thus, though she had some sensitivity to light, she was for all practical purposes blind.

Merrill and Kewman decided to try to improve her sight by reinforcing appropriate responses to visual stimuli. The training procedure was fairly complicated, but basically involved asking the girl to identify objects of various shapes and colors. After each attempt, the therapists told her whether she answered correctly. Under such circumstances, positive feedback is typically a powerful reinforcer. The result was that she began to improve. As she did so, Merrill and Kewman gave her increasingly difficult tasks.

After two years of training, which included rehabilitation of intellectual and motor deficiencies as well as blindness, she returned to school. Amazingly, she was able to see well enough that she did not require special visual aids. The researchers admit that some recovery of vision would likely have occurred even if the girl had received no special training. But they also believe that, to some extent at least, their patient actually learned to see again.

A Lesson in Crime from D. B. Cooper

On Wednesday, December 1, 1971, a passenger on Northwest Airlines flight 305 handed a stewardess a note demanding that the airline give him $200,000. Then he opened his briefcase and revealed what looked very much like a bomb.

The passenger, registered under the name D. B. Cooper, had thought things out carefully: The airline would have the cash, and four parachutes, ready when the plane touched down at Seattle-Tacoma International Airport in Washington, or the airline would lose one Boeing 727, 36 passengers, and a crew. The airline came up with the money and the parachutes. Cooper let everyone deplane in Tacoma except the cockpit crew and one stewardess; then he ordered the pilot to head for Mexico. Once aloft, however, Cooper made his escape 10,000 feet above the forested countryside of southwestern Washington. He was never captured, and is now presumed to have died while making his escape.

Naturally, Cooper's very clever crime got a lot of coverage in the news media, so much so that anyone who cared to follow his lead had access to all the pertinent details. And follow his lead they did. Albert Bandura (1973) later wrote that ``within the next few months . . . a number of hijackers, emboldened by the successful example, copied the specific tactics, including threats of bombing unless passengers were exchanged for ransom money and parachutes'' (p. 107).

This incident demonstrates very nicely the role vicarious learning can play in crime. It also raises two intriguing questions: If people were not so adept at learning from models, would crime cease to be an important social problem? And if so, would we gain more than we would lose?

Questions like these are not easily answered. Except, perhaps, by D. B. Cooper.

Sniffy the Virtual Rat

The following manual is designed to assist instructors in using *the Sniffy the Virtual Rat™, Pro Version* (henceforth referred to as "Sniffy Pro" or simply "Sniffy") software package in psychology courses at the university and college level.

In writing this manual I have drawn on my experiences with Sniffy as a pedagogical tool in second and third year psychology courses I have taught at the University of Alberta. However, I recognize that conditions at other universities and colleges may make some of the ideas provided here unfeasible, or may suggest entirely new uses for the Sniffy material. I encourage instructors to modify the information provided herein to suit their particular needs.

For ease of use I have divided the manual into the following sections:

There are a number of pros and cons to using any information technology in teaching, and Sniffy Pro is no exception. In the "Why use Sniffy Pro?" section I describe the advantages of Sniffy, but also comment on some of its drawbacks. In particular, Sniffy Pro can never take the place of a laboratory course in which students work with live animals. Nevertheless, Sniffy does provide students with a valuable understanding of the underlying elements of conditioning protocols which can be applied to other situations. Sniffy uses an operant chamber environment to explore issues of both operant and classical conditioning. As a result, the Sniffy Pro text covers operant conditioning before classical conditioning. In "The Order of Sniffy Pro" section I address some of the consequences of this. The third section of this manual, "Sniffy Assignments and the Nature of the Course," discusses ways to fit Sniffy into your course format. Psychology courses take a variety of forms, from small discussion-based classes to giant lectures with hundreds of students; Sniffy can be integrated into almost any course, although the material should be used differently for different course levels and sizes. The next two sections cover some of the more common technical difficulties and problems that students experience when using the Sniffy software with the aim of avoiding problems before they begin. The "Assignments" section is by far the largest portion of this manual. In it you will find a series of additional questions which you can assign to your students. A marking key follows the questions. Although the questions are structured around the 40 exercises provided in the Sniffy Pro text, instructors should feel free either to use them as they are, or to modify them to suit their particular needs.

Sniffy Pro is a useful pedagogical tool, but it must be carefully tailored to a course to be most effective. Hopefully this manual will help first-time users, as well those who are already familiar with Sniffy, in getting the most value out of the Sniffy materials.

Dr. Michael R. Snyder
Department of Psychology
University of Alberta

Why Use Sniffy Pro?

The Sniffy Pro software package is a useful and powerful pedagogical tool in the teaching of university level psychology courses in the fields of learning, conditioning, and behaviour. In 1949 Beach could criticize the overemphasis on the white laboratory rat in psychology courses; today, due to growing class sizes and budgetary cutbacks, psychology students are fortunate if they receive any hands-on exposure to conditioning paradigms. Sniffy offers psychology instructors a means of training their students in the basics of laboratory research methodology with the Sprague-Dawley rat. More generally, the skills, techniques, and theoretical issues explored in the Sniffy Pro software are easily applicable to other areas of the behavioural sciences, both under laboratory and "real-world" conditions.

If you are fortunate enough to be an instructor at a university or college that offers live animal laboratories, Sniffy Pro can still be useful in precursor courses, to give students some preliminary experience with shaping and conditioning techniques. Although the Sniffy Pro simulations are, obviously, somewhat restricted in the types of techniques used, the general principles are more than sufficient to offer students a significant increase in their knowledge and appreciation of traditional operant chamber methodological techniques. Previous experience with Sniffy will allow students in live-animal courses to devote more time to the hands-on work with animals rather than focusing on the basic methodological techniques of shaping and conditioning.

The Sniffy Pro text is also helpful in offering alternative explanations for topics covered in many learning and behaviour courses. Instructors can direct students to work through relevant sections of the Sniffy exercises or to read the explanatory material in the Sniffy text to increase understanding of specific topics. For example, Sniffy is an excellent resource for giving students first-hand exposure to conditioned emotional response (and the related suppression ratio) and peak shift, two topics with which students often have difficulty. Additionally, the Sniffy material offers instructors opportunities to direct students to significant primary sources from the field of learning and behaviour, such as Estes & Skinner (1941), Honig, Boneau, Burstein, & Pennypacker (1963), and Rizley & Rescorla (1972). Instructors can easily assign these (and other) articles to be read in conjunction with the appropriate Sniffy exercises, thereby increasing students' exposure to groundbreaking research in the field.

Obviously, there are differences between a simulation of a rat and a live rat. Besides those already alluded to, here are a few more. First, unlike live rats, Sniffy does not bite, defecate, or escape from his cage. One can argue that this does not provide students with the "full experience" of working with live animals. On the other hand, it has been my personal experience that there are a number of students who experience mild to strong phobic reactions when confronted with a live rat. The animated nature of Sniffy does not appear to elicit this fearful response. When you also consider concerns over allergies and the possibility of tetanus shots and stitches due to rat bites, the Sniffy software looks very appealing.

Unfortunately, students do not learn a sense of responsibility for the care and maintenance of laboratory animals when working with Sniffy. Such experience is, arguably, one of the more valuable aspects of having students work with live animals. Given public concerns with the treatment of experimental animals, making students responsible for the well-being of a laboratory animal is an excellent way of instilling in them knowledge of the ethical treatment of research animals.

Although most students do not become as bonded to Sniffy as they do to live rats, a minority of students do become quite fond of their synthetic rat and, as with the Tamagotchi craze (the small, Japanese produced, "virtual pets" which owners had to feed, exercise, and play with to keep "alive") of a few years ago, become quite affected when Sniffy eventually "dies." This is a point that is not made clear in the Sniffy Pro text. On page 29 the text notes that "...there is a maximum of 10 Cumulative Record windows.... After that program time limit has been reached, you can examine and save your results; but you cannot add any additional stages to that particular Sniffy Pro file." Regrettably, the text neglects to explain that Sniffy appears to die when the end of the tenth Cumulative Record is reached. Sniffy lies down and curls up, apparently as if asleep, and a text box appears with a comment to the effect that the simulation, like the rat, has reached its end. I know of one instructor who used Sniffy with an introductory class and received frantic phone calls from distraught students who desperately wanted to bring their rat back to life, disturbed by the possibility that something terrible they had done had caused Sniffy's demise. While this did afford the instructor an interesting lead-in to the topic of grief counseling, you may wish to warn the students in advance that the simulation has a limited "life expectancy."

Another difference between Sniffy and live rats is the issue of variability in behavioural response. As anyone who has worked with Sprague-Dawley rats can attest, individual animals can be quite different in their behavioural repertoire, learning rates, and food and response preferences. While the software does use a randomization function in the selection of Sniffy's behaviours, individual copies of Sniffy will perform fairly similarly. There are, of course, exceptions. For some exercises, particularly in chapter 5, a minority of students will get results quite different from those of their classmates. From a learning perspective this is not a problem. In fact, I would argue that this is actually a beneficial feature of Sniffy, demonstrating to students the variable nature of working with animals. However, it can raise some difficulties in producing marking keys if you have students turn in Sniffy exercises for grades. The best solution I have found is to structure assignments in such a way that students have an opportunity to comment on or explain their results. The assignment section later in this manual further addresses this issue.

Finally, as stated earlier, while Sniffy's behavioural repertoire is fairly representative of a rat in an operant chamber, it does lack the greater behavioural range seen in live animals. The most significant result of this is the software's reliance on the Conditioned Emotional Response (CER) as a means of demonstrating classical conditioning. Although the CER is a perfectly acceptable means of studying classical conditioning paradigms, it is probably not the technique most students will be familiar with. Students are generally far more used to the traditional Pavlovian "ring a bell, see the dog salivate" methodology. For a variety of reasons this technique does not work well with rodent subjects. There are other ways of demonstrating classical learning with rodents; Holland (1977), for example, used different food-related behaviours to show that conditioning had occurred. However, given the constraints of the software and the focus on the operant chamber, the Sniffy developers opted to use the CER technique. As will be discussed in the next section, this may result in some problems when trying to use Sniffy in parallel with your course textbook.

The Order of Sniffy Pro

The Sniffy Pro text is somewhat unusual in that it moves from operant conditioning to classical conditioning before finally dealing with habituation and sensitization. Within the context of the Sniffy software this is probably the most logical sequence to follow. Given that Sniffy uses the CER for all of the classical conditioning exercises, it is necessary for the rat to be magazine shaped before any other studies can be conducted. Hence, operant conditioning needs to be dealt with before classical conditioning. In and of itself, there is nothing wrong with this. In fact, one could make a strong argument that this is a more sensible way to teach learning and behaviour, as students are likely most familiar with operant conditioning paradigms from everyday life (e.g., reinforcement and punishment from school or home life, training pets to perform tricks, etc.). However, learning and behaviour textbooks generally follow the reverse sequence: habituation, classical, then operant conditioning. The challenge, therefore, will be for you to work Sniffy into your class material.

If you are using Sniffy for a "second tier" course (i.e., your students have already had one course on learning and behaviour), this may not prove to be especially problematic. With luck your students will remember the basic properties of, and distinctions between, operant and classical conditioning, and can begin working through the Sniffy chapters sequentially while you are teaching material from the course textbook in a different order.

If, on the other hand, you are using Sniffy with a "first tier" (i.e., introductory learning and behaviour) course, your job is going to be somewhat more difficult. Students will have to work through Sniffy material at least somewhat out-of-phase with the material in the course textbook. Although the explanatory content in the Sniffy Pro text does a relatively good job of introducing relevant concepts, instructors should expect to spend additional lecture time introducing basic background material concerning operant conditioning to help students cope with the initial few chapters in Sniffy. By the time students reach the classical conditioning chapters instructors will probably have covered this material in detail. I do recommend, however, that instructors of first tier courses do not have students work through chapter 5 (stimulus discrimination and generalization) until this material has been covered in course lectures. Instructors' confidence in their students' abilities to work through material on their own, the amount of teaching assistant support, and whether or not course lectures are accompanied by seminar or laboratory sessions will guide decisions as to how much lecture time needs to be spent preparing students for the Sniffy material that is out of sequence with the course textbook.

Finally, if you are using Sniffy in a course dedicated to teaching conditioning principles (i.e., a laboratory-style course), the order of Sniffy's assignments is not problematic at all as you will, presumably, be centring the course around the Sniffy exercises, using supplemental readings to support the students' progress through Sniffy.

A related question is how much of the Sniffy content you need to include in your course. With a few minor exceptions, this is almost entirely up to the instructor. Students do need to work through the initial shaping exercises, but beyond this instructors may pick and choose the specific chapters and exercises they want their students to complete. The habituation or peak shift material, for example, can easily be omitted should your course have limited focus on these concepts.

Alternatively, instructors can use Sniffy for demonstration purposes only, in which case the order of the material in the Sniffy text is largely irrelevant. In a classroom equipped with a computer projection system Sniffy can serve a useful function as a means of showing students concrete and real-time examples of cumulative records on different reinforcement schedules, shaping techniques, extinction bursts, etc. The animated nature of Sniffy is typically more interesting to students than a static image in a textbook. Also, the artificial nature of Sniffy guarantees more consistent results than demonstrations with live animals can provide. Just one word of warning: test the Sniffy program on the room's computer projection system before class.

Sniffy Assignments and the Nature of the Course

Sniffy can be used with a wide range of course sizes and types. The central issue is that of motivating students to work through the assigned Sniffy chapters and exercises. This is, of course, the same problem that confronts the assignment of any material in a course. Unless you have a small class in which it is readily apparent who has done the assigned work, or a course of especially dedicated students, you will likely need to assign a portion of your course grading scheme to Sniffy assignments.

How you handle Sniffy assignments will be largely dependent upon three things: the size of your class; whether it is lecture, lecture and laboratory, or laboratory only; and the amount of teaching assistant/grading support available. For example, in the past I have assigned questions 1-28 listed in the "Assignments" section of this manual to a second tier lecture-based course of 160 students with one teaching assistant. However, in retrospect, unless you have a lot of time to devote to marking I do not recommend this.

One solution for large classes (e.g., classes of over 100 students) is to allow students to work in groups on Sniffy assignments. Groups of two or three students seem to work well. The logistics of scheduling meetings if more than three students are in a group sometimes presents problems; there is also the difficulty of arranging more than three students around a computer terminal, but use your own judgement in this matter. If you choose to allow group work on assignments, how you assign students to groups is up to you. You may use a random assignment of students from the class list or allow students to pick their own groups. Any form of group work can lead to problems with interpersonal dynamics. Random assignment may increase incidents of interpersonal friction. On the other hand, allowing students to pick their own groups may result in some students (e.g., those without friends in the course) being left without a group. Alternatively, you may stress the value of group work in terms of individual work reduction, but allow those students who wish to work individually to do so. All options present their own strengths and weaknesses.

Another issue to consider with group work is how assignments are to be graded. Generally, groups should hand in one assignment and all members of the group should receive the same grade. In large classes one of the main advantages of group work is that it reduces the number of assignments that must be marked. Allowing members of groups to turn in individual assignments defeats this advantage. In the event of interpersonal conflict between group members, however, it may be advisable to allow students the option of turning in an individual assignment.

If you are using Sniffy in a course with an assigned laboratory period then you can easily assign Sniffy exercises as weekly laboratory assignments. In this case individual laboratory sections will probably be relatively small (e.g., 30 students or less) and the laboratory assistant can be set the task of grading the weekly assignments. Within laboratory sections group work is relatively common, and this structure can be used to further reduce the marking load.

With smaller classes the time constraints and work load of grading are proportionally reduced. Smaller classes also offer greater potential to use Sniffy as a means of generating class discussion. Students can be instructed to complete Sniffy readings and/or be prepared to offer discussion in class on the assigned sections. To help promote student participation in class discussion some instructors find it useful to break their class up into small groups of five to ten students and allow the groups to debate the topic amongst themselves for a short period of time. Afterwards the groups can be asked to tell the class as a whole their views on the particular questions they were posed with. For example, once students become familiar with the Sniffy software, instructors can ask groups (or individuals) to propose experimental designs to test different research questions.

An alternate approach which may be used to motivate students to work through Sniffy assignments is to organize in-class presentations. Divide students into groups and set the groups a research task (e.g., several Sniffy exercises) using the Sniffy software and have each group present its results to the class. Alternatively, you might organize a class "research conference" in which groups present their research findings either as oral or poster presentations. Instructors can use this approach to teach students the essentials of scientific methodology and the formal presentation of research findings. Similarly, instructors may assign specific research topics based on the Sniffy assignments and require students to turn in a research paper, using APA format, discussing their results. This approach generally works best with smaller classes, due to the time required to mark papers.

Finally, Sniffy assignments could be worked into midterm and final examination questions. Instructors could inform students that one of a selection of questions based on Sniffy exercises will be asked on their examination. Students will have to prepare the Sniffy exercises for the examination. Depending on the nature of the questions you ask, you may also allow students to bring some prepared materials to the examination, such as Cumulative Records, Suppression Ratio graphs, etc., to help them answer the examination questions. If the examination questions are similar to those presented in the "Assignments" section of this manual, the amount of additional work required to grade the written answers should be manageable, even for fairly large classes (e.g., of several hundred students) that are usually dependent on multiple-choice questions. This technique forces students to work through the

Sniffy material, think about the answers to the questions in advance, and complete a written examination question, all for a minimal increase in marking time and effort.

Technical Issues

Despite the best efforts of the Sniffy production team, students may encounter a variety of technical problems when using the software. Many, although not all, of these problems appear to involve software/hardware interaction difficulties. While highly regrettable, given the speed with which new computer hardware (e.g., video cards, graphics accelerators, printers) and software (e.g., updated operating systems, printer drivers) are being produced, it is very difficult to test the Sniffy software fully for compatibility with all computer configurations. From my own experience, I would say that Macintosh users experience fewer difficulties than Windows users, but this is a subjective observation from a limited sample size.

The majority of difficulties appear to involve abnormal screen displays and/or printing problems. I strongly recommend that if you intend to have your students use Sniffy on your laboratory computers that you first test the software/hardware compatibility yourself. If students are going to be using Sniffy on their personal computers (which is more likely), you should stress that they should test the software early on and, if any difficulties arise they should immediately contact Technical Support at 1-800-423-0563. This number is printed on the back of the Sniffy text, although most students fail to notice it; announcing the number in class or putting it on the course syllabus is probably a good idea.

Technical Support has provided the following list of technical questions and answers related to problems most often encountered by users of Sniffy.

Q: My Cumulative Record doesn't print.

A: Sniffy can print information from a variety of windows. For example, you can print the Cumulative Record information, the Suppression Record information, the Mind Wind, etc. In fact, the only window you can't print is the operant chamber window which has Sniffy in it. If you have the operant chamber window active, you don't have any information selected that can be printed, so you will not get a print-out. In fact, the "Print" menu item will be grey, indicating that you don't have any information available for printing in the active window. In order to let the Sniffy program know which information you want printed, you must have the window you want printed "active". To make the window active, simply click on it.

Q: The Cumulative Record is displaying poorly on my machine.

A: There appears to be a conflict with certain high end 3D graphics accelerator boards. Technical Support is working to isolate the problem and to determine if this is a Sniffy problem, a conflict with Windows, or a setup problem. If you have this problem, please call our support line and provide as much information about your system as possible (Technical Support will ask about the type of graphics board in your computer, the amount of memory on the board itself, the version of Windows you are running, and your monitor settings). If you don't know this information, please be near your computer when you call and Technical Support will help you find most of the information required.

As a temporary solution, use the scroll bar to move forward manually on the Cumulative Record. This should stop the display problems until the pen next reaches the right hand side of the record.

Q: I have a cursor animator installed and some of my windows/print-outs are messed up.

A: There appears to be a conflict with Sniffy and some third party novelty software. Technical Support is working to resolve this and suggests you uninstall these novelty programs when running Sniffy.

Q: I have my monitor set to 16 colours and some of the windows are not displaying properly.

A: Try a different setting. Set your screen to 256 colours or higher and see if the problem resolves itself. For help on how to set the depth of your monitor, consult your system operating manual.

Q: I've installed Sniffy on our server and it runs fine when signed onto through the administrator's account, but there are a lot of problems when running the software from a normal user's account.

A: Sniffy is designed to be run from local machines and not servers. You may be able to get around some of these problems by ensuring there is write permission on the Sniffy.ini file. However, installing Sniffy locally is a better approach to correcting this problem.

Q: I installed OS X Public Beta and, when I run Sniffy, the operant chamber window appears messed up after the monitor settings' dialogue appears.

A: Preliminary testing indicates that Sniffy runs better in Classic mode under the release version of OS X. You might want to try upgrading. We are putting the finishing touches on a version of Sniffy which will run "native" on OS X and should have an updater available for download in the summer of 2001. In the meantime, you may be able to work around this if you launch Sniffy and set the Sniffy Preferences (under the File menu) so that "Limit Colours" is unchecked, then quit Sniffy; set your monitor to either 256 or thousands of colours before launching Sniffy the next time.

Student Problems

Despite the fact that many, if not most, students own or have access to personal computers, their actual computer knowledge is generally quite limited. Consequently, if your students encounter a technical problem of the sort discussed in the preceding section, they may be incapable of making the necessary corrections. Unfortunately, there is relatively little you can do about students' lack of computer knowledge. As more software (and hardware) moves towards a "plug-and-play" format it should not be surprising that an increasing number of people lack basic understanding of how their computer's software and hardware actually works. Perhaps the best you can do is to be prepared for such difficulties. Spending an extra bit of time early in the course demonstrating how the Sniffy software should work, how it loads, and ways of fixing some of the more common problems may be well worth it in the long run. If you have a teaching or laboratory assistant in your course, this would be a good task to turn over to him or her; you should (if possible) ensure that your assistant is well versed in the Sniffy software before the course begins so that you can direct your students to the assistant if or when they encounter difficulties.

Another problem students have, and one which is not specific to using the Sniffy software, is that they generally do not read material carefully and often follow instructions poorly. Admittedly, some of the instructions in the Sniffy text are a bit dry; who wants to read when they can play on a computer with a virtual rat? Nonetheless, many problems student might encounter can be avoided if they read the Sniffy instructions. The authors of Sniffy Pro have done quite a good job of providing inclusive and explanatory material to guide the user through the exercises.

Failure to read explanatory material can cause particular problems in understanding the Sniffy graphical display; awareness of the potential for misunderstanding can help both instructor and students when confusion arises. As you will quickly discover upon running the Sniffy software, there are a number of graphs which provide information about Sniffy's behaviour, his rate of learning, and his internal states. The first thing that is important for students to know is that graphs with a light blue background represent inferred mental states; only those graphs with a white background present actual behavioural data. For example, the Cumulative Record and Suppression Ratio graphs depict behavioural data, whereas the Operant Association and Discriminative Stimulus Response Strength graphs represent theoretically-inferred information designed to give the user some sense of Sniffy's internal mental state.

A second problem related to the graphs is that many students never seem to gain an understanding of how the Cumulative Record works. It would be well worth your while to take part of a class to discuss the workings of the Cumulative Record in some detail. To start with, the fact that it is cumulative is often lost on them. Many students fail to grasp the concept that the Cumulative Record (being *cumulative*) never decreases; the only time the line drops is when the top of the "paper" is reached and the pen resets to the bottom. Other key points to stress include the fact that each upwards movement of the cumulative record line represents one response by Sniffy, and that a diagonal tick mark indicates a response that was reinforced. All of this material is covered in some detail on pages 27-30 in the Sniffy Pro text; stress to your students the importance of reading this section. Similarly, students also often lack a basic understanding of the Suppression Ratio graph, depicting the CER. Suppression Ratios and the CER are covered at length on pages 84-87 of the Sniffy text.

The final graph-related problem that I will mention comes from the classical conditioning section of the Sniffy exercises. Pages 87 to 93 of the Sniffy text give detailed instructions on the mechanics of using the classical conditioning experimental design screen. Students should be encouraged to read this section carefully so that they understand how the system works. The most common misunderstandings seem to revolve around the categorization of stages and trials in classical conditioning designs. In Sniffy, classical conditioning studies involve one or more stages with each stage consisting of one or more trial types. On the CS Response Strength and Suppression Ratio graphs, stages are represented by numbers and trial types by letters. For example, the Suppression Ratio graph below shows the results of a two-stage study with two trial types in both. In stage 1 a low intensity shock is paired four times with a medium intensity tone and a high intensity shock is paired four times with a medium intensity light. In stage 2 both the light and tone are presented independently three times to determine the strength of conditioning. Unfortunately, a key is not provided with the graphs to determine whether the A or B refers to the tone or the light. However, it is easy to go back into the Design Classical Conditioning Experiment screen and move through the design to determine which is which. A more extensive example of interpreting this sort of graph is found on pages 94-97 of the Sniffy Pro text.

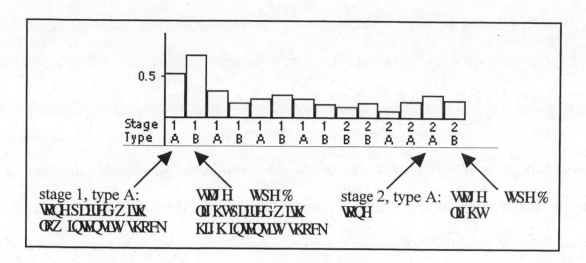

The last common problem that occurs with students is that of time management. If you are using Sniffy as part of a weekly laboratory session, this is probably less of an issue as students will likely have the opportunity to work on exercises during the scheduled laboratory period. However, if you are assigning work outside of class periods students often fail to leave sufficient time to complete the work. A frequent question from students is, "How long will it take to run this exercise?" The answer will depend on the speed of the computers they are using and the speed setting of the Sniffy animation. For example, on a Macintosh G3 Powerbook with Sniffy's animation set to its highest speed, it took 5 minutes to run 10 minutes of Sniffy time. Under accelerated time conditions (i.e., the door is closed on the operant chamber isolating Sniffy), this dropped to 21 seconds for 10 minutes of Sniffy time. If additional software is running in the background, or if Sniffy is running in the background, the times will be longer.

The actual time it takes to run the Sniffy simulation is generally not really the issue. With the exception of the initial shaping exercise and some of the exercises in chapters 5 and 12, most exercises take relatively little time to run. The greater problem is that students fail to allow sufficient time for reading and understanding the textual material and coping with unexpected difficulties, such as computer problems or anomalous behaviour produced by the randomization function of the Sniffy software designed to make the virtual rat appear more life-like. One of the most disappointing aspects of students' lack of time management is that they generally fail to leave time to play around with the software; they tend to be highly goal-oriented, intent on completing the exercises in the shortest amount of time, rather than on using Sniffy as a pedagogical tool to explore issues in learning and conditioning. If you can instill in your students the desire to experiment with the Sniffy software, investigating different conditions and situations not specified in the text's exercises, you will have gone a long way towards exposing them to one of the most exciting and rewarding aspect of the sciences: learning for its own sake.

Assignments

One of the major strengths of the Sniffy Pro package is that it comes equipped with 40 separate exercises for students to work through, either on their own or as class assignments. While instructors can have students work through the chapter exercises exactly as they are laid out in the Sniffy manual, others may wish to tailor the exercises to their class. Fortunately, Sniffy exercises are quite amenable to this sort of modification. At the simplest level, all one need do is alter some of the numbers. For example, in exercise 9 one could simply change the final schedule of reinforcement from VR-50 to VR-75. In other cases more elaborate modifications may be desired. For example, instructors could have students work through an exercise and then combine their data with that of several other students. A comparison could then be made between the individual and grouped data to demonstrate the advantages of increased sample size.

To demonstrate the sorts of questions that instructors can ask their students, I provide a series of questions that I have used successfully as assignments in my own classes. Instructors should feel free to adjust the individual questions to reflect their particular class structure, course content, or teaching style.

The following questions are structured around the chapters in the Sniffy text. In some cases the questions simply ask the students to complete an exercise from the Sniffy text and print out some of the graphs; sometimes the Sniffy material does not lend itself readily to further elaboration. More often, though, additional questions, modifications of exercises, and opportunities for students to comment on topics related to learning and behaviour that go beyond the scope of the Sniffy software are included. Generally, these questions follow the order of those exercises listed in the Sniffy text.

I have also included a set of questions structured around observing Sniffy's behaviour. These questions do not correspond to any of the exercises in the Sniffy text itself, rather it involves students observing Sniffy's behaviour before they have begun any conditioning protocols. Given that there are no specific instructions in the Sniffy text for students to follow, I have provided a much more extensive series of notes and instructions for the observation-based questions. In the following list of assignment questions I have put this material first under its own subheading of "Observational Study". In the marking key that follows the questions, I have provided an example of how behavioural observations can be analyzed using percent agreement scores, time budgets, transition matrixes, and Markov chains.

An answer guide for the rest of the questions is also included. Again, instructors are encouraged to modify the answers to reflect the specifics of their course design and textbook. By cutting and pasting the provided questions, you can easily produce class assignments of varying length and difficulty.

Observational Study

The first part of this assignment focuses on describing Sniffy's behaviour during a 1000-second (16.6 minutes) observation period. This is called a time-based sampling procedure. Although the observation procedure is straightforward, analysis of time-based sampling procedures can be more complex. First of all, there is the issue of reliability of measurement. Are the observations consistent? This can be assessed by looking at whether two observers agree with respect to the behavioural observations. A simple way to measure agreement is to look at the percentage of observations in which two observers classify the behaviour in the same way. This is called an inter-observer reliability score.

Another aspect of the data is the time budget. That is, what percentage of the time does Sniffy spend in different activities? When behavioural observations have been classified into mutually exclusive categories this measure is easy to compute.

At a more complex level, one can ask how different behaviours relate to each other. For example, given that Sniffy is engaged in a bout of behaviour X, how likely is it that he will next do behaviour Y? One way to answer this question is to develop a transition matrix, in which behaviours are examined one at a time and then related to the behaviour in the next time interval. This type of analysis can be used to develop a "Markov chain" that describes behaviours over successive episodes.

Here's what you have to do to complete this part of the assignment. First, start a new Sniffy file. You can follow the instructions on page 18 of the Sniffy text to start the Sniffy program. Next, select "Preferences" from under the "File" menu. When the Preference window appears, set the "Animate Sniffy" option to the slowest position. This will reduce Sniffy's speed of behaviour to a manageable level for this assignment. Click "OK" to return to the Sniffy program.

Here's what you have to do to complete this part of the assignment. First, start a new Sniffy file. You can follow the instructions on page 18 of the Sniffy text to start the Sniffy program. Next, select "Preferences" from under the "File" menu. When the Preference window appears, set the "Animate Sniffy" option to the slowest position. This will reduce Sniffy's speed of behaviour to a manageable level for this assignment. Click "OK" to return to the Sniffy program.

You and your partner(s) are going to have to agree upon operational definitions of Sniffy's behaviour. I suggest that your group spend awhile watching Sniffy in his cage to see what sorts of behaviours he performs. Once you have identified the predominant behaviours, assign each behaviour a simple name and provide a definition of the behaviour. It is important that you and your partner(s) agree upon the operational behavioural definitions so that you will be in agreement when you begin recording Sniffy's behaviours.

Once you have your operational behaviour definitions you can begin recording data. You will observe Sniffy for 1000 seconds. During each 5-second interval, each of the observers is to independently record the dominant behaviour of that interval. When you are ready, start the timing and record on a sheet of paper with 200 spaces (a ruled sheet with different columns will suffice) the dominant behaviour exhibited during successive 5-second intervals. Make sure you stay synchronized with your partner(s).

After the 1000-seconds of observation are up you can exit the Sniffy program.

Your group needs to complete the following:

Question O-1:

A. Provide your group's list of operational definitions and the inter-observer reliability score.

B. Do you think that your observations are reliable? (Note: for groups with 3 members, pick two of the three behavioural observation sheets for analysis.)

A. Provide the time-budget, showing your calculations. B. Briefly comment on how Sniffy spent his time.

Question O-3:

A. Provide your transition matrix and Markov chain. B. Use the transition matrix and Markov chain to comment on how Sniffy's behaviours relate to one another; are there any obvious trends?

Part 1 (Chapter 3)

1. Magazine Training and Shaping.

Question 1:

Follow the steps in Exercise 1 (pp. 21-23) to magazine train Sniffy. Save your magazine-trained version of Sniffy. Next, following the steps in Exercise 2 (pp. 23-26) shape Sniffy to lever press. Make sure you save a new copy of Sniffy once he is fully conditioned to press the lever.

Answer the following question: Throughout the lever pressing shaping process, why should you try to deliver a pellet of food as soon as possible after Sniffy does the desired behaviour?

Question 2:

It is also possible to use "autoshaping" to condition Sniffy to press the lever. Load the first saved version of Sniffy from Exercise 1 (i.e., Sniffy is magazine trained, but not trained to lever press). From under the "Experiment" menu select "Isolate Sniffy." This speeds up the rate at which program time passes. Pay attention to the Cumulative Record and the Operant Association window (specifically the Bar-Sound measure). After a while the Cumulative Record will indicate that Sniffy has pressed the lever and received a food pellet. Eventually, Sniffy will press the lever more frequently and you will see the Bar-Sound graph rise, indicating that Sniffy is learning the appropriate association.

Compare the Cumulative Record from when you shaped Sniffy by hand (i.e., in Exercise 2) with the Cumulative Record of the autoshaped Sniffy. How do they differ with respect to the development of the Bar-Sound association and in terms of the amount of program time required to produce a fully conditioned rat?

Question 3:

Sniffy is a simulation, or model, of a live rat. As such, he lacks certain cognitive features of real rats. Given this, why might it be much harder for autoshaping of the lever pressing response to occur in a real rat, especially given the longer time frame over which autoshaping takes place?

2. Extinction.

Question 4:

Complete Exercise 5 (pp. 34-38) to extinguish Sniffy's lever pressing response and answer the following: How many responses did Sniffy make after the extinction criteria was imposed but before he actually extinguished his lever pressing response and how long (in program time) did this take?

Attach to your assignment a printout of the portion of Sniffy's Cumulative Record showing the five minute period (of program time) before and after the extinction burst. On this Cumulative Record circle (or otherwise identify) the extinction burst.

Question 5:

Complete Exercise 6 (pp. 38-40) to extinguish Sniffy's lever pressing using the alternate technique in which the "Mute Pellet Dispenser" option is turned off.

Answer the following: How many responses did Sniffy make under this condition before he extinguished his lever pressing response and how long did this take? How does this differ from your results in Question 4? Why?

Question 6:

Does the difference in extinction time and number of responses made under the two extinction conditions (i.e., pellet dispenser sound muted or not muted) seem realistic given that Sniffy does not receive any food once the extinction protocol is put in place in either case? What does this imply about the strength of secondary reinforcers in controlling behaviours?

3. Spontaneous Recovery.

Question 7:

Complete Exercise 7 (pp. 40-42). Make sure you use your saved version of Sniffy from Exercise 5. Also, save a version of Sniffy after his responding has extinguished following the spontaneous recovery procedure. You will need this for Question 8 below.

How many responses did Sniffy make and how much program time was required for him to reach the extinction criterion?

Question 8:

Using the version of Sniffy you saved in Question 7, give Sniffy another time out so that he will show spontaneous recovery and extinction a second time. Finally, give Sniffy a third time out and allow him to extinguish his responding again. Print the Cumulative Record showing the initial extinction and the two spontaneous recoveries following the two time outs that you delivered. (Follow instructions described in step 16a on p. 36 to print the Cumulative Record.) Your Cumulative Record should show the initial extinction of Sniffy's bar pressing, followed by Sniffy's response patterns after the three time outs. Attach your Cumulative Record to your assignment and use the information on it to complete the following question:

Calculate the number of responses made and the time required for Sniffy to extinguish lever pressing for the initial extinction phase and for each of the three subsequent extinguished spontaneous recoveries. Using this data, fill in the line graphs below. Be sure to add the numeric scale to the Y-axis of each graph.

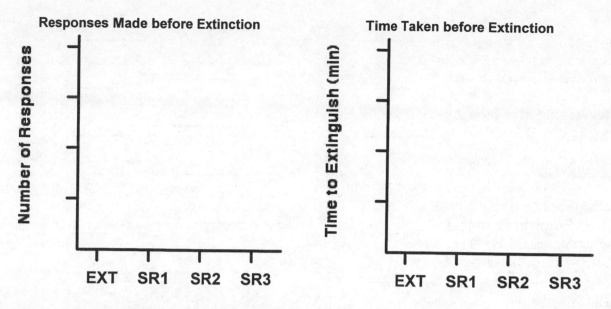

Responses Made before Extinction

Number of Responses

EXT SR1 SR2 SR3

Time Taken before Extinction

Time to Extinguish (min)

EXT SR1 SR2 SR3

Key: EXT = initial extinction trial, SR1 = first spontaneous recovery, SR2 = second spontaneous recovery, and SR3 = third spontaneous recovery.

Part 2 (Chapter 4)

4. Reinforcement Schedules.

<u>Question 9</u>:

Following the instructions in the Sniffy Pro text, complete Exercises 8, 9, 10, 11, and 12 with the aim of achieving the following:
1. Condition Sniffy to VR-5, VI-5, FR-5, and FI-5 reinforcement schedules.
2. Condition Sniffy to VR-25, VI-25, FR-25, and FI-25 reinforcement schedules.
3. Condition Sniffy to VR-50, VI-50, FR-50, and FI-50 reinforcement schedules.
Be careful that you do not extinguish Sniffy as you move to higher schedules of reinforcement.

Complete the following: Calculate the response rates for each of the four schedules at each of the four rates of reinforcement. To calculate the response rate you need to find the slope of the Cumulative Record for each reinforcement schedule. This will require you to print the Cumulative Record for each schedule, or to use the cut and paste functions (see pp. 42-43 for instructions) to transfer representative samples from the Cumulative Records into a word processor for printing. The slope of a line is its "rise" divided by its "run", that is, the increase in the vertical distance divided by the horizontal distance covered. For example, if Sniffy presses the lever 75 times in 10 minutes then his response rate is 75 resp./10 min., or 7.5 responses/minute.

Complete the calculations in the chart below. Also, attach a copy of the Cumulative Records that you used to calculate the response rates to your assignment. On the Cumulative Records indicate what sections you used in your calculations.

$$\frac{\text{resp.}}{\text{min.}} = \underline{\hspace{2cm}} \text{ resp./min.} \qquad \text{FR-5: } \frac{\text{resp.}}{\text{min.}} = \underline{\hspace{2cm}} \text{ resp./min.}$$

$$\text{VR-25: } \frac{\text{resp.}}{\text{min.}} = \underline{\hspace{2cm}} \text{ resp./min.} \qquad \text{FR-25: } \frac{\text{resp.}}{\text{min.}} = \underline{\hspace{2cm}} \text{ resp./min.}$$

$$\text{VR-50: } \frac{\text{resp.}}{\text{min.}} = \underline{\hspace{2cm}} \text{ resp./min.} \qquad \text{FR-50: } \frac{\text{resp.}}{\text{min.}} = \underline{\hspace{2cm}} \text{ resp./min.}$$

$$\text{VI-5: } \frac{\text{resp.}}{\text{min.}} = \underline{\hspace{2cm}} \text{ resp./min.} \qquad \text{FI-5: } \frac{\text{resp.}}{\text{min.}} = \underline{\hspace{2cm}} \text{ resp./min.}$$

$$\text{VI-25: } \frac{\text{resp.}}{\text{min.}} = \underline{\hspace{2cm}} \text{ resp./min.} \qquad \text{FI-25: } \frac{\text{resp.}}{\text{min.}} = \underline{\hspace{2cm}} \text{ resp./min.}$$

$$\text{VI-50: } \frac{\text{resp.}}{\text{min.}} = \underline{\hspace{2cm}} \text{ resp./min.} \qquad \text{FI-50: } \frac{\text{resp.}}{\text{min.}} = \underline{\hspace{2cm}} \text{ resp./min.}$$

Next, plot the information as a the line graph. The X-axis should depicts the value of the reinforcement schedule (i.e., 5, 25, and 50) and the Y-axis the rate of response. Make sure you label your graph fully and use appropriate scales. Finally, *briefly* explain the differences in Sniffy's response rates for the four schedules.

5. Extinguishing Schedules.

Question 10:
Complete exercise 13 (pp. 58-59) in the Sniffy text. Place Sniffy on extinction for VR-25, VI-25, FR-25, and FI-25 schedules and answer the following question:
Determine how many responses and how much time it takes Sniffy to extinguish on each of the four schedules. Rank the schedules from easiest to hardest to extinguish, and explain your results.

Part 3 (Chapter 5)

6. Stimulus Discrimination/Generalization.

In preparation for the questions in this section read the background material in chapter 5 (pp. 61-73) in the Sniffy Pro text, and then complete Exercises 14-19.

Question 11:
Answer the following: for the generalization gradient tests in Exercises 15, 17, and 19, why do you need to restart from a saved version of Sniffy for each of the nine tone frequencies that you present for the complete generalization gradient test?

Question 12:
Print out and include the DS Response Strength graphs from exercises 14, 16, and 18 (ensure that you label the graphs clearly). Explain the differences between these three graphs.

Question 13:

Produce a graph of the three generalization gradients from exercises 15, 17, and 19 and include it with your assignment.

Question14:

Answer the following: Draw what a hypothetical stimulus generalization gradient would look like if you trained Sniffy on an S+ of 2.0 kHz and two S- of 1.75 and 2.25? (Unfortunately, you can't actually do this with the Sniffy software.) Explain your generalization gradient in terms of Spence's theory of peak shift.

Question 15:

Complete the following:
1. Run discrimination learning trials for the following pairs of S+/S- stimuli: 1. S+ = 2.0 kHz, S- = 1.0 kHz; 2. S+ = 2.0 kHz, S- = 1.5 kHz; 3. S+ = 2.0 kHz, S- = 1.75 kHz. (You can follow the general instructions from Exercise 18 to complete these S+/S- learning trials; simply replace the values in step 4 with those listed here.)
2. Run stimulus generalization tests for the nine tones (i.e., 1.0 kHz to 3.0 kHz) for each of these three discrimination learning sets. (You can follow the general instructions from Exercise 19 to complete these stimulus generalization gradients.)
3. Generate a graph, of the sort depicted on p. 81 of Sniffy Pro, showing the generalization gradients for these three discrimination learning sets; also include the generalization gradient from Exercise 15 on your graph (i.e., S+ = 2.0 kHz, no S-).
4. Explain the results shown in your graph in terms of behavioural contrast and peak shift. Use data from the DS Response Strength graphs to help explain results shown in your traph.

Part 4 (Chapters 6-7)

7. Classical Conditioning:

Read chapter 6 carefully. Although there are no exercises in this chapter it explains how to run classical conditioning studies with the Sniffy program.

Question 16:

Complete Exercises 20, 21, and 22 (pages 104-112) on acquisition, extinction, and spontaneous recovery, respectively. Follow the instructions in the Sniffy text with *one* exception. For these exercises, type "20" in the text box located to the right of the Present Each Trial Type instead of "10". That is, you will present the CS-US pairing 20 times to Sniffy. Use the copy of the VR-25 file located on the Sniffy Pro CD for questions in this section. Follow the instructions on p. 105 to use this VR25 file.

Print both the Suppression Ratio and CS Response Strength graphs after you have completed exercise 22 and attach them to your assignment. Make sure you label the graphs so that they can be identified by the marker.

Question 17:

As it turns out, it does not matter whether you use the tone or the light as the CS for these studies; both stimuli give the same CS Response Strength numbers. In other words, the tone and the light are treated by Sniffy as being equally salient and relevant. We have discussed differences between real rats and the Sniffy model of rats in class. Given that the model may not be a completely accurate representation of a live rat, would you expect similar results (i.e., that the stimulus used as the CS is irrelevant) from real rats? Why? Explain your answer (hint: consider issues of stimulus salience).

Question 18:

Complete Exercise 23 (pages 112-119). As with the exercises in Question 16, for both the low and high CS intensity conditions present 20, instead of 10, CS-US pairings. Follow the instructions on pages 115-119 to produce a line graph of the CS response strength for the three CS conditions (i.e., low, medium, and high intensity tone).

Attach the CS Response Strength graphs for the three intensities of CS to your assignment. Ensure that you title and label the graphs appropriately.

Question 19:

Exercise 24 (pp. 120-122) deals with the influence of US strength on the learning of the CS-US association in classical conditioning.

As in Questions 16 and 18, run 20 instead of 10 CS-US pairings.

Using the instructions from Exercise 23, produce a line graph of the CS Response Strength of the three levels of US intensity (i.e., low, medium, and high) with a medium intensity CS. Label the graph completely. Attach the graph to your assignment. Using this graph, answer the following: For the low strength US, is there a point of diminishing conditioning? Explain this in terms of habituation. According to your results, what is the point of diminishing conditioning for Sniffy?

Question 20:

How is the habituation of a medium-intensity CS and low-intensity US pairing like or unlike the extinction of a medium-intensity CS and medium-intensity US pairing? Explain what happens to Sniffy's values of the Suppression Ratio and the Pain Sensitivity measure in both of these conditions?

Question 21:

Suppose you only have a record of the Suppression Ratio of Sniffy's performance and do not know what conditioning situation Sniffy has been exposed to (e.g., you've mixed up your data files, lost your labels, etc.). Using *only* the behavioural data of the Suppression Ratio, is it possible to determine if Sniffy has been learning an association between a medium-intensity CS and a low-intensity US, or if he had a medium-intensity CS, paired with a low-intensity US, extinguished? Explain your reasoning.

Part 5 (Chapter 8)

8. Compound Conditioning, Blocking, Overshadowing, and Overexpectation.

Question 22:

Complete Exercise 25 (pp. 124-130). Because of the random variability built into Sniffy, you can sometimes get some rather peculiar results in the final testing phase. For this reason, students should test the appropriate stimuli three times, rather than once. The easiest way to do this is to set the Present Each Trial Type to "3", instead of "1". This will allow you to test the CS of interest three times and take an average value.

Print the Suppression Ratio and CS Response Strength graphs from the Compound-Conditioning Experiment Condition (pp. 124-127) and the Compound-Conditioning, Separate-Pairing Control Condition (pp. 127-130) and attach them to your assignment. Label the graphs appropriately so that the marker can identify them.

Provide the values of the averaged Suppression Ratios (i.e., the average of the three test trials you conducted for each stimulus) for the tested stimuli from the two parts of Exercise 25. That is, present the values for the CS_{ML} and CS_{MT} for both the Compound Conditioning and Separate Pairing conditions.

Question 23:

Answer the following: In experiments with real animals researchers might use a technique similar to the one used in Question 22 (i.e., presenting test trials more than once) to control for an animal's response variability. The drawback of this approach is that the animal may begin to extinguish to the CS because it is not followed by the US on testing trials. Describe another technique that could be used to control for response variability?

Question 24:

Complete Exercise 26 (pp. 130-135) on blocking. As in Question 22, test each CS three times. Complete the following: Print, label, and attach to your assignment the appropriate Suppression Ratio graphs from Exercise 26. Provide the values of the averaged Suppression Ratios for the tested stimuli (i.e., for the CS_{ML} and CS_{MT}) from the Blocking Experimental and Compound Conditioning Control conditions.

Note: essentially, you are being asked to provide the actual values from your data for the Stage 3 section of the chart on the top of page 131.

Question 25:

Complete Exercise 27 (pp. 135-138). Print and label the Suppression Ratio and CS Response Strength graphs and attach them to your assignment. How might your results have differed if you had used a low-intensity light and a medium-intensity tone, instead of the high-intensity tone that you did use? Support and explain your answer.

Question 26:

Complete Exercise 28 (pp. 138-141) on the overexpectation effect. Print and label the Suppression Ratio and CS Response Strength graphs and attach them to your assignment. What would happen if you had used a high-intensity shock instead of a medium-intensity shock in stage 3 of the chart on page 139? Provide support for your answer. Hint: the easiest way to answer this is to actually test the condition using Sniffy.

Part 6 (Chapter 9)

9. Inhibitory Conditioning.

Question 27:
        Complete Exercise 29 (pp. 144-148). Print and label the Suppression Ratio and CS Response Strength graphs from Exercise 29 and attach them to your assignment

Question 28:
        Complete Exercise 30 (pp. 148-152). Print and label the Suppression Ratio and CS Response Strength graphs and attach them to your assignment. Consider the results from Exercises 29 and 30. Both provide measures of conditioned inhibition. Discuss the importance of both of these techniques in explaining the working of conditioned inhibition.

Part 7 (Chapters 10 and 11)

10: Associations in Classical Conditioning.

Question 29:
        Complete Exercise 31 (pp. 154-160). Then run the following exercise.
        Open the VR25 file, then use the Save As command to give the file a new name (e.g., Ex31-SPCMOD). Choose the Change Nature of the Association command from the Experiment menu and select the S-S association for CS used as US; click OK. Choose Design Classical Conditioning Experiment from the Experimental menu. Under Stage selection, set the Interval Between Trials to 5 minutes and the Preset Each Trial Type to 5 times. In the First Stimulus section of the dialogue box, select both medium-intensity light and medium-intensity tone. In the Second Stimulus section of the dialogue box, select none. Click the New Stage command button (you should now be editing Stage 2, Trial Type A). Set the Interval Between Trials to 5 minutes and the Preset Each Trial Type to 10. In the First Stimulus section of the dialogue box, select the medium-intensity tone and in the Second Stimulus section of the dialogue box, select the medium-intensity shock US. In the Stage section of the dialogue box, click the New Stage command button (you should now be editing Stage 3, Trial Type A). Set the Interval Between Trials to 5 minutes and the Preset Each Trial Type to 3 times. In the First Stimulus section of the dialogue box, select the medium intensity light and in the Second Stimulus section of the dialogue box, select None. Click the Save command button and then execute the Run Classical Conditioning Experiment command.
        Print the CS Response Strength and Suppression Ratio windows and attach them to your assignment. Label the graphs clearly so the marker can identify them.
        How do your results compare to those in the Unpaired Control Condition and Experimental Condition of Exercise 31 in the Sniffy text? In Stage 1 of the Experimental condition the light is designated as the CS and the tone as a US. That is, the light turns on by itself to be followed at the end of the presentation period by a simultaneous presentation of the tone. Consider the difference in the modified exercise you have just run. In this case the tone and light come on simultaneously for the entire CS presentation period. However, your results are probably quite different from the Experimental condition results. Comment on your results in terms of sensory preconditioning. What associations are being formed? Do the results of this modified exercise agree with the sorts of results you would expect from live animals exposed to various forms of sensory preconditioning?

Complete Exercise 32 (pp. 160-163). Exercise 32 demonstrates higher-order conditioning, specifically what is called second-order conditioning. Third-order conditioning can also be produced. In third-order conditioning an additional CS is subsequently associated through pairing with the second-order CS. The following instructions will allow you to conduct a third-order conditioning test with Sniffy. Fourth and even higher-order conditioning is possible with live animals, but in practice it becomes progressively more difficult to form the higher-order associations. With Sniffy we are limited by the number of stimuli available in the operant chamber (i.e., light, tone, bell) to testing third-order conditioning.

Follow the instructions for Stage 1 of Exercise 32. Then make the following changes. Click the New Stage button (you should be in Stage 2, Trial Type A) and set the Interval Between Trials to 5 minutes and Present Each Trial Type to 5 times. In the First Stimulus section of the dialogue box, select the Bell and in the Second Stimulus section of the dialogue box, select the medium-intensity Tone as a CS Used as US. Click the New Stage button (you should be in Stage 3, Trial Type A) and set the Interval Between Trials to 5 minutes and the Present Each Trial Type to 5 times. In the First Stimulus section of the dialogue box, select the medium-intensity Light and in the Second Stimulus section of the dialogue box, select the Bell as a CS Used as US. Click the New Stage button (you should be in Stage 4, Trial Type A) and set the Interval Between Trials to 5 minutes and the Present Each Trial Type to 3 times. In the First Stimulus section of the dialogue box, select the medium-intensity Light and in the Second Stimulus section of the dialogue box, select None. Click the Save button and then select Run Classical Conditioning Experiment from the Experiment menu.

Print and include your CS Response Strength and Suppression Ratio graphs in your assignment. Label them clearly so the marker can identify them.

Answer the following: Do your results agree with what you would expect for third order conditioning? Why or why not?

Question 31:

Read pp. 165-168 and then complete Exercises 33-34 (pp. 168-174). Explain your results in terms of S-S and S-R theory. More specifically, how does the nature of the association when the CS is paired with the US determine the experimental results?

Part 8 (Chapter 12)

11. Habituation, Sensitization, Background Conditioning, and Pre-exposure Effects.

Question 32:

Read the material on pp. 187-188 and run Exercise 38 (pp. 189-194). Answer the following:

Why does a suppression ratio not provide useful data for the interpretation of background conditioning (i.e., conditioning of contextual stimuli)?

Print, or examine on the computer screen, the Cumulative Record of conditioning trials 1-5, 21-25, and 46-50 for each of the three US strength conditions (i.e., low, medium, and high intensity). Calculate the average time that the US suppresses Sniffy's bar pressing for the three periods of each of the intensity conditions. Remember that the Cumulative Record represents ten minutes of time by the space between two solid vertical lines. To calculate the time of suppression, measure the length of the Cumulative Record's line that remains flat following the termination of the US (note that each pen movement upwards on the Cumulative Record represents one bar press by Sniffy). Then measure the length of Cumulative Record between the ten-minute marker lines. Divide the length of your first measure by the length of the second and multiply by 10 to produce a value in minutes. Plot your averaged results on the graph below. Fully label your graph.

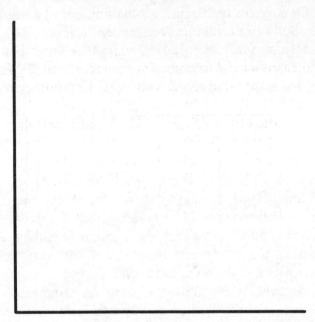

Question 33:

Read the material in the Sniffy text related to exercise 39 (pp. 194-197) and complete this exercise.

Explain why the CS pre-exposure effect slows the acquisition of learning. How is the CS pre-exposure effect similar to habituation?

Question 34:

Read the material in the Sniffy text related to exercise 40 (pp. 197-200) and complete this exercise.

Using the graph shown on the bottom of page 199, propose an explanation for why both the CS pre-exposure and US pre-exposure effects result in an asymptotic maximum CS Response Strength that is less than that for the control condition. Also, see if you can theorize a reason for why the US pre-exposure effect has less of an effect on the speed of conditioning than the CS pre-exposure effect. Note that the data presented in the graph is generated from the Sniffy software and, as the text states on p. 200, the data may not be representative of live rats. (If you are particularly keen you may wish to construct your own graph; note that you should probably run Sniffy at least three times through each of the conditions [i.e., control, CS pre-exposure, and US pre-exposure] and average the results for each trial to control for variability.)

Marking Key

Observation Section

Question O-1

A. Operational definitions of behaviours should be specific enough to prevent/limit ambiguity about what actions constitute a particular behaviour. Also, I think the absolute minimum number of behaviours used is 5; any less than this and they are misrepresenting the range of behaviours Sniffy engages in. Similarly, anything over 10 behaviours is probably too many; some behaviours, like water drinking, food eating, or lever pressing will occur so rarely that students would be better served to combine them into an "other" or "food-related" category.

They also need to calculate the interobserver reliability score. For example, the observational data might have appeared as follows (note: I'm only giving 20 observations here):

Period	Ob 1	Ob 2	Agree?
1	S	S	Y
2	S	S	Y
3	G	S	N
4	H	H	Y
5	G	G	Y
6	S	S	Y
7	S	S	Y
8	G	G	Y
9	G	S	N
10	S	H	N
11	G	G	Y
12	H	H	Y
13	H	H	Y
14	S	S	Y
15	G	G	Y
16	S	H	N
17	S	S	Y
18	G	G	Y
19	S	S	Y
20	H	H	Y

For this example,
> 20 samples
> 16 agree
> 4 disagree
> Percent agreement = 16/20*100 = 80%

B. The students are asked to comment on how reliable they think their performance was. Note that we are not going to penalize them if their score was very low. It is the nature of their commentary and interpretation that is the issue. This is going to call for a judgement call on your part. Do the students offer a plausible explanation for their interobserver reliability score?

Question O-2

A. Students need to provide a time-budget of Sniffy's behaviour. For example, from the sample data above, using the data of Observer 1:

9 Sniff
4 High Sniff
7 Groom

Convert to percentages:

$9/20*100 = 45\%$ of time sniffing
$4/20*100 = 20\%$ of time high sniffing
$7/20*100 = 35\%$ of time grooming

B. Students are asked to comment on how Sniffy allocates their time. Note that this should not simply be a repetition of the numbers from the time-budget; students should "comment", not parrot.

Question O-3

A. Students have to produce a transition matrix and Markov chain from their data. For example, from the sample data above, the transition matrix should look something like this (keep in mind, of course, their matrix will be bigger, as they should have more behaviours):

	S	H	G	
S	⦙⦙⦙ $3/19*100$ = 15.8%	⦙ $1/19*100$ = 5.3%	⦙⦙⦙⦙⦙ 26.3%	9
H	⦙ 5.3%	⦙ 5.3%	⦙ 5.3%	3
G	⦙⦙⦙⦙ 21%	⦙⦙ 10.5%	⦙ 5.3%	7
	8	4	7	19/19

or this, if they just provide percentages (either is acceptable):

	S	H	G
S	15.3%	5.3%	26.3%
H	5.3%	5.3%	5.3%
G	21%	10.5%	5.3%

The Markov chain will look something like this:

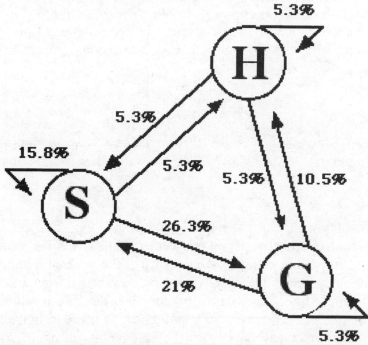

Again, keep in mind that I've only included 3 behaviours; students will have included more.

     B. Students are asked to comment on how Sniffy's behaviours relate to one another. Again, I'm asking for commentary and interpretation, not a regurgitation of the raw data off the matrix or chain. They should be commenting on trends; does one behaviour commonly lead to another, are there particular "loops" in behaviours that Sniffy might be getting stuck in, etc. They might also comment on whether or not these sorts of behaviour patterns seem realistic; is it simply a random number generator that controls Sniffy's activity, or does it seem to be more complicated (e.g., in live rats, certain behaviours go together and won't appear in isolation; how about in the Sniffy model of rat behaviour?).

Part 1 (Chapter 3)

<u>Question 1:</u>
    Contiguity promotes the association made between the behaviour and the reinforcer.

<u>Question 2:</u>

The Bar-Sound association only increases with autoshaping; it doesn't decrease. Autoshaping Sniffy usually takes longer (note: this might not hold for students if they are not particularly adept at shaping).

Question 3:
  Forgetting; cognitive associations formed with extraneous distracters; no frustrations; no environmental distractions; no satiation.

Question 4:
  The averaged result of three trials produced 65.6 responses in 14.3 minutes. Note that this could be quite variable across students.
  Students should produce something resembling the following:

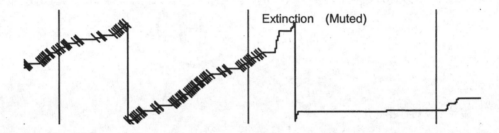

Question 5:
  Generally, extinction should take much longer than in Question 2-1 and probably more responses will be made. Note that the actual number of responses will vary from student to student. Also, unfortunately, due to the variable nature of the random number generator that drives Sniffy's behaviour, a few students may even get results that are the opposite.
  As to why, the more likely result of taking longer is due to the value of the sound from the pellet dispenser acting as a secondary (or conditioned) reinforcer. In Question 2-1 the sound was muted, so that Sniffy was receiving neither the food pellet (primary reinforcer) nor the sound of the dispenser (secondary reinforcer); in this case, Sniffy is at least receiving some reinforcement from the sound which should probably prolong the extinction process.

Question 6:
  This seems somewhat unrealistic. The program specifications set the strength of the secondary reinforcer very high. Real animals are unlikely to take so long to extinguish if they are only receiving the secondary reinforcer (i.e., the sound) but no primary reinforcer (i.e., the food). Note that some students may argue that the secondary reinforcer is sufficient to make extinction more difficult.

Question 7:
  This will be highly variable across students.

Question 8:
  Student graphs should resemble the following (refer to the student's attached Cumulative Record to confirm the specifics):

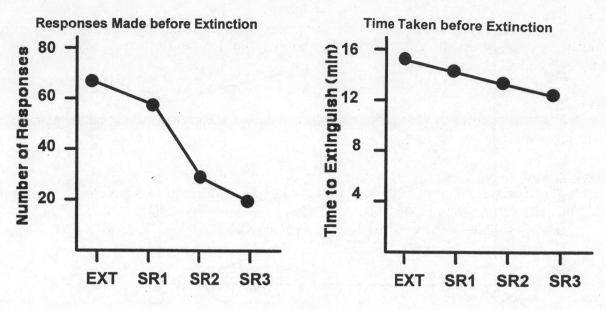

Responses Made before Extinction

Time Taken before Extinction

Part 2 (Chapter 4)

4. Reinforcement Schedules.

Question 9:

Here is an example of results students may produce in the chart and graph:

$$\frac{\text{resp.}}{2.5 \text{ min.}} = \underline{60.7} \text{ resp./min.} \qquad \text{FR-5: } \frac{225 \text{ resp.}}{4.9 \text{ min.}} = \underline{45.5} \text{ resp./min.}$$

$$\text{VR-25: } \frac{225 \text{ resp.}}{2.5 \text{ min.}} = \underline{89.0} \text{ resp./min.} \qquad \text{FR-25: } \frac{225 \text{ resp.}}{6.8 \text{ min.}} = \underline{33.0} \text{ resp./min.}$$

$$\text{VR-50: } \frac{300 \text{ resp.}}{3.8 \text{ min.}} = \underline{79.8} \text{ resp./min.} \qquad \text{FR-50: } \frac{300 \text{ resp.}}{9.2 \text{ min.}} = \underline{32.7} \text{ resp./min.}$$

$$\text{VI-5: } \frac{150 \text{ resp.}}{5.9 \text{ min.}} = \underline{25.5} \text{ resp./min.} \qquad \text{FI-5: } \frac{75 \text{ resp.}}{8.2 \text{ min.}} = \underline{9.1} \text{ resp./min.}$$

$$\text{VI-25: } \frac{150 \text{ resp.}}{5.2 \text{ min.}} = \underline{29.0} \text{ resp./min.} \qquad \text{FI-25: } \frac{150 \text{ resp.}}{13.7 \text{ min.}} = \underline{11.0} \text{ resp./min.}$$

$$\text{VI-50: } \frac{150 \text{ resp.}}{14.6 \text{ min.}} = \underline{10.3} \text{ resp./min.} \qquad \text{FI-50: } \frac{150 \text{ resp.}}{14.6 \text{ min.}} = \underline{10.3} \text{ resp./min.}$$

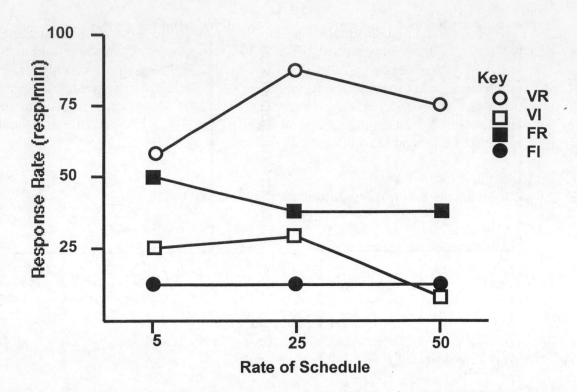

Students may provide a variety of explanations for their results. In general, make sure that their explanations support their findings. In some cases, due to the randomization feature in the Sniffy software, students could have somewhat atypical results. This offers students the chance to explain differences between theoretically predicted values and the results they achieved.

5. Extinguishing Schedules.

Question 10:

Ratio schedules often take longer than interval schedules to extinguish. More significantly, variable schedules take longer than fixed schedules due to the non-predictive nature of the variable schedules.

Students may also comment on their choice of how to judge the difficulty of extinction of responding (i.e., tome or number of responses). This is something of a judgement call, allowing students an opportunity to develop critical skills in supporting an argument.

Part 3 (Chapter 5)

6. Stimulus Discrimination/Generalization.

Question 11:

If you don't restart from a saved version of Sniffy, he just extinguishes his responding, since all generalization tests are extinction trials. Consequently, you don't get an accurate representation of Sniffy's generalization/discrimination abilities.

Question 12:

The DS Response Strength graphs should closely resemble the examples in the Sniffy text on pages 74, 77, and 79. For exercise 14, with an S+ = 2.0 and no S- you would expect to have an excitatory gradient centred on the S+ of 2.0, gradually dropping off on either side. For exercise 16, with an S- = 2.0 you will get an inverted pattern, with a negative inhibitory gradient forming, centred on the S- of 2.0. Finally, for exercise 18, where there is an S+ = 2.0 and an S- = 2.25, you will generate both an excitatory and an inhibitory gradient. The excitatory gradient will be centred on the S+ of 2.0 and the inhibitory gradient on the S- of 2.25.

Question 13:

The following are two ways that students might present their graphs:

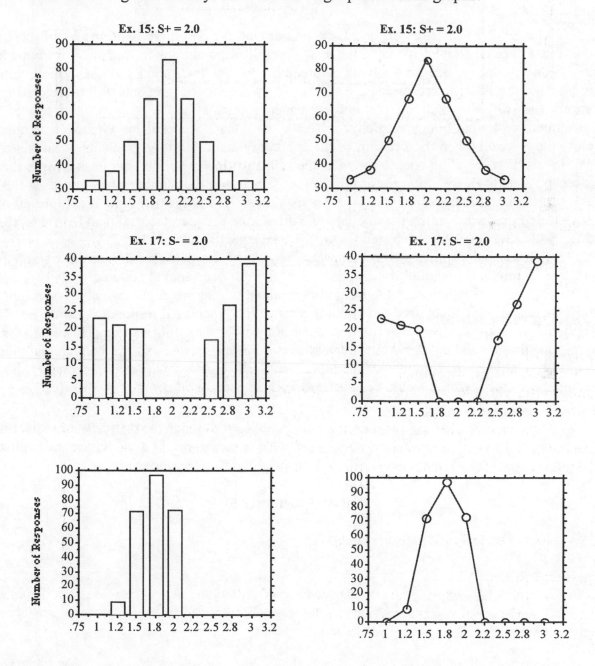

Question 14:

When you train with an S+ of 2.0 Hz and an S- of 1.75 and a second S- of 2.25 you will get a narrow generalization gradient centred on the S+. The two S-s will "dampen" out the tails of the generalization gradient. According to Spence's theory of peak shift, you will have formed one excitatory gradient (centred on 2.0) and two inhibitory gradients (one centred on 1.75, the other on 2.25). Consequently, while there will be some suppression of responding at 2.0, this is still where the maximum responding should be, and the inhibitory gradients will reduce responding on either side of the S+. Hence, you will see a narrow, focussed generalization gradient centred on the S+.

Question 15:

The S+ 2.0 line is, as expected, centred around the S+; there is no peak shift here. The other three lines all show peak shift; the peak point of responding is moved away from the S+ in the direction opposite to the S-. This is predicted by Spence's theory because the excitatory gradients will all be centred on the S+ of 2.0 and the inhibitory gradients will be centred on the various S-s, all of which are of lower frequencies than the S+ (i.e., to the left of S+). Consequently, the inhibitory gradients will have the greatest suppression effects on frequencies below the S+, and when the net sum of the excitatory and inhibitory gradients is calculated the peak levels of responding should move to the right. A second point about peak shift is that the closer the S- is to the S+ the greater the difference between the number of responses at the new peak and the number of responses at the S+ should be. This holds true quite nicely for all of the peak-shifted gradients. In the graph below the difference between the peak and S+ are 8, 12, and 16 for S+2.0/S-1.0, S+2.0/S-1.5, and S+2.0/S-1.75, respectively.

Behavioural contrast argues that the "height" of the peak for an animal trained on an S+/S- discrimination should be higher than that of an animal trained only on an S+ discrimination. This is because the inhibitory gradient is interpreted as extinction of responding to the S-, resulting in a positive behavioural contrast (i.e., increased responding) to the S+. In the graph below, only the S+2.0/S-1.0 line does not conform to this pattern. However, for this condition, the S+ and S- show the greatest separation in distance, so the behavioural contrast would be relatively small anyway. The other two S+/S- trials show greater responding than the S+ alone condition, which would be predicted from a behavioural contrast perspective.

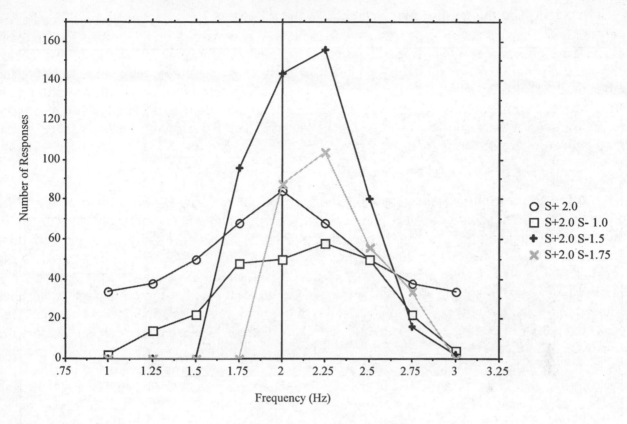

Comparison of Four Generalization Gradients

Legend:
- ○ S+ 2.0
- □ S+2.0 S- 1.0
- ✚ S+2.0 S-1.5
- ✕ S+2.0 S-1.75

X-axis: Frequency (Hz)
Y-axis: Number of Responses

Part 4 (Chapters 6-7)

7. Classical Conditioning:

Question 16:

The students' Suppression Ratio and CS Response Strength graphs should resemble the following:

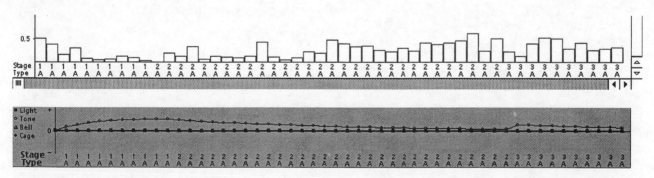

Question 17:

No. Rats' visual and auditory systems are not equal; generally rats' vision is worse than their hearing. One would expect that the tone would be more salient than the light and should condition more easily.

Students should produce a graph similar to the following:

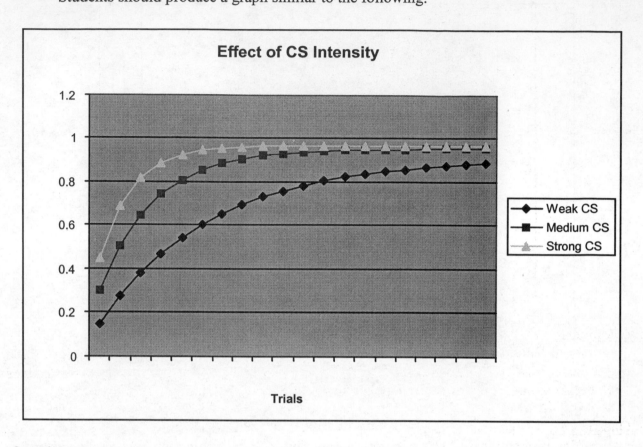

Effect of CS Intensity

Legend:
- Weak CS
- Medium CS
- Strong CS

Trials

Question 19:
Yes, there is a point of diminishing conditioning. Sniffy begins to learn the CS-US association, but the US is weak, so Sniffy begins to habituate, thereby losing CS response strength. According to the graph below, the point of diminishing return is at trial 5 or 6.

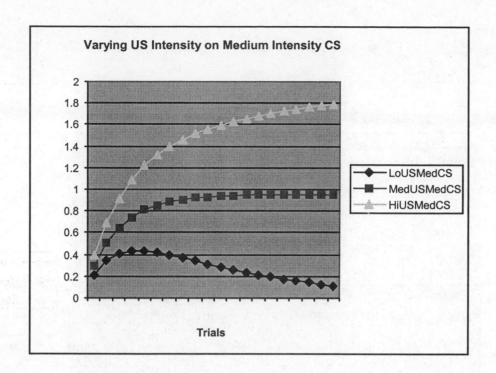

Varying US Intensity on Medium Intensity CS

Question 20:

Both habituation and low-intensity US show increases in the Suppression Ratio (after a previous decrease). The fear measure is near zero for both. Pain sensitivity values are reduced from the maximum in both, but are near zero with low-intensity US (higher for extinction).

Question 21:

You probably can't tell them apart very easily. Theoretically, you should see a decrease in the Suppression Ratio for both early on followed by an increase in Suppression Ratio in low US due to habituation or extinction.

Practically, there is some difference. The Suppression Ratio doesn't seem to decrease as much in the low-intensity US condition as in the medium-intensity CS condition before heading back up to 0.5.

Part 5 (Chapter 8)

8. Compound Conditioning, Blocking, Overshadowing, and Overexpectation.

Question 22:

Suppression Ratio for Compound-Conditioning condition:

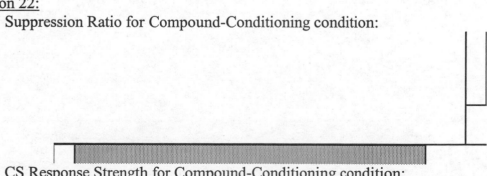

CS Response Strength for Compound-Conditioning condition:

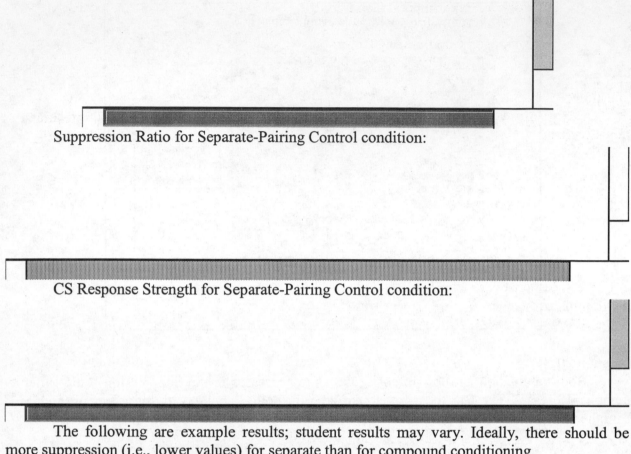

Suppression Ratio for Separate-Pairing Control condition:

CS Response Strength for Separate-Pairing Control condition:

The following are example results; student results may vary. Ideally, there should be more suppression (i.e., lower values) for separate than for compound conditioning.

Compound Conditioning
CS_{ML}: 0.1990 CS_{MT}: 0.2346
Separate Pairing
CS_{ML}: 0.1826 CS_{MT}: 0.1311

Question 23:

Run multiple animals instead of one subject; use a large sample size and average the results across animals instead of running a single subject multiple times and averaging the single subject's results.

Question 24:

Example of Suppression Ratio:

The following are example results based on the Suppression Ratios provided here; student results may vary.

Blocking Experimental Condition
CS_{ML}: 0.4784 CS_{MT}: 0.1344
Compound Conditioning Control
CS_{ML}: 0.1990 CS_{MT}: 0.2346

Question 25:
Suppression Ratio (Overshadowing). Note: 2A = medium intensity light, 2B = medium intensity tone:

CS Response Strength (Overshadowing). Note: 2A = medium intensity light, 2B = medium intensity tone:

There will not be as great a difference in salience, so there should not be as much of an overshadowing effect. That is, there will be less of a difference between the Suppression Ratios in the testing phase.

Question 26:
Suppression Ratio:

CS Response Strength:

With a high-intensity shock rather than a medium-intensity shock underexpectation will result. The animal would learn to expect a greater US when the two CSs are combined. Given that high-intensity may not be twice as strong as medium-intensity in the Sniffy software, what we might expect is to see some degree of decrease in Suppression Ratio in the underexpectation condition.

Part 6 (Chapter 9)

Part 6 (Chapter 9)

9. Inhibitory Conditioning.

Question 27:
   Suppression Ratio:

   CS Response Strength:

Question 28:
   Suppression Ratio (2A = bell, 2B = bell + tone):

CS Response Strength (2A = bell, 2B = bell + tone):

   Exercise 29 showed that a CS- will inhibit conditioning to a stimulus with which the CS-is paired in training, whereas Exercise 30 showed that a CS- can also inhibit responding to a novel CS+. This is significant because it demonstrates that the inhibitory power of the CS- is not limited to stimuli with which it has been previously paired, but that its inhibitory properties can be generalized to new conditions.

Part 7 (Chapters 10 and 11)

10: Associations in Classical Conditioning.

Question 29:

In terms of the CS Response Strength and Suppression Ratio it does not appear to matter whether the two CSs are initially presented sequentially (as in the Unpaired Control Condition of Exercise 31) or simultaneously (as in this modified training version). This is because the two CSs are initially presented together without the US. Consequently, no initial CS-US association is formed. Subsequently, the tone CS is associated with a shock US, but the light CS is not. Therefore, when tested the light CS does not result in a suppressed CER. It is not the association between the two CSs that matters, but the subsequent association between one of the CSs and a US. This is, actually, rather peculiar, as one would expect a sensory preconditioning association to form between the two CSs. This suggests that in the Sniffy software, the rat only forms associations between stimuli when presented in a CS-US format.

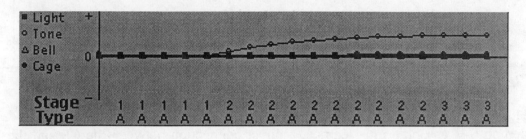

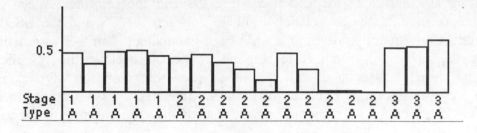

Question 30:

The CS Response Strength graph shows that there is some increase in the associative strength of the light (third-order CS) after it is paired with the bell (second-order CS). There may be some suppression of the response to the light, but it is not particularly strong. This is in keeping with the theory of higher-order conditioning. One expects the associative strength to decrease as the number of associations increases.

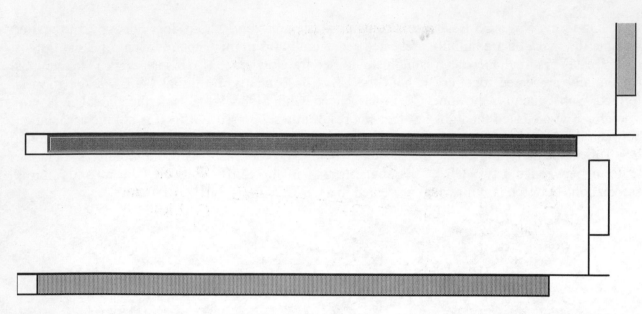

Question 31:

When an S-R association is learned, a direct connection between the CS and the UR is formed; that is, the association is made between the CS and the response. When an S-S association is learned, though, the association is made between the CS and the US, that is, between two stimuli. Consequently, after the US has been habituated, if an S-R association was initially conditioned, Sniffy will continue to respond to the CS because the CS elicits the inhibitory elements initially associated with the shock (i.e., the inhibition of response). In contrast, with an S-S association, habituation of the US eliminates the CS's ability to elicit a response; now the US produces no response, so because of the stimulus-stimulus association neither will the CS.

Note: this is a relatively simple answer which students could produce based only on the material in the Sniffy text. Depending on the level and nature of the course, a more elaborate answer with a greater reliance on S-S and S-R theory could be required.

Part 8 (Chapter 12)

11. Habituation, Sensitization, Background Conditioning, and Pre-exposure Effects.

Question 32:

Because contextual stimuli are always present; no baseline measure (i.e., CS absent) of responding can be taken for comparison to the CS present condition.

The following is an example of the sort of graph students should produce.

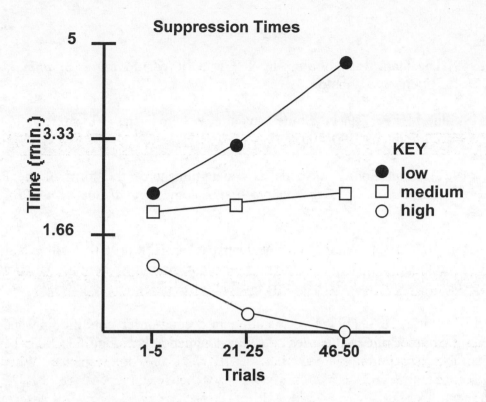

Suppression Times

KEY
● low
□ medium
○ high

Time (min.)

Trials

Question 33:
Essentially, through pre-exposure to a CS not paired with a US Sniffy learns to associate the CS with nothing. That is, the CS is not representative of any following US. Subsequently, when the CS is paired with the US, Sniffy must overcome his earlier conditioning while learning the new association. The CS pre-exposure effect is similar to habituation in that both effects tell the animal that the stimulus it is exposed to has no particular consequence.

Question 34:
This question allows students to speculate and theorize about the principles of learning and conditioning based on what they have learned from the Sniffy exercises and their other course work. Because of the highly hypothetical nature of this question, the answer could be quite open-ended. This could be turned into a short paper (e.g., 1-2 pages) in which students are required to use at least one or two references. Alternatively, students could be given this question several days in advance of an in-class written examination. This would allow them time to play around with Sniffy and formulate the outline of their answer, while the in-class writing of the answer would keep their responses relatively brief, thereby making the grading less onerous. Another option might be to use this question to generate class discussion, perhaps in small groups if the class is large. Students could also be encouraged to comment on the value of modeling behavioural processes with computer simulation. For example, "Can simulations lead to new research directions in the field of learning and behaviour, or are they only useful for teaching purposes?"

References

Beach, F.A. (1949) The snark was a boojun. In: T.E. McGill (ed.) *Readings in animal behavior.* New York: Holt, Rinehart & Winston.

Estes, W. & Skinner, B.F. (1941) Some quantitative properties of anxiety. *Journal of Experimental Psychology,* **29:** 390-400.

Holland, P.C. (1977). Conditioned stimulus as a determinant of the form of the Pavlovian conditioned response. *Journal of Experimental Psychology: Animal Behaviour Processes,* **3:** 77-104.

Honing, W.K., Boneau, C.A., Burstein, K.R., & Pennypacker, H.S. (1963) Positive and negative generalization gradients obtained under equivalent training conditions. *Journal of Comparative and Physiological Psychology,* **56:** 111-116.

Rizley, R.A. & Rescorla, R.A. (1972) Association in second-order conditioning and sensory preconditioning. *Journal of Comparative and Physiological Psychology,* **81:** 1-11.